INTEGRITY

INTEGRITY

MY SLOW AND PAINFUL
JOURNEY TO SUCCESS

GLENN STEARNS

WITH LAURA MORTON

Forefront
BOOKS

Published by Forefront Books.
Distributed by Simon & Schuster.
Library of Congress Control Number: XXXXXXXXXX

Print ISBN: 978-1-63763-043-3
E-book ISBN: 978-1-63763-044-0

Cover Design by Bruce Gore, Gore Studio, Inc.
Interior Design by Mary Susan Oleson, BLU Design

Dedication
TK

CONTENTS

CHAPTER ONE

NOTHING TO LOSE, EVERYTHING TO GAIN

Obstacles don't have to stop you. If you run into a wall, don't turn around and give up. Figure out how to climb it, go through it, or work around it.
—MICHAEL JORDAN

GROWING UP, I was labeled "The biggest loser" and "most likely to fail." The odds were clearly stacked against me. Everyone knew it too. My parents were alcoholics, as was much of my extended family, many of whom ultimately passed away from drug and alcohol related deaths. I had Dyslexia, failed 4th grade, I fathered a child at 14 and basically had very little structure or supervision growing up. So yes. I WAS a loser and as far as everyone was concerned, destined for certain failure.

Except for one thing; that didn't happen.

Life is all about timing. I have always had timing. Both good and bad, but for whatever reasons, despite the obstacles meant to stand in my way, I have managed to create amazing outcomes-- even when those results weren't clear from the start.

As I write this book, I have to pinch myself. As a matter of fact, I pinch myself often. Why? There are some days, even I can't believe where my life has led me.

I have dined with world leaders, become friends with notable music and sports figures. I have owned all the luxuries one could imagine; exotic cars, a luxury yacht complete with a personal helicopter, private jets, a home in Fiji, properties in South Africa, Jackson Hole, the British Virgin Islands (co-owned with Sir Richard Branson) and one of the largest estates in Newport Beach, California.

My name has adorned buildings, I have starred in several successful TV shows, have traveled all over the world and slept in palaces. I've sat at the table with the most famous actors, singers and dignitaries.

This all sounds pretty cool right?

I sure thought so. For a long time.

But, then life slapped me in the face, hard, every time I started to buy into my own bullshit. And it was easy to get caught up in all of that, only to discover none of it mattered more to me than my life, family and health.

Please allow me to share the story of my rise and fall and the journey along the way that led to my ultimate success.

Hopefully, along the way, I can provide you with insights that demonstrate how everything we do always has the potential for a positive or negative impact. Ultimately, it is up to us to choose how we navigate through the challenging times and not let our heads get too big when it comes to success.

I will share how *integrity* played an active role in the story of my life through all the ups and downs and how *grit* and yes, *pressure* along the way polished this unimpressive lump of coal into a shiny example of what is possible.

Like many successful people before me, I have been accused of being lucky. Really lucky. Ok, sure. That may be true, but luck only plays a small part of success. Even a lottery winner isn't guaranteed success. It's all how you manage your luck—good or bad.

I became curious about the word luck, especially because I hear it—a lot. So I looked it up in the dictionary.

luck

/lək/

noun

1. success or failure apparently brought by chance rather than through one's own actions.

For me, a more accurate description of luck was coined by Roman philosopher Seneca, who said, *"Luck Is What Happens When Preparation Meets Opportunity."*

Now, *that* I could relate to, as there's no question, we each make our own luck. The difference between lucky and unlucky people though, is all in one's perspective.

This got me thinking about success, how its defined and achieved.

suc·cess

/səkəses/

noun

1. the accomplishment of an aim or purpose.

One definition of success I can really relate to comes from American author Christopher Morley, who wrote: *"To be able to spend your life in your own way."* For me, success also has to do with the impact we make in other people's lives. It took me years to understand that being crystal clear about how you define success will reap immeasurable rewards. I don't think this. I know it.

Hopefully, my journey will enlighten you that being successful isn't predicated on being born with a silver spoon, hitting the lottery, or having a great mentor base to start with. I had none of those things. And, to be certain, it isn't how we start this game of life. It is all about how we finish.

In 2015, I sold a majority stake in Stearns Lending, the mortgage company I founded in 1989. The buyer was Blackstone, one of the world's most prominent investment firms. At the time, it was one of the largest acquisitions of a private lending company ever made in the US. When the sale closed, Stearns Lending was a leading provider of mortgage lending services in the wholesale, retail, correspondent, and strategic alliance sectors throughout the country, and our wholesale lending division was ranked number one nationwide. With more than 2,700 employees, Stearns originated loans in all fifty states. We also operated more than one hundred retail branches, where we provided loans directly to consumers. I was excited about aligning with a strong financial partner like Blackstone and believed they would provide us with the resources needed to continue executing the strategic plan we already had in place to increase both market share and profitability.

After the sale, I was no longer involved in the day-to-day operations. But I remember talking with Blackstone about many of the decisions the new team was making and how I believed they were headed in the wrong direction. It was then that they told me I needed to look at the big picture as a board member and investor and not as someone entrenched in the everyday details. I understood, but I couldn't help myself. I knew too much. My name was still on the door—actually, on the building—but you get what I'm saying. Stearns Lending was my legacy, and I cared deeply about the people I had left behind. I became extremely worried about the company's prospects and its future.

From the start of this new relationship, I frequently found myself trying to explain the mortgage business to a room full of investors who looked only at numbers and the bottom line. I was the only person in those meetings who understood the business from the inside out. I had grown the company from a mere seedling into a forest of mighty oaks. I knew the people who worked for me, their families, and our customers. Those relationships were irreplaceable. I put people above profits, whereas the suits cared *only* about the profits.

A few years before I sold the company, I took a week-long

Harvard Business School class through YPO, a global leadership group I belonged to that was composed of chief executives. The organization is driven by the shared belief that the world needs better leaders. During that week, we studied other businesses, their platforms, their leadership, and how they operated and thought. It felt as if I were in a room surrounded by giant brains whose thoughts were powered by supercomputers, while my thoughts were being powered by an endlessly spinning hamster wheel. I've always believed that all business is relational, but when you're the bank funding the largest single purchase most people will make in their entire lives, it's not just personal, it's intimate. There's so much more to successfully operating a business, especially *this* business. When all you do is crunch numbers in an effort to make the biggest buck, you can't possibly understand that there's a cost to that approach.

The culture dramatically changed over the next five years. In my opinion, the pressures the company faced were due mainly to a change in management style. This caused a domino effect that ultimately led to cash issues. No matter the cause, those pressures led Blackstone to think their only option was to file for reorganization. I saw things differently, of course. You see, Stearns Holdings, the parent company of Stearns Lending, still owed me tens of millions from the sale, which made me the company's biggest creditor besides its bondholders.

They filed for bankruptcy on July 9, 2019, the very same day the Discovery Network announced my new television show, *Undercover Billionaire*. I'll never forget the phone call I received from the *Wall Street Journal* asking if I was the new undercover billionaire or the man who had just filed for bankruptcy at Stearns Lending. My heart dropped to the floor when I heard that question. Once again, everything is all about timing, isn't it?

Whenever I've been faced with a sudden, unexpected change, I've acknowledged it but never dwelt on it. All you can do is live in the moment and plan for the future, whatever it may bring.

I've never thought of myself as a victim, in business or in life. Maybe it's a defense mechanism, and perhaps it isn't the healthiest way to look at things in some people's minds, but for me, it's the only way.

Blackstone did what they do. It wasn't personal; it was just another transaction.

Life is transactional.

Business is transactional.

That's just the way it is.

But I'm not that way. I am all about relationships.

Some deals go the way we want them to, but many don't. And that's okay. It wasn't going to do me any good to twist the knife in my own stomach by belaboring the point. And besides, I didn't want the negative outcome clouding my thoughts about my next steps. I felt horrible about what had transpired, but I refused to think about it for more than a few minutes. That's my limit when things like this happen.

Why?

There's always a silver lining. Even if you can't see it in the moment, it's there.

Here's what I mean.

When the company filed for bankruptcy, I was back in the game. I was no longer a shareholder, so my non-compete agreement was over. I had the chance to start anew. Instead of making me angry, beginning again excited and inspired me. In fact, it became the fuel in my rocket. They say success is the best revenge, and I believe that can be true. I now had the opportunity to show those suits in New York how it's really done.

In forty-eight hours, I packed up my family and moved from our home in Jackson Hole, Wyoming, back to Southern California, where it had all started. My two youngest daughters, Brooke and Taylor, weren't very excited about the sudden change, because it meant leaving their friends behind and starting in new schools. I'm not sure my wife, Mindy, was ready for the change either. One thing I can count on, though, is the unconditional love and support of my family, even if my spontaneity sometimes creates havoc.

I was ready, willing, and eager to get back into the mortgage business. To be clear, I wasn't taking over Stearns Lending. That ship had sunk. I wanted to start something fresh, do it differently, and build a new business from the ground up. I would call it *Kind Lending*. After everything I'd been through, I was ready to put kindness back into the mortgage business.

In late 2019, the economy was strong, the stock market was at an all-time high, and real estate all over the country was booming. I'd never felt better or surer of myself than I did then. After a five-year absence, Glenn Stearns was getting back into the business, and word quickly spread. I was stunned by the response, and even more surprised by the press coverage. I remember one headline referring to me as, "One of the biggest names in the mortgage business in the past thirty years."

Whoa.

Reading that practically took my breath away.

Maybe I had an impact after all.

When I heard something like that from people I didn't even know, I couldn't help but feel proud of what I'd accomplished, the company we'd built, and the lives I had a small hand in changing for the better.

So, yeah, I wanted to do that again—only *better*.

With the help of my friends at New American Funding, we were set to open March 16, 2020. I quickly staffed up with people I'd worked with in the past. Hundreds of applicants wanted to join the team, but I was being selective. I only wanted players who were happy about the opportunity we were creating.

In interviews, they'd ask, "Why is this company different?"

It wasn't about lower rates. Everyone had access to those.

We wanted people to laugh, enjoy themselves, and have a good time. If they couldn't have a good time and keep their sense of humor during the business's high-stress days, then we wouldn't be the right company for them. That's why I called our loan portal the "KWIKIE." It's fast and efficient. Other catchphrases that can be heard around our office include "It doesn't have to be this hard" and "We're easy." All are obvious plays on words. My wife, Mindy, is the CKO, or Chief Kindness Officer—although her original title was Chief Happiness

Officer, aka the "Chief Ho." As she says, "We're making sure we provide happy beginnings and happy endings." It didn't hurt that she was sleeping with the boss.

Okay, so you get the picture. We weren't planning to be your typical lender. We wanted to disrupt the industry in a positive way. We were developing this philosophy of fun, and everything we needed to support it, right up to our proposed opening date. We'd created a unique brand, assembled a new team, and written new software for our services when something truly unexpected brought the world to a screeching halt. You guessed it: COVID-19.

Interest rates were the lowest they'd been in years. Then, the government dropped them even further. When that happened, mortgage companies were suddenly inundated with refinancing applications. You'd think that would be great for lenders, but most couldn't handle the demand.

As the world stood still, so did our new business. We were set to open our doors in the same building, on the same floor, and in the same offices Stearns had left behind. We'd taken over the space, removed the old sign, and put up the new Kind Lending sign. Was it personal? You bet it was. But on the day we opened our doors for business, Gavin Newsom, the governor of California, closed down all nonessential businesses. While the mortgage industry was on fire, we would have to find new ways to work with staff members who were now sequestered at home. I had signed a lease for twenty-five thousand square feet, and only a handful of us were physically there during the early days of Covid.

It felt like the housing crisis of 2007–8 all over again.

Except for one thing.

The fact that I hadn't yet officially entered the market might have been the *best timing* of my life. Sure, I was missing out on a lot of business, but that business came with great fluctuations in the secondary market for certain types of loans, the need for huge amounts of cash to hedge swollen pipelines, and additional volatility in loan program stability.

I couldn't open.

No way, no how.

My competitors were all scrambling to navigate the situation, but we were able to slow down and assess how and when we would move forward. Talk about an exercise in patience. The easy choice would have been all systems go; the more challenging decision was holding back and waiting things out until we had a clearer picture of how we could effectively proceed.

I knew our people were worried, scared, and unsure of the future. What they needed was leadership. They deserved that. And that put a lot of pressure on me, because I knew they were relying on me to be that leader.

I wrote an email to my team. I reminded everyone that our main currency was our health, and that, *this too shall pass.*

I set this tone for my team and myself because I knew firsthand that life has a funny way of being a great equalizer, especially when it comes to our health. It can level us without a moment's notice. You see, five years earlier—when I sold Stearns Lending to Blackstone—I had retired, ready to see the world. And then… I was diagnosed with throat cancer. It was serious; I was even told it could be fatal. After battling cancer twice in five years, I decided to come out of retirement and get back into the game. And I was fired up.

Who could have predicted that I would return at the start of a pandemic? Let's face it, I thought cancer and a bankruptcy was enough. But, now, on the very day I was set to open, the Governor shut everything down?

Puhleeze.

Even I couldn't make this up.

Even with all I'd endured throughout my life—much of which you'll read about in the pages that follow—I had never experienced something like this and an economic collapse no one saw coming. No one had—at least not in my lifetime.

We were all trying to dodge an invisible enemy, one that didn't discriminate or care about what was happening in our lives or who we were. *That* I'd had some experience with during the previous five years. While I calmly reassured my team that everything would be all right and that we'd get through this, I knew I had to fly to Houston to see my doctors at MD Anderson Cancer Center, one of the top cancer hospitals in the country. I go there several times a year to stay on top of my condition—if not ahead of it.

As my plane took off from John Wayne Airport, I stared out the window, deep in thought. Life is about perspective. I was feeling tremendous pressure, measuring each circumstance by its level of concern, whether it was launching a new company, watching the catastrophic losses in the stock market, or managing my health. As the plane banked left over Santa

Ana, I could see the office building that, once bore my name at the top and now it said Kind Lending. I couldn't help but wondered just how kind the days ahead would actually be? With that thought, I lowered my window shade and sat back as the plane continued to climb. My ears popped, and I took a deep breath and swallowed hard.

My superpower has always been overcoming adversity. Give me a challenge and I'll give you solutions. I enjoy figuring things out. It's like a puzzle. I love being able to see a path from start to finish. It isn't always clear at first, but I always find a way forward. Sometimes I meditate in the shower, especially when I really need to think things through. I'm not sure I'm truly meditating so much as deeply thinking, trying to sort all the pieces out. I'm quiet and alone with my thoughts, looking for those evasive answers. I ask myself, "What's going on? What can I do? How can I make this work?" I address whatever issue is at the forefront. To me, that's time well spent. I believe our minds are so much more powerful than we know. We see and hear things every day that maybe we don't want to see and hear but that data is imported into our mind, where it ultimately helps us formulate answers, and make decisions. *Worry prides itself on its ability to co-opt our imagination.* Giving myself this solitude slows down my thoughts, focusing them on the present. No wild rides into the future, full of what-ifs and big projections. I'm in control of my thinking, which means that I can choose to concentrate on the things that, even in small doses, help me feel steadier.

When life gets tough, you have two choices: you can get

in the game or you can sit out. I've been called a lot of things over the years, but no one has ever accused me of running away from the fire. I'm the guy who not only runs toward it, I want to battle it, hose in hand. (A lot more on that later!) As a result, I've come to realize that every challenge is just a situation that can be figured out. It's a simple question, really: Can I do it or not? If it's going to kill me, then the answer is a quick and self-assured no. Otherwise, there's always a way to prevail.

To be certain, for many years in my youth, the idea that something *might* kill me was often my reason for doing it. Not that I had a death wish. I didn't. But I always wanted to prove that my mind and body were stronger than any pain the situation could present. Giving up, throwing in the towel, and calling it quits have just never been options.

That's the definition of grit—at least for me.

I was unusually tense when I arrived at MD Anderson that day.

I had never been nervous going into these types of appointments. But I was that morning. I was on pins and needles as I waited for my results.

Since I started treatment, I'd always told my doctor it was okay if he wanted to mess with me when giving me test results. I was serious, too; there was a part of me that thought if he walked into the room and said, "Glenn, I've got bad news," and then said, "I'm just kidding," it would be a big relief. As many times as I asked, my doctor just wouldn't comply with my slightly twisted request. He'd walk into the room and say, "Glenn . . . ah, I can't do it."

On this morning, he hesitated, but then he said, "Glenn, your tests look great. See you in six months." He smiled.

I think I let out an audible sigh of relief. I don't know for sure. But it definitely felt like the heaviest weight had been lifted off my shoulders—at least for another six months, anyway. And that was a good feeling. I had a lot to. I couldn't let anything get in my way.

CHAPTER TWO

THE ART OF GETTING LOST

Not till we are lost . . . do we begin to find ourselves.
—HENRY DAVID THOREAU

"LET'S GO, KIDS. We're getting in the car and we're going to drive until we get lost," my mom called out from our tiny kitchen.

Mom had a great love for adventure. She never needed a plan—she just wanted to get up and go. When she wanted to take those drives, my sister, Sue, and I piled into her Volkswagen Bug and off we went.

I was born on December 30, 1963, which was significant because Mom loved to sing "December, 1963 (Oh, What a Night)" by Frankie Valli and the Four Seasons, especially the part that went "Late December back in '63 . . ." as she drove us to who knows where. I was conceived on April Fools' Day, which set me up to be a practical joker for life. I loved that people teased me about being an April Fools' baby. I never thought of it as people laughing *at* me—I thought of it as people laughing *with* me. I never took it personally. I made a joke out of it. For me, sparring is fun. I think laughter and pranks are great ways for people to come together.

On those rides, Mom would drive to a farm or somewhere else out of the way, pull over to the side of the road, and turn to face the two of us in the back seat. Then she'd say, "Oh no—guess what, kids?"

"We're lost," we'd gleefully shout back.

And then we'd try to find our way home.

Sue and I were little then, and we loved every minute of it.

So many people live in fear, especially of things they don't understand or control. The idea of not knowing what's going to happen next is debilitating for them.

When I was eight, my family moved from our tiny apartment in Silver Spring, Maryland, to a small, eight-hundred-square-foot house near the railroad tracks in Rockville, Maryland. My dad wanted to get us out of the low-income neighborhood we were living in. The apartment had bars on the windows, there were dealers openly selling drugs on the streets, and I was never allowed to play outside after dark. My dad was a printer who often worked the graveyard shift, and over the years he was able to save enough money to buy a $14,000 house.

My younger sister, Sue, and I were born three years apart. We were close as kids, despite the fact that I picked on her relentlessly. I used to feed her gerbil turds, telling her they were candy. My mom whipped me with a belt when she caught me doing that. I was six years old—what did I know? At the time, I thought it was hilarious. When I was a teenager, I constantly coaxed Sue to loan me money to buy beer. Every time she ponied up, I'd call her a sucker and run out of the room, clutching the cash. I was mean to her, and those two incidents really stuck in her mind. I didn't know until many years later how much they really hurt her.

Even though I was a horrible brother early on, Sue always had my back, especially as we got older. Whenever someone—whether friend or foe—came after me, Sue would jump on their back and pummel them, despite her four-foot, eleven-inch stature. She didn't care how big they were. Sue didn't want anyone messing with me. One time there were some kids picking on me at the bus stop. Sue yelled at them to quit it, but they wouldn't. Everyone had put their books down as they waited for the bus, and Sue grabbed their books and threw them in the sewer. Afterward, I was so mad at her for doing that. While I appreciated her sticking up for me, I didn't think it was that big a deal. I could take the hazing. I didn't care if kids were harassing me, not at all. But she did.

By fourth grade, I was really struggling in school. I didn't really understand why, but letters and numbers were getting all jumbled up in my head. When we started studying mythology, I couldn't read the big words. All the letters flowed together and didn't make any sense. It was extremely frustrating. My teacher, Mrs. Kernan, tried to help me by giving me extra homework to do over the summer. She encouraged me to learn to recognize and read words like "difficulty" and "organization" as exercises to help train my brain. I remember going over those words and more all summer long, but I just couldn't seem to get it, so they held me back. I was humiliated when I flunked the fourth grade and had to repeat it the next year. I thought everyone would look at me and think I was stupid. I wasn't; I just couldn't seem to focus and retention was nearly impossible.

When I went back to school in September, I saw my previous classmates, all of whom were now in fifth grade. They were standing together while I was grouped with the rising third graders, bracing myself for repeating the fourth grade. At the time, this was by far the worst moment of my life. I felt like such a loser. It was hard to go to school because I felt as if people were always looking down on me.

Thank God for my mom. She was the neighborhood favorite. She genuinely cared about people and was kind and loving to everybody. She absolutely adored every girlfriend I ever had like they were her own daughters. She was so accepting and always did her best to steer me in the right direction, which wasn't easy because I spent most of my youth pretty lost. She had no problem telling me when I was wrong, but always in a way that prevented me from feeling like I had disappointed her. The mere thought of letting my mother down was utterly unbearable. And yet I know there must have been many times throughout my life when I did. Sometimes I'd be pissed about what she was saying, but deep down I knew there was great truth to the adage "Mom knows best." Certainly my mom did. She wasn't perfect, but she was perfect to me.

Mom may have always been fun and the life of the party,

but she was also my touchstone, my go-to person, especially when I needed a shoulder to lean on or an ear to bend. There were so many times I broke down in front of her without ever feeling judged or misunderstood. She would take my calls anytime, day or night. Even when I was drunk off my ass, Mom would stay on the phone for as long as it took until I fell asleep and she knew I was safe. I could call her at three in the morning, and she never once hung up on me.

As I grew up, there weren't many moments of joy in our home, but those car rides with Mom always stuck with me.

Why?

They taught me not to be afraid of the unknown. So often, we fear what we don't know. Not me. I learned at an early age to be excited for whatever was around the corner. We can't always see what's ahead, but oftentimes it's full of opportunity and hope, even if we can't feel it in the moment. It's a simple choice, really: Are you afraid or excited about what's coming next? Mom somehow understood the value in that and passed the lesson along to my sister and me at a very early age.

As I got older, I began to understand that she also took us on those long car rides to get us out of the house and away from my dad. He wasn't a very happy man back then. You see, my dad was an alcoholic and a drug addict. And he also had a mean temper. That's the guy I knew growing up. While I don't recall him ever hitting me, he would get in my face and yell as loud as he could; he threatened me, too. Often. There was an incident when I was in high school when things got so heated that we choked each other out. Neither of us backed down.

I knew one of us was going to get seriously hurt—or worse. I remember thinking, *Man, that guy is strong.* I didn't expect my dad to go at me like that. I thought he was going to kill me, or I was going to kill him unless one of us caved, so I eventually surrendered—something I rarely did back then.

My general refusal to back down, a trait I inherited from my dad, became an issue for me as I grew up. My friends used to say, "The problem with Glenn is that he won't give up." I didn't see that as a problem. I prided myself on never stopping. I looked at it as fierce determination.

My dad worked at a local printing house where magazines such as *Architectural Digest* were printed. Since he usually took the overnight shift, he was gone by the time I got home from school and asleep by the time I left the following day, so I didn't really see him a lot growing up. When I did, he was usually drunk or high. We hunted and fished together sometimes, mostly on weekends. A lot of the money Dad made—which wasn't much—went up his nose.

Whenever I traveled with my dad, it was usually just a reason for him to party with his friends Leonard and John. Occasionally he'd take me to a remote mountain cabin in West Virginia where we could hunt. My dad had an old Ford pickup with a cap over the bed. He put two cots in the truck bed, and I slept next to the tiny cabin while he and all his buddies were inside. It was freezing. I can remember asking, "Why can't I go inside?" through chattering teeth.

I didn't know it then, but my dad didn't want me to see him and his friends doing drugs. Eventually, he'd have mercy and allow me to come in out of the cold. I would have to sleep on the floor in another room while he and his buddies snorted cocaine and drank until they passed out.

One time we were at the cabin with Leonard, who brought his daughter. She and I were playing outside together when, out of nowhere, she bit me. We were little, maybe eight years old. Crying, I went inside to tell my dad and Leonard what had happened. Leonard motioned for his daughter to come inside, and he bit her. I was completely shocked.

"Don't ever bite anyone," he said wagging his finger in her tiny face.

That was his way of parenting.

A couple of years later, while on another hunting trip at the same cabin, I was sleeping on the couch when I woke to see Leonard get up and go outside to pee in the middle of the night. He was so drunk that he fell forward and passed out in the snow. I waited for over half an hour for him to get back up, but he never did. I opened the sliding door, grabbed his feet, and dragged him into the cabin, where he slept on the floor. Leonard awoke the next morning having no idea what had happened.

John once fell asleep at the wheel and plowed his car under a tractor trailer, spending more than a year in the hospital recovering from his injuries. Even that didn't slow him down. After he got out, he would still sometimes fall asleep while driving after he'd partied.

These guys were hard-core—and they were my influences at a very young age.

Every year, my dad and I went on a fishing trip to the Shad Landing area of Pocomoke River State Park in Snow Hill, Maryland, about 150 miles away from our home. We would leave early in the morning and spend the whole weekend on the river in the small aluminum boat my dad hauled behind his pickup truck. I'd fish and swim while my dad drank and drank, until he was so drunk that he could barely keep his head up. On one trip, he got behind the wheel of his old Ford and attempted to drive us home. I sat next to my dad, watching him nod off as the truck veered across the centerline and into the oncoming lane. I was scared for my life. This wasn't the first time he'd done this. It was all too common. Only this time, I could tell he was actually going to pass out. When I saw his head lean against the window and his eyes close, I grabbed the wheel and steered.

"Dad, Dad . . ." I kept saying, hoping to wake him.

He would open his eyes for a minute or two and then he'd passed out again, never taking his foot off the accelerator.

Route 50, the road we were traveling on, was relatively straight for most of the trip. All I had to do was keep the truck in our lane. I did a pretty good job until we reached the Chesapeake Bay Bridge. The Chesapeake is just over four miles long. Even seasoned drivers go white-knuckled when driving across it. I was petrified I would steer our truck off the bridge as it bounced off the guardrails. I did the best I could to keep us on the road, but eventually we crashed.

Thankfully, no one was hurt, but the police took Dad away in handcuffs. I was horrified to see him being escorted off by the cops to a waiting patrol car, his hands bound behind him. I even pounced on one of the officers, trying to beat him up, screaming, "Leave my dad alone!" as they placed him in the back seat. It was no use. They drove him away in one car and took me to the station in another. My mom wasn't very happy when she got the call saying Dad had been arrested for drunk driving with me in the car. Nor was she surprised.

Watching my dad get arrested that night was traumatic. And it made me angry. I despised him for being drunk all the time, and for his fierce temper. His drinking had almost killed us. If that wasn't enough to make him think about where his life was going, then what would be?

My mom refused to bail Dad out of jail. She was so mad at him. Perhaps a few days in the clink would help him come to his senses, to see what he'd almost lost.

And it did.

Dad quit drinking for four years after that. Then one day, I came home, walked through the front door, and found my mom and dad sitting on the couch watching TV. There was an open can of beer on the coffee table in front of him.

"What's that?" I asked, pointing at the beer can.

"It's one beer," my mom said. "He can have a beer, son. It's just one."

I was devastated. How could she? How could *he?*

"No, he can't. One beer will lead to a thousand beers. He cannot drink!" I shouted at both of them.

My mom did her best to calm me, but I wasn't buying into her enabling. How could she have allowed this?

In a moment, my dad went from being sober to being a full-fledged drunk all over again. That's when my world changed completely.

What I didn't fully realize then was that my mom was also an alcoholic. In fact, alcoholism and addiction ran through both sides of our family. Mom drank like a fish, although I never saw it as unhealthy, mostly because she wasn't mean like my dad. She was fun. When she drank, we would laugh all the time. Mom and her sister, my aunt Joy, just seemed happy to me. They were always together and seemed like they were having a good time. My dad, on the other hand, drank and then got nasty.

By the time I was fifteen years old, my dad's challenges with drugs and alcohol embarrassed me to no end. I used to have friends over all the time, but after one too many incidents, I stopped. Other kids' parents weren't smoking pot or doing lines in front of their kids or their kids' friends. My dad sort of tried to hide it from me, but he wasn't very good at it. One time I was at Lake Needwood with a friend. I had my dad's bow and quiver. We dumped the arrows out on the grass, and a bag of weed fell out with them.

"Your dad smokes pot?" my friend asked.

"No!" I denied the obvious. I was mortified. The older I got, the more I started to understand that he was riddled with addiction. I didn't excuse it. By then I was just really disappointed.

The only behavior I knew was from watching my parents. So, of course, it didn't take me long to start following in their footsteps, especially when it came to alcohol.

THE ART OF GETTING LOST

Some of the best days of my adolescent years were spent at Congressional Roller-Skating Rink in Rockville. The rink was once an old airplane hangar, which Betty and Louie Bargmann bought and converted into a roller rink in 1956. There they coached up-and-coming skaters and welcomed amateurs during open skating. Business boomed. There wasn't a better place in town to learn to skate. And it cost only a dollar! As far as I know, they raised the price just once, by a whopping fifty cents, still making it affordable fun for everyone.

Congressional turned out more national champions than any other rink in the country. The Bargmanns were especially successful in coaching pairs and freestyle skaters. I admired the beautiful choreography and the extreme athleticism required to spin around the floor in a controlled and precise manner. I would watch the couples twirl and flip and think to myself, *Wow, someday that might be me.*

The idea of holding a pretty girl's hand, gently sliding my arm around her waist during a couples skate, and gliding around the wooden floor together to the beat of whatever music was playing seemed really cool. So, I started spending a lot of time practicing at the rink. I would skate as often as possible during the two open sessions they had on weekends and at night. Like everybody in 1977, I spent every Friday and Saturday night boogying down to Donna Summer, Yvonne Elliman, and Earth, Wind & Fire. Roller disco was very popular back then.

By the time I was thirteen, I had actually gotten pretty good and began competing with a partner, Tracey Earhart. We skated cha-chas, tangos, and all sorts of dances. Tracey and

I practiced six nights a week, although she was much more dedicated than I was. She used to get so mad at me during competitions, especially when I wasn't doing what she wanted. She'd smile a great big grin, and through her teeth she'd say, "Point your damn toe!" just before the music would start. I was having fun. I didn't care about being a great skater; I just loved being in the room with my friends.

In the mornings, I'd go to the rink before school for lessons, and then again after school to skate in the open sessions. Afterward, a bunch of us would pile into the car of the manager of the roller rink. We'd grab a bite to eat at a local hangout and then come back to skate the eight-to-ten-thirty session. We did that six or seven days a week for two years.

As much as I loved skating, there were other reasons I enjoyed being at the roller rink. On weekends, it had the best action in town. There was nothing better than sitting on one of the wooden benches next to the water cooler, lacing up my skates, and checking out all the pretty girls. Kathy Ellis and Mimi Callahan were there every weekend. They were two of the hottest girls I'd ever seen. They both wore shiny pink lip gloss that smelled like bubble gum. I fantasized for months about what it would taste like. Then one day at the rink, Kathy leaned over and kissed me. I was shocked and excited by her boldness. They say you never forget your first kiss, and it's true. I was instantly smitten. I fell for her fast and hard. I'd had the biggest crush on this girl, and now here she was, kissing me. And for the first couple of months, everything was great. Then, about a year later, a new girl caught my eye. Her name was

Kathy, and I thought was cute. Kathy Kuehl was a fantastic skater. She skated with Mike Minimum. I looked up to both of them because I really respected their talent. I was attracted to that winning mentality—and I won't deny it, I was very attracted to Kathy. I broke up with Kathy Ellis so I could date Kathy Kuehl. I knew my decision to move on would hurt Kathy Ellis, but what I didn't realize was how much I would regret that choice, or how quickly.

Kathy Kuehl and I instantly became girlfriend and boyfriend. She was almost sixteen, and I had just turned fourteen. So, yeah, you could also say she was my first older woman. To be fair, she was also my first, well, everything. It feels pretty darn great when you're a fourteen-year-old boy on the receiving end of an older girl's attention. It certainly had its perks. Before I knew it, we were sneaking behind the roller rink to mess around all the time. I was doing stuff I'd never done before, and I liked the way it felt.

I began spending time at Kathy's house, and she would come over to mine. Within weeks we were having sex—often. My parents never actually had "the talk" with me, at least not that I recall. I was young and naive, and honestly, I didn't care about anything but skating and getting laid. All I knew about the birds and the bees was that girls had periods, and if I had sex with Kathy just before her time of the month, there was a chance I could get her pregnant. As far as I knew, any other time was fair game. At least, that is what I thought.

What we were doing felt risky and fun. I didn't think there was anything wrong with it. I thought I was living the life.

A few months after I started dating Kathy Kuehl, I realized that I really missed Kathy Ellis. I desperately wanted her back. It got to the point where I didn't want anyone else but her and didn't want her being with anyone else but me, and I told her that. Seeing how happy she was when I confided that was the best feeling I'd ever had. Kathy Ellis had big, beautiful eyes. That look of joy was something I've never forgotten. I thought I'd be with her the rest of my life. Okay, sure, I was only fourteen, but that was how I felt.

I had to break it off with Kathy Kuehl, and fast. We'd been dating for only a short time. I wasn't emotionally involved, and I didn't think she was, either. When I told her it was over, she looked me right in the eye and blurted out, "I'm pregnant."

My heart sank like an anchor.

Was she serious?

I knew she'd kept talking, but after she said "I'm pregnant," I felt as if the walls of the room were closing in on me. There was no sound except for the heavy, loud thumping in my chest. I didn't know what to do or say.

"Whoa." I think that was the only word that came out of my mouth until I asked, "What are we going to do?"

"What do you mean? I'm having the baby," she stated. In fact, she was almost defiant about it. She gave me no choice— no say in the matter whatsoever. I was stunned and scared.

I wasn't ready to be a father at fourteen.

I'd been plotting my way out of that relationship for weeks, and now we'd be inextricably connected forever. I pleaded with Kathy to think it through.

Was this really what she wanted?

I didn't think she could corral me back into her world until she said, "You've got responsibilities."

And then she began to cry.

Here's a little secret about me: I'm utterly helpless in front of women who cry. I turn to mush. And it was clear that Kathy wasn't going to change her mind. I didn't know what to do. I felt lost and terribly afraid. I also wasn't ready to tell my parents about Kathy being pregnant. I wasn't sure how they would react. And for the moment, I didn't want to know.

I didn't know it at the time, but this wouldn't be the only occasion when a woman's courage would change my life.

Instead of going home, I met up with a couple of buddies who could tell something was wrong. These guys were my older friends, all of them sixteen or seventeen years old. When I told them about the baby, I thought they'd have some good insight about how I should handle things. Yeah, not so much.

That weekend, the guys and I drove to Triadelphia Lake, about an hour from my house. It was a place where we could swim and relax. I found it really comforting to be there. Even so, it didn't take long for my bravado to turn into tears. I didn't want the guys to see me crying, so I hid my angst as best I could.

A week before, I'd heard the guys talking and using the word "impotent." I didn't understand what that meant. I thought it was street slang for "important." When they told me what it meant, all I could do was laugh. They started calling me "Impo." Ironically, when we all went to the lake, they gave me a tight-fitting T-shirt with my new nickname plastered across the torso. I thought it was funny—sort of. There was a certain irony in wearing those scarlet letters on my chest. The relentless teasing went on for nine months. I was now known as the kid with a baby on the way. When you're fourteen, there are much more desirable ways to stand out in a crowd.

When I got back from the trip to Triadelphia Lake, I thought the best thing to do was to stick with my routine. That included going to a school dance, where I knew I would see Terri Lonon. Terri and I were in eighth grade together. I'd always thought she was attractive, and hey, I wasn't dating anyone at the moment, so why wouldn't I try to meet up with her? Okay, I know what you must be thinking, but I was confused. And I certainly didn't want to accept the reality of what was happening, so I did what a lot of people do—lived in denial. If I didn't acknowledge the elephant in the room, maybe—just maybe—I wouldn't have to deal with it.

After the dance my mom picked me up. She could tell something was on my mind. For weeks she'd been saying to me, "If there's anything you want to talk about, Glenn, I'm here for you." She'd noticed that I'd been sinking into a deep depression, but she didn't know why.

My mom was a very intuitive woman. She was the kind of mother who always enjoyed getting to know my friends and girlfriends. She wouldn't go to bed, even when that was exactly what we wanted her to do—especially when I had girls over. But she and I were very close, and she could always tell when something was wrong. This time, though, I had to come clean and tell her what was happening.

"Mom, Kathy is pregnant, and I don't know what to do," I said in a voice just louder than a whisper. As I said before, the last thing I ever wanted to do was disappoint my parents, especially my mom.

She began to cry, which made me feel even worse.

"Please don't tell Dad," I pleaded.

She didn't say a word for the rest of the drive.

The next morning, I could hear my parents talking in the kitchen as I lay in bed. Our house was eight hundred square feet, so there wasn't a lot of privacy. When they finished their conversation, I heard my dad walking toward my room, and then he opened my door.

I stood up and said, "I don't care what you do to me. If you want to put me up for adoption or stop feeding me, no matter what you do, you can't hurt me."

Those were my exact words.

Just for a moment, Dad was quiet; then he said, "Look, son, the one thing I can tell you is it's all going to blow over. You just need to realize that. I know you're in a dark place now, but this too shall pass."

I was dumbfounded by his reaction and his words of wisdom. I hadn't seen that coming, and I didn't really under-stand why he reacted the way he did.

Looking back, I can see that he was right. It's often very hard to see the light when you're in the middle of the storm. Ever since Kathy had told me she was pregnant, I'd been seeing only blackness. I hadn't considered that the feeling might someday pass. My dad, who'd lived a lot more life than I had, understood that no matter how hard things might appear in the moment, eventually the storm lets up and the sun comes out. It would take me some time to understand what he meant, but I've never forgotten those words or his support.

As he walked out of my room, he stopped, turned back toward me, and said, "I'll tell you one thing: if it ever happens again, I'll knock your block off." And I knew he meant it.

He also made it clear that I was an adult now. I'd have to figure out how to take care of the baby and provide for it.

There was no hiding from the truth. Kathy was pregnant, and we were going to have a baby together. I was going to have to accept that fact.

My top priority was figuring out how I was going to tell Kathy Ellis. I knew it would break her heart, because it was breaking mine.

I met her at the roller rink later that day. I asked if we could talk for a moment. She was so happy and said yes. We walked out to the parking lot, where we got into a friend's car.

"There's something I need to tell you. You know I'm no longer with Kathy Kuehl and I want to be with you; however, something's come up," I said. I was afraid to tell her the truth. I didn't want to ruin the moment, though I was about to.

"What is it, Glenn?" she asked.

"Kathy is pregnant." The words just fell from my lips.

Tears filled her eyes. Those big, beautiful eyes.

I could tell she was trying not to cry. She just looked at me with the most pained expression. I sat there, knowing our future had evaporated that very moment. I never stopped loving Kathy Ellis. She was the first love of my life. What was I going to do?

CHAPTER THREE

A YEAR, A MONTH, A WEEK, AND A DAY

*The only reason for time is so
everything doesn't happen at once.*
—ALBERT EINSTEIN

AS THE MONTHS went by, Kathy Kuehl stopped skating but still came to the roller rink every day to socialize. It was a constant reminder of what was to come. I did my best to be kind and supportive, but I'm sure it wasn't enough.

Like my mom and dad, Kathy's parents accepted our situation. No one in our families gave us a hard time about her being pregnant or choosing to have the baby. My mom and her mom became friends over the impending arrival of their first grandchild.

Kathy gave birth to our daughter, Charlene, on December 29, 1978—one day before my fifteenth birthday. Back then, people weren't allowed to be in the delivery room with the mother to be until after the baby was born. So, like most first-time fathers, I paced the length of the waiting room until a nurse came out holding the baby.

The new grandmas ran over, both reaching for the newborn. I was bobbing my head to the left and right, darting around them to try to get a glimpse of my daughter. I felt more like an older brother than I did a new dad. I don't believe the nurse realized I was the father. She showed the two mothers the baby, all but ignoring me. They cooed over this tiny little thing, talking their best baby talk. I never really got a good look at Charlene, let alone a chance to hold her.

I'll admit, I was very confused. Only a few hours earlier, I was at the roller rink hanging out with a group of my friends. And now, here I was, in the hospital meeting my *daughter*. It felt like it wasn't real. But it was. Very.

A few weeks after Kathy gave birth, I bumped into one of her best friends at the rink. She walked up and slapped me in the face. She hit me harder than I'd ever been hit.

"What did you do that for?" I asked.

"I slapped you because you won't acknowledge that you have a child," she screamed.

At first, I was shocked. She didn't know what she was talking about. The baby had been coming to my house regularly, and I was now working part-time at the local movie theater to help pay for diapers and other necessities. I thought I was doing all the right things. Many years later, I finally grasped why Kathy (and, ultimately, Charlene) felt that I had never paid my way. While I was working to provide for them,

I gave my parents (not Kathy) the money to buy necessities. As a baby, Charlene was at our house during the day on Mondays through Fridays. Kathy would take her home at night. My parents used the money I earned to buy Charlene whatever was needed when she was with us. Kathy was never aware of this—certainly not then. What I realized, though, was that people were judging me more for choosing not to be with Kathy. And they were probably right. In my mind, I had moved on.

After my daughter was born, everywhere I went, I thought people expected me to be an adult. I felt like they were pointing at me and saying, "Look at the little kid who already has a kid." The jokes were endless, and sometimes really hurtful—and not just for me but for my mom, too. Everyone knew I'd gotten Kathy pregnant. Suddenly, my family was also marked, not just me. Mom was working as a gym coach at our school and often felt as though the nuns looked down on her, especially for having a messed-up son. While walking down the hall one day, she heard someone call out, "Janet, come in here." It was Sister Bonifice. She was reputed to be the meanest nun at school. Her hands were arthritic, so she used to hold a ruler with just her thumb and pinkie and threaten to beat us for any reason. She could hit hard, too. When my mom was summoned into that classroom, she panicked. While almost everyone else ignored or shunned our family, Mom knew that wouldn't be the case with Sister Bonifice. She always acted very intentionally. Mom gulped, took a deep breath, and walked into the classroom.

"Close the door," Sister Bonifice demanded.

My mom's heart was beating out of her chest. She did

what she was told and then turned to face the sister. "All of these families, teachers, and students who are passing judgment and laughing behind your back: screw 'em," the nun said. "Hold your head up high. Don't let them get you down."

Mom was speechless. She had expected the wrath of God. Instead, she received unexpected support.

It was years before my mom told me that story, but it has become one of my favorite examples of why you should never judge a book by its cover. You don't always know the reasons why others build walls around themselves. What you can be sure of, though, is that those walls are usually built for self-protection, making their prickly behavior more about them than us. This realization has come back to me so many times in my life, and it has always helped me see things through the other person's lens, not just my own.

After Charlene was born, I was drinking all the time. I had just turned fifteen, had become a father and was trying to find my way. I guess it was how I hid my pain. Like my dad, I would drink every night until I passed out. I woke up in laundromats, in parking lots, and on random lawns around the neighborhood. What did I know about responsibility, parenting, and good decision-making?

Apparently not much. I was becoming a seriously dysfunctional human. I had a lot of issues to resolve, especially my drinking and the inevitable anger that followed. I was doing my best to drink my problems away, but the trouble was, my drinking only created more problems. It complicated everything, which I couldn't understand while I had a bottle in my hand. Rational thinking went right out the window. Turning to drugs or alcohol to solve your problems is like drinking poison and thinking your enemy will die. It was self-destructive behavior. If you ever get to a place where you don't care anymore, know that the way you respond will define you *and* the outcome. We all make choices. Each decision sets the path we walk. And at that time, I was making some pretty poor choices.

When Charlene was born, I suddenly had huge responsibilities, but my parents never set any boundaries for me. It didn't matter what I did; nobody cared where I was or what I was doing. Worse, I also had uncontrollable rage brewing inside me that I didn't know how to manage. I was mad at the world. I didn't know how to handle everything that was happening around me. I'd get into fistfights all the time. Sometimes they were harmless, but other times they were born out of fury. I felt like I'd become the laughingstock of the community. Even so, I had a lot of friends.

The first time I met Shane and Cliff, two guys who became lifelong friends was in ninth grade. They both came up through the public school system. I had just transferred from St. Mary's, a Catholic school in Rockville. My parents had wanted to keep me in Catholic school, but after I'd gotten Kathy pregnant, they felt it wasn't a great fit for me anymore. Shane, Cliff, and I didn't know one another well, but soon enough it was clear that we all had a lot in common—mostly that we were wild and reckless. Cliff had endured a lot of trauma as a kid. He and his brother witnessed their grandma shoot and kill their grandpa with a shotgun. To say they'd experienced some really bad things growing up is an understatement. Their dad was an alcoholic and a rough, mean man. Their lives were really dysfunctional. But I loved Cliff, because under his tough exterior, there was a really great person.

When Shane found out I had a daughter, he was totally freaked out. Once the shock wore off, however, we clicked, and we've been best friends ever since. Shane has a way about him that's just *fun*. He celebrates life and lives it to the fullest. I appreciate that.

Shane, Cliff, and I were inseparable. We partied together; we drank and experimented with drugs, although drugs were never really my thing. Shane and I would get into fights all the time. My dad would say, "Go outside and duke it out." That's how we settled things back then. It didn't mean anything. When we were done beating on each other, we'd usually end up hugging it out and having a drink. On more occasions than I can count, one of us actually worried that we'd hurt the other. There was one time when we broke my mom's kitchen table during a particularly heated fight. Shane had a cast on his arm and was choking me out, pushing against my throat until I almost couldn't breathe. I still have the scar from where he gashed my neck with his cast. I was bleeding all over the place. In self-defense, I bit his nipple. I clenched down and wouldn't let go. My teeth actually met. I know it must have hurt, but he didn't give up. He earned a lot of respect from me for his perseverance that day. In a way, our scuffles were how we showed each other we cared. They usually started when one of us said something stupid, and before we knew what was happening, punches were thrown. But the anger would never last. We'd rough each other up, throw each other against a wall, and five minutes later we'd be eating burgers together. We lived in a rough world back then. Fighting was just part of what guys did. It was mostly about reputation, honor, and not being a wimp. So many of the experiences Shane and I lived through bonded us for life.

During this period of my life, the more judged I felt, the harder I partied. And the boys were always right there by my side. And when people weren't making fun of me, it felt like every pedophile in town was coming after me. I'm not sure why, but everywhere I went, men would hit on me. I had really long hair and was, I suppose, cute. I was sexually active, and everyone in town knew it. I guess something about the way I moved through the world invited come-ons from men, especially older guys. I was never interested, and yet I found myself in these awkward situations more times than I could count.

One night I was hanging out with an older friend. He had a Mustang and would drive us around. On that particular evening, it was just the two of us cruising through town. He started laughing.

"What's so funny?' I asked.

"My friend and I have a bet to see who can give a blow job to a guy first," he said.

I just rolled my eyes. He wasn't going to win with me, that was for damn sure.

"I just want to win the bet, man. I hate losing. I'll even give you the money." He was doing his best to entice me, but I wasn't having it.

We drove to his house so he could change into his work uniform. He had a job at the local pinball arcade, where a lot of kids liked to hang out.

"Glenn, come on up here," he yelled from his bedroom.

"No, it's okay," I shouted back.

"Come on, it's cool."

I didn't know how to say no, so I reluctantly trudged up the stairs. When I got to his bedroom, he was holding a girlie magazine. It might have been *Playboy* or *Penthouse*.

"Have a look at this!" He was so excited to show me the naked pictures that I thought for a moment I'd misread his intentions. He didn't bring up the bet again, so I shrugged it off.

We drove to the pinball arcade, where he dropped me off.

A week later, I met Cliff at the arcade. Cliff and the guy with the Mustang went for a ride and I stayed back to play a game, as I had by this point completely written that guy off as a bad dude. When they returned, Cliff stood in the middle of the place, pointed at the other guy, and yelled, "He's a fag. He tried to suck my dick."

The guy ran out the door.

I started laughing. Maybe it was a douchey response, but that's what happened.

"Did he say he wanted to win a bet and that he'd give you the money?" I asked.

Cliff hauled off and punched me in the face.

"What the fuck? You knew about it, Stearns?"

I did. At the time, I didn't really think it was that big a deal. I didn't see them as pedophiles or as people who would hurt kids, at least not back then. I knew they weren't the most stable guys, but I didn't think they were dangerous. Cliff had been exposed to some pretty awful things in his life, events no kid should ever witness. I suppose I cut Cliff some slack for hitting me because of that. Sadly, his life continued to be mired in pain and he has since spent most of his life in and out of jail.

The manager of the Congressional roller rink would host a skate-a-thon once a year to raise money for us kids who skated. We'd go for twenty-four hours, dancing, free skating, and playing broom hockey. He would act as a chaperone. He was the local host for the annual *Jerry Lewis MDA Labor Day Telethon*, too, so he was a hometown celebrity in Rockville. He was talented and very articulate, and everybody liked the guy. I thought he was really cool. If you were a kid in Rockville, you looked up to him.

He must have been in his thirties when we were hanging around the rink. Sometimes on weekends after open skate we'd go to Bob's Big Boy. If you were lucky enough, you got to pile into his car. He had a Chevy Malibu that could seat two kids up front and three in the back. Another kid and I always rode shotgun. It was like we were anointed kings, and that was our throne. The kids in the back rotated out, but this one kid and I were always up front. I felt so privileged, and thought the other kids saw us as his favorites.

One day, out of the blue, the roller rink manager came up to me and said, "Glenn, you're going to be a leader one day. I can tell." Coming from him, that meant the world to me. My dad wasn't the kind of man who would give me that type of encouragement. Given my behavior, I wasn't sure I believed him, but it sure felt good to hear. It made me feel really proud that this man, whom I respected and admired, thought of me that way. Oddly, it also embarrassed me because I didn't believe I deserved the compliment. I was such a screwup. How could he see leadership qualities in the way I'd been acting?

Right around the time Kathy had the baby, that manager left Congressional to take a job at another rink thirty miles away. A lot of us would skate there one or two nights a week just to see him. One time, he suggested that my buddy and I spend the night at his place so we could be at his rink all weekend.

"Okay," I said. Again, I didn't think twice about it.

We went to his house and ate dinner. When it came time to go to bed, he said, "Why don't you two share the bed, and I'll sleep on the floor." Again, it didn't really strike me as odd. In fact, I thought it was a kind gesture—that is, until I woke up in the middle of the night to find this guy touching my ass. He was rubbing it like a masseuse, which was weird and very disappointing. He was my idol, my mentor. I didn't want to make a big deal out of it, but I pushed his hand away—many times—until I finally shoved him so hard that he fell off the bed. I wasn't into it. I pretended like I was sleeping the whole time because I didn't want to embarrass him. I was annoyed and worried about what might happen next, but I didn't confront the situation.

I never said a word about it the next morning, either. When we got to the rink later that day, I kept my distance. After that, I pretty much never talked to him again. I didn't realize it at the time, but now I can see clearly that the roller rink was a place where a lot of young people gathered, so it was a magnet for pedophiles. What better setup for someone who liked to prey on young children? It was the 1970s, and society was naiver than it is today. I don't think it's ever okay to sexually assault children or anyone else. I'm certain I wasn't the only boy who was touched. It's never a one-time thing. And maybe I should have spoken up so it wouldn't happen to another kid. I was just a kid myself and at the time, I didn't understand the bigger picture. What he did was wrong, and I know it today. Pretending nothing happened doesn't mean nothing happened. It's never okay to put your hands on someone if it isn't consensual. Never.

These were strange days indeed. And through it all, I never did give up on Kathy Ellis. Despite all the crazy stuff that was happening in my life, I missed her. One night, I called her on the phone at around two in the morning and told her I wanted to see her. She said I couldn't come over, but I did anyway. I didn't have a car at the time, so I ran the nine miles from my house to hers. In my mind, I envisioned a romantic embrace. I imagined that everything would go back to normal. I had dated her for exactly one year, one month, one week, and one day. All I wanted was one more day.

When I got to her home, I gently tapped on her window.

She didn't respond.

I knocked a little harder.

She never opened her window.

That was her way of saying goodbye.

That hurt my heart in ways I didn't expect, and in ways I had never felt before.

Twenty-five years later, Kathy Kuehl called to tell me that Kathy Ellis had called her out of the blue. "You ruined my life," she'd said. She explained that if Kathy hadn't gotten pregnant and had the baby, she was certain that she and I would have ended up together. A year later, Kathy Ellis died. And when she did, I have to admit that a piece of my heart died, too.

By the time I graduated high school, my mom had had enough of my dad's drinking. She decided to leave him, and she did—that very day. I came home and found my sister and mom crying so hard. Through her tears, my mom told me she was done. Seeing my dad slumped in his armchair, I seized the moment and said, "Let's go. Let's get you out of this house. Go to Uncle Bernie's." Bernie was my mom's brother.

After I got my mom and Sue to leave, my dad stood up and stumbled toward me. He could barely stand, let alone walk.

"You're a fucking disgrace," I said right to his face. "You make me sick." I was ready to kill him, I was so mad. "Do you realize why no one comes over anymore? Because I'm so embarrassed by you. You're a fucking drunk." At this point I was nose to nose with the old man.

My dad took a deep breath and, spitting in my face, he yelled, "HA, HA, HA!" as loud as he could.

"Do you know why you're laughing?" I asked. "Because you know I'm right."

He stopped, took a long hard look at me and mumbled, "You're absolutely right."

"Go to bed." It's all I could think to say. He looked so sad and pathetic.

Dad turned around, went to his bedroom, and landed face down on his mattress.

My mom and sister were sitting on the front porch and had heard the entire exchange. When I walked outside, my mother pleaded with me to come with them, but I didn't. With tears streaming down my cheeks, I told them to just go. They left and my mom never came back. Ever.

After Mom walked out that day, Dad never drank or did drugs again. He started going to AA and attended meetings ever since.

While helping my mom and sister out of that house was a good call, my teenage years were filled with, well, a lot of bad calls. At one point, I lost my driving privileges because my license had been suspended so many times for speeding. I didn't care. I still drove. I had the coolest baby-blue 1969 302 Camaro Z28 Rally Sport with white racing stripes up the hood and down the back. Chevrolet made only twenty of the Z Sports with a 302 engine like the one I had. That car was the envy of everyone in my high school. At the time, I had no idea how rare it was or how valuable it would be someday. I got it from my dad's friend, who sold it to me for $1,500 when the engine broke. I was working at King Pontiac GMC at the time. When I showed the car to the mechanics there, they offered to fix it for me. I drove that car everywhere. That Camaro was the ultimate muscle carl; I felt like a total stud driving it. I wasn't going to let it sit there and not be driven.

INTEGRITY

When you're young and stupid, you think you're invincible.

One weekend, Shane and I decided to drive to Ocean City for a party. We met a group of girls who wanted to have a good time. We were game, so we got a bottle of grain alcohol and spiked a jug of punch, which got all of us drunk. When we reached the rental house where one of the girls was staying, we poured the punch into a large silver bowl we found in their dining room, thinking we'd be fancy. The girls got so wasted that they were throwing up all over the place. We were grossed out and decided to leave. We were pretty tanked ourselves, but we drove anyway. Shane wasn't leaving the booze behind, so he took the silver bowl, which was still half full. He was wearing white pants and didn't want anything to spill.

"Drive slow," he said.

Right.

When I hit the gas, the punch splashed all over Shane's pants, which were now pink. He got so mad and insisted on changing his clothes. We were staying in Delaware, which was a twenty-mile drive along the ocean. I knew it was a bad idea, but what choice did I have? I stepped harder on the gas, pushing the pedal all the way to the floor. We were going 120 miles an hour, driving as fast as we could. We were making our way around Ocean City toward Delaware when I encountered a roadblock set up to catch us. Police cars were everywhere.

Shit. We were definitely busted.

The cops took one look at Shane and me and pulled us out of the car. I insisted that I was fine, but the police officer kept saying, "You can't even talk."

I pointed to a nearby house and said, "That's where I live. C'mon, man."

Much to my surprise, the officer handed me a ticket for $149, charging me with driving at a speed greater than was reasonable and prudent, and let me go. "Get home and sleep it off, son," he said.

Things were different back then. Driving drunk was stupid, but people weren't as aware of the consequences as they are today. Of course what I did wasn't right, but at the time I didn't even think about it.

A week later, I was headed to orientation at Salisbury State College, on the Eastern Shore of Maryland. I was attending that school because, naturally, I was following a girl I was in love with. Okay, so it probably wasn't the most ideal reason to pick a college, but at least I was going. In fact, I was the first member of my family to attend a university. Given my struggles with school and life, that was a pretty remarkable achievement.

Shane and I decided to go to the bars in Georgetown that weekend. We always wanted to be where the action was, and Georgetown is the ultimate college party town on the weekends. We closed down the bar at two in the morning and did what we always did: drove home.

All of a sudden, I saw a cop in my rearview mirror. He was coming up fast right behind me.

"Shane, whatever you do, don't turn around. There's a cop following us," I said in a slightly panicked tone. Immediately, Shane turned around and started yelling "Fuck you!" at the cop.

I knew I was driving drunk on a suspended license. There was no way this would end well if we got stopped.

When I drove into Shane's neighborhood, I was hoping I could make it to his house without a problem. Shane was looking left and right, trying to see if the cop was still behind us. He was totally flipping out, which was making me really uptight.

"Stop, man. Just be cool," I kept saying.

When we reached the cul-de-sac where Shane lived, the cop was right behind us. I got out of the car and walked around to Shane's side. As he got out, I immediately punched him in the face. I thought, *If I'm going to jail, I want to get one good shot in at this guy before I go.* We fell into the bushes and kept going at it. All five of his sisters came running out of the house, trying to break things up. They were pulling our legs to try to get us off each other.

The cop was just sitting there. He didn't do anything.

By the time we were done with our scuffle, the police officer had backed up and pulled away. He never even got out of his car. Man, did we get lucky that night.

The next day, I went to Salisbury to get my meal card. When my picture was taken for the card, I had a shiner from the night before. That would be my identification all semester— me and my black eye. I suppose it was appropriate.

Not long after that, my girlfriend, April Caputo, convinced me to sell my beloved Camaro. She thought I should get something more fuel-efficient. Besides, a lot of my driving troubles seemed to stem from that car, so I agreed to sell it. I put an ad in the paper and was inundated with calls. The first guy I spoke to drove over in his 1964 Corvette. He loved the car. I told him I wanted $2,500 for it, and before I knew it, I was holding the cash and he was driving away in my Z28. Later that day, a tow truck came to fetch his Corvette. I remember thinking, *That guy must be rich!* I felt sick to my stomach. What had I done?

When I walked back inside the house, my phone was still ringing off the hook with people inquiring about the Camaro. One caller asked if I understood how rare that car was. At the time, I didn't. There was no Google back then. With every call, I slowly realized I had made the *biggest* mistake of my life.

I ended up with a light-blue Volkswagen Rabbit. Hardly the same impact as that Camaro. And I hated driving it. The Rabbit was always breaking down. After I installed a new radiator in it, the engine blew. I was so pissed that I left the car on the side of the road. When I heard it had been towed to the local junkyard, I went over to tell the guy he could keep the car, but I wanted the radiator because it was brand-new. He just laughed and told me to get out of there.

I'VE ALWAYS LOVED dinosaurs and the era in which they lived. One of the courses I took in college was paleontology. I had never been a great student, and I was really struggling academically in that class. Just like in the fourth grade, all the big words were hard for me to understand. The letters would become scrambled, and I couldn't see them in the proper order. Even a word like "Hawaii" was difficult for me. It wasn't until then that someone finally told me why I labored so much over words. One of my professors explained that I had a classic case of dyslexia—but instead of giving me resources to help me overcome it, he sent me to a counselor who said I should probably quit college.

I was completely confused by his advice.

Why would I quit college?

My surprise quickly turned to anger. "I'm not a quitter. Why would you tell me to leave?" I asked.

"Glenn, I'm merely suggesting you take some time off. Maybe a year or two to regroup."

I knew if I did that, I would never go back to school. I was paying my own tuition. My parents weren't footing the bill. I also knew that there was nothing more important than getting an education. I wasn't flunking my classes. I was struggling, but I wasn't failing. The counselor could see how upset I was.

"You know, when I was your age, I wanted to be a doctor. I ended up becoming a teacher. Sometimes we don't get what we want," he said.

While I know he was trying to console me, I realized that he was also mad that he hadn't gotten as far as he wanted to in his own life, and that was why he was telling me to quit. I thought that was the worst advice he could have given me.

Instead of dropping out, I became highly motivated to prove him wrong. Up until then, my usual routine had been to hit a local pub immediately after my last class, especially one that offered free food during happy hour. I would stay out until at least one or two in the morning. I was drinking all the time, following the same trajectory as my mom and dad. But now, determined to overcome this obstacle—which was how I saw this thing called dyslexia—I began studying my ass off. When my classes ended, I would go directly to the library until eight o'clock every single night, Monday through Friday. I had no idea there were other kids in college who did that. Up until then, I'd never stepped foot in the library. There were beautiful girls there, studying, taking their work seriously, and I liked it.

I studied as hard as I could, trying to understand the material, which wasn't easy. I worked on memorization, just like my fourth-grade teacher had encouraged me to do so many years before.

I never wanted to be defined by dyslexia. In fact, I don't even like saying the word. People learn to compensate for areas they're lacking in. I'm not a great reader, even today, but I'm 100 percent sure my dyslexia helped me learn how to communicate and think in other ways. For me, it's as though I see sound and hear color. My brain processes cadence and presents it in a way that helps me connect with people. So instead of using it as a crutch, I consider it a gift. It's a constant reminder of how far I've come.

I stayed at Salisbury for only a year. April and I transferred to Towson University for my sophomore year, and I spent the rest of my college years there. When I graduated in 1987, I became the first member of my family to earn a degree.

CHAPTER FOUR

ALWAYS GIVE MORE THAN YOU TAKE

Success is finding satisfaction in
giving a little more than you take.
—CHRISTOPHER REEVE

THE FIRST JOB I ever had was delivering a free local newspaper to 150 homes in our neighborhood. I was paid a penny a paper, which earned me six dollars a month. I was eight years old and thought I was doing great. One day, I met a boy who did the same thing in a different area. He asked why I was delivering all the papers. I didn't know how to answer until he said, "I just throw mine in the sewer. No one cares about those free papers, man." I was shocked by his admission. I didn't understand why someone would take on a job and then choose not to do it. Worse, he was deceiving the people who had trusted him with this task.

A few years later, I got a job selling the *Montgomery*

Journal, the county newspaper. I credit this job with honing my sales skills. I learned about preparation, reading, client relationships, the power of levity, and closing the deal. My boss rewarded us with trips to McDonald's. For every three sales we made, we could pick one prize from a hat.

A bunch of kids would pile into his VW bus, and he'd drive us to a large apartment complex, where we would canvass from six in the evening until nine at night. I would take a stack of papers and go knock on doors. When someone answered, I would immediately say "Hi!" while stepping over the threshold as I handed them a paper. It was a literal foot in the door every time. I did this so they couldn't slam the door in my face. They'd have to listen to my spiel. I had my message down so well that I could pick up on all the cues that would tell me whether I'd make the sale or not. My speech went something like this:

"Hi, my name is Glenn Stearns. I work for the *Montgomery Journal.* You can help me win prizes and cash bonuses by getting more readers for our paper. It covers all your local news, like sports, editorials, classified ads, wining and dining, and other interesting articles. And you can help me win a brand-new ten-speed bike!"

By knowing my speech so well, having my foot in the door, and gaining 100 percent attention from the clients, I could focus on them and their facial expressions to know how close I was to making the sale. At times I would use humor, even getting down on my knees and begging, "Please!" I would do whatever it took—and that sometimes included eating at their homes. I often look back on this and thank God I never knocked on someone like Jeffrey Dahmer's door.

By the time I was fourteen, I was paying taxes on the money I earned working part-time at the KB Georgetown movie theater. I had to take a bus to work. I was a new dad by then, and a full-time student juggling part-time jobs. I never stopped moving.

ALTHOUGH I HELD many part-time jobs throughout high school, I didn't get my first full-time job until I was in college, when I worked at TGI Fridays. The training program was much harder than I'd expected it to be. It took three weeks to learn every last ingredient of their famous seven-layer dip, and to become familiar with all the other items on the restaurant's vast menu. Being a waiter isn't just about taking orders and bringing food; it's about learning how to sell and connecting with your customers. It's being out on the floor with enthusiasm for your product. It's learning time management and delegation among the cashier, the bar, and the kitchen. There wasn't a better training ground for business.

I had no idea what I was getting myself into.

On my first day on the floor, I completely froze in fear when I was unable to prioritize what I needed to do. There were drinks to be picked up, food to be run, orders to be placed, and checks to be cashed out. *What should I do first? Should I make someone who wants to leave wait for the bill? If I don't, I might end up delivering cold food to the person whose dinner is ready now.* I panicked.

People were whizzing by me, doing their thing, and I

was just standing there. Mark, one of the other waiters I barely knew, came over and said, "What are you doing? What's going on?" I couldn't even answer him. Not a single brain cell would properly fire. I just had a blank stare and a handful of tickets with people's orders that needed to be filled.

Thankfully, Mark grabbed the tickets out of my hand and took charge: "Mary, take these drinks to table nine. John, take these fries to table ten," and so on.

Suddenly, I realized I had nothing left to do—and that's when I discovered the art of delegation, one of the most powerful tools to scale and grow. In that one moment, I learned so much. I was in the middle of great chaos, which could have been disastrous. Mark showed me that even in the worst circumstances, there's always a way to turn things around if you're willing to pitch in. Regardless of the challenge, there can be resolution.

In general, people want to feel needed, and a lot of people are afraid to ask for help. They don't want to appear weak or vulnerable. But that's a mistake; asking for help makes you strong. We don't always know what we don't know. And for some, it's hard to acknowledge that. Even so, I was never the guy who wanted to put someone out, be a burden, or not carry my weight. That's why I freaked out that first day.

From then on, I got it. I was the first to pick up other people's checks or bring out food and drinks for them. It made me feel needed, and that was a gift to the people I was helping and to myself. It was about building camaraderie and a strong team.

TGI Fridays had a saying: "Full hands in, full hands out."

It meant that you never walked into or out of the kitchen with empty hands. I learned so much from Mark during the entire time that I worked at TGI Fridays, but nothing was more important than this: *Always be willing to give more than you take.* This simple lesson would become my primary way of doing business throughout my career.

I had been at TGI Fridays for about a year and a half and thought things were going well when I got called into the manager's office with some other staff members one day. He claimed that people were stealing money. Whenever a server put in a large bill for change, the bill would somehow go missing. To get to the bottom of things, the manager decided to bring in a polygraph operator, and some of us would have to meet with him. I didn't think anything of it because I knew I hadn't taken any money.

"Glenn, we want you to take the test," the manager said as he pointed straight at me.

At first I was shocked. But my emotions turned to anger when he added that he'd heard there was a lot of drug use going on at the restaurant and again singled me out. I was very taken aback by the accusation.

I was now twenty-one years old, and though I'd mastered the art of drinking alcohol, drugs just weren't my thing. I could drink just about anyone under the table, but I was appalled that my boss thought I was on drugs. When I went to the back office, which was just a storage room in the mall where the restaurant was located, I was met by a burly man. He was sitting at a table with a lie detector on it. There was an empty chair opposite him. As the man hooked me up for the test, he said, "Do you want to know the real reason you're here? It's not because we think you do drugs. You're here because you know who does, and if you know what's good for you, you'll tell me right now." The man was in my face, being far more aggressive than he needed to be.

The man kept coming after me, asking who was doing drugs, until I finally snapped. "You're right," I said. "I know who's doing drugs here. And it isn't me. You can ask me if I'm the guilty party."

"Tell me right now—who's doing drugs?" he repeated.

"Nope," I said. "You can hook everyone else up and ask them. It's not my place to tell on them." I was no snitch.

The general manager walked in while the man and I were having our discussion. He was there to check on how things were going. "Glenn says he knows who's doing drugs, but he won't tell me," the man said in a far more polite tone than the one he'd been using with me.

I looked up at the manager, shook my head, and threw my hands up in the air in frustration. But the manager didn't defend me; he just shrugged his shoulders, said he had to get back to work, and headed out the door toward the dining room.

Admittedly, it was a little unnerving to be interrogated like that. All I could think about was getting back to my shift. I didn't have time to play this game. I stood up and said I was going back to work.

"Don't let the door hit you on the way out," the man said.

I hadn't planned on quitting that day, but when he yelled

that last line, something inside me changed. "You know what? Take this fucking job and your fucking machine and shove it up your fucking ass. I'm outta here."

I was so mad that there were actually tears in my eyes as I left the room. By then, the general manager was in a meeting with the other managers. I busted in on them and said, "I quit. This place is a bunch of bullshit."

I could see they were all stunned. When I told them how rudely I'd been treated, the general manager walked back to the room where the lie detector test was set up. He grabbed the guy by his collar and walked him out the door.

I became a reluctant hero that day because I stood up to the polygraph operator and didn't spill the beans on anyone. The general manager asked me to reconsider and stay, which I did—for a few weeks, anyway, until they brought in another lie detector.

This time, though, the operator's demeanor was completely different. He wasn't screaming at me or making wild accusations. He was actually nice, understanding. He didn't even turn the machine on at first.

"Glenn, we know you're not the one stealing or doing drugs. I'm not here to talk about the little stuff. I mean, have you ever taken a cup of soup without paying for it?" he asked.

"Sure, when my shift is over, sometimes I'll sit down and have a salad or a cup of soup." I didn't really think anything of the comment at the time.

"Yeah, who doesn't do that, am I right? It's not a big deal. But over the past year and a half, say, how many times do you think you've done that? Like, how many cups of soup?"

I didn't answer right away, but then I took a guess and said, "Twenty-five."

"Yeah, I get that. But again, we aren't worried about the little stuff here. Tell me something—have you ever left with a glass?" he asked.

"Yes, sure. When I work a late shift, sometimes I'll have a drink afterward, and I've taken a roadie or two—maybe even five," I said.

"Again, Glenn, we're not worried about that type of thing. What we want to get to is the big stuff. Have you ever done anything you think might be viewed as stealing from the restaurant?"

"No way," I said with great conviction.

"Okay, I've got all the information I need from you. Shall we turn on the machine?" he asked with a sheepish grin. Once I was hooked up, he said, "Okay, so is it true you've stolen at least a hundred dollars' worth of product from the restaurant?"

Well, I'd already told him the truth, so what choice did I have but to answer him affirmatively? "Yes," I said. "I just told you that. You said none of it was a big deal." I never lied to him. And because of that, the eleven people who told the truth, including me, were fired. The people who lied through their teeth kept their jobs.

When this happened, I wasn't really upset. I was ready to move on. I was beginning to learn about people and their behavior in the work environment. There were a lot of politics in that restaurant, and there was a definite pecking order. If you didn't play by their rules, you were out. In this case, it was a blessing in disguise. One of the managers who was also fired that day said a bunch of the others had taken jobs at Country Fare Inn, a high-end restaurant about twenty minutes away. She said I'd make triple the money as a waiter, and I wouldn't have to bus another table. I was in heaven. Of course I took the job, and I loved it.

Even though I was making really good money, I knew waiting tables wasn't my calling. I had big dreams. I wasn't even sure if I wanted to stay in Maryland or explore other parts of the country. Here's when I knew for sure:

I was sitting in a dive bar with a buddy when a girl slapped him and threw her beer in his face. I belly laughed as he fell off his stool onto the dirty, sticky floor. It was two in the morning, and there I was, hysterically laughing at his expense. As I did so, I thought, *Man, I laughed at the same dumb stuff last night, the night before, and the night before that. I'm so bored. What am I doing with my life?* I was caught in a cycle and didn't want to be doing this anymore.

I was drunk, and my thoughts were rambling. But I couldn't shake the feeling that it was time to make some changes. In the deepest of fogs, I had my strongest moment of clarity.

The next morning, I woke up and called my friend Parker.

"Let's go," I said.

"What do you mean?" he asked.

"Let's get out of here. Let's see the United States, drive to California."

"Okay, when do you want to leave?" he asked.

"Tomorrow. Let's just go. We can drive south and then make our way west."

As usual, Parker was game.

The next day we loaded up the BMW I'd bought from a doctor for $1,000 and headed to New Orleans. When we arrived, we stopped at a bar to watch Washington crush Denver 42–10 in the 1988 Super Bowl. John Elway was the Broncos' quarterback. He was the man. But that day, Doug Williams got the better of him. Little did I know that many years later, John Elway and I would become great friends and business partners.

Parker and I downed hurricanes until we were so drunk we couldn't see straight. We'd been in the bar all day. So much for making changes. By the time the game was over, we'd met some girls who invited us to go with them. When we walked outside toward my car, we saw that someone had bashed in the window and stolen all our things. I was really bummed, but Parker was pissed. The thieves had stolen his boom box and all his cassette tapes.

"C'mon, man. The girls are waiting. Let's just go have some fun," I said. There wasn't much I could do about what had been taken. I brushed the pieces of glass off the seat, shrugged my shoulders, and thought, *What's gone is gone.* Whenever things like that have happened in my life, I never gave them a lot of thought. I mean, what's the point? It wasn't going to change the outcome. There was no way I would file a police report for a missing boom box. The cops would laugh me right out of the station. All you can do is move on. So that's what I did.

Besides, we'd met some cute new "friends." That was a lot more interesting to me than being angry about a broken window.

"Get in the car, man. Let's go. There's a bar up the road," I said.

Parker angrily got in.

We drove toward the levee, where there was a string of bars along the water. As we parked the car, I could see that Parker was still extremely agitated.

"Are you just leaving everything here?" he asked.

"What do you want me to do, Parker? We're going to leave it here, go into the bar, and hang out with those pretty girls," I said nonchalantly.

Before I knew it, Parker and I were brawling. It was, well awkward. He's a lot taller than I am, which gave him an extreme advantage. I was swinging at him and mostly missing. We were punching each other until a large crowd gathered around us and started chanting, "Fight! Fight! Fight!" It was at that point when I turned to the crowd and said, "Leave us alone. This is my best friend," and kept swinging. Here he was, beating me up, and I was trying to defend him to everyone surrounding us. That was the last fistfight I can remember having.

Something clicked for me around that time. It was the second night in a row that I told myself I no longer wanted to be *that* guy. As I've said before, my dad was that guy for years. He drank himself into oblivion, got angry, grabbed me by the hair, and threw me into my room more times than I can count. That's just how he disciplined me. It's all he knew, and therefore it was all I knew, too.

The older I got, though, the less I wanted to be like him. Since that night, I cannot remember laying a hand on anyone ever again. I threatened to many times, but the physical aspect of beating the crap out of someone was no longer appealing to me. Instead, I learned to funnel that energy, harness it, and use it for good. I let it fuel my success and help me face whatever challenges came my way. I would emerge victorious thanks to my actions—not my reactions.

My dad once told me that everyone has a blind spot in life. Back then, mine was obviously alcohol. I drank like nobody's business. And when I did, I would find myself in trouble—often. My other blind spot was sex. I just wanted to get laid as much as possible. Neither addiction is something I'm proud of, but that was who I was back then. I looked at it as setting a goal and not stopping until I achieved it. To be fair, some of my choices were better than others. The older I got, though, the more I realized that my penchant for fighting was just pent-up energy. I wondered what would happen if I learned how to channel that energy into something productive. Was it possible that I could accomplish anything I wanted to? I suppose that's why I left Maryland.

When Parker and I arrived in California, our first stop was Long Beach. We went to see the *Queen Mary* and the Spruce Goose. As we sat on a stoop and stared out at the Pacific Ocean, we realized that we couldn't go any farther. We had driven as far west as possible. All I could think was, *Now what?*

I was broke, had nowhere to stay, and had no real plan. My mom took pity on me and agreed to wire fifty dollars through Western Union, so at least I had a little spending money in my pocket. To be clear, it was the *only* money I had.

ALWAYS GIVE MORE THAN YOU TAKE

I remembered that Brendan Moriarty, a buddy of mine from Towson, had moved to California. I wasn't sure where he was living; it could have been San Francisco or San Diego. I found his number through some friends and gave him a call. He was in Costa Mesa, near Newport Beach. That wasn't too far from where we were, so we drove south to meet up with him.

Brendan was living in a one-bedroom apartment with four other guys. They were all from Maryland, but none had gone to Towson. Brendan said we could crash at his place for as long as we wanted. My designated spot was on the linoleum floor in the kitchen. I slept there with only a thin blanket every night. It didn't really bother me. I was so grateful to have some-place to stay. And the guys were great. We partied like we were still in college. Clearly, I was still in a rut, because things didn't really feel any different than when I'd left Maryland.

My manager from Country Fare was also in California then. I'd always thought she was attractive, so I called her. It turned out that she was living with her boyfriend in Corona del Mar, which was very close to Brendan's. When I told her I was sleeping on the kitchen floor in a house with a bunch of guys, she said, "You can stay at my place tonight if you want."

I was surprised by her offer, and really grateful. A night anywhere but on the kitchen floor sounded pretty good to me.

I went to her place that evening. When I awoke the next morning, she had already left for work. Her apartment was one block off Ocean Boulevard, so I headed down there to check things out.

I walked along Ocean Boulevard until I came to a cliff overlooking some large oceanfront estates and the bright blue sea. I noticed a nearby stone bench, so I sat for what felt like hours. I took in the sights, the fast cars, and the fancy homes.

Man, this is the life, I thought.

Behind me I noticed a man cutting roses in his yard. I walked over and asked, "What does it take to own a house like this? What do you do for a living?"

"*Señor*, I'm the gardener," he replied. But then he said, "I think the owner is in real estate."

Real estate? I could do that. Yeah, that's what I would do: I would go into real estate. I had no doubt I could succeed.

About a week or two after we'd arrived, Parker told me he was ready to go home.

"I think I want to stay," I said.

I could see that Parker was surprised, and a little worried about how he was going to get back to Maryland. His parents helped him book a flight, while I set off to find my future.

January and February came and went. By March, I was easing into the California lifestyle. I suggested to Brendan and the other guys that we get a larger place, and said I would find it for us. I located an affordable three-bedroom apartment that was in a less-than-desirable area of Costa Mesa. We agreed to draw straws to see who would have to share a room and who would get the single. I drew the long straw, meaning I got my own room—or so I thought. The others sat me down and said they didn't think it was fair that I had my own room because I was the new guy. So, I went from having my own room to sharing a tiny bedroom with Mark, one of the other room-mates. We slept on the floor in sleeping bags because we didn't have the money to buy mattresses. The only pieces of furniture we had were a milk crate and a lamp. We lived like that for almost a year.

The guys and I would go out to the local bars every night and drink until we couldn't stand. There were plenty of times when I hung in there like a champ, but a few months in, I found myself wanting to leave early while my friends would want to stay. There was always some girl I wanted to go see, so I usually had an ulterior motive. On one particular night, though, I left when I probably shouldn't have.

As I exited the parking lot, I immediately noticed that I was being followed by a cop. Déjà vu. I pulled over, rolled down my window, and asked, "What's the problem?"

"First problem, sir, is you've pulled over in the fast lane. That's likely a problem, don't you think?"

"Sounds like a problem to me," I said. I mean, what else could I say?

"So, what do you want to do—take a blood, breath, or urine test? It's up to you," the cop said.

In Maryland, if you didn't take the test, they could suspend your driver's license for up to six months. That sounded like a much better plan than giving the cop an answer, so I said, "Well, something tells me I don't think I should take a test. It wouldn't be a good idea."

"Have it your way," the officer said before taking me in.

When we got to the station, they placed me in a holding

cell. I was in there for about an hour before five burly cops came in, held me down, and beat the crap out of me. I suppose when you're a jerk like I was, that's how they got you to take the test, because a nurse came in and began to draw blood from my arm despite my continued refusals. "Stop," I pleaded. I didn't want a needle breaking off in my arm. But the cops kept beating me.

Once the nurse drew the blood, I was booked for a DUI and thrown into a cell for two days. My arm turned purple where they took the blood. Throughout my stay, they'd shove a tray of unidentifiable food in a holding area, and then slam the door shut. The food sat for an undetermined amount of time, but always until it got cold. I could hear other guys begging for their food, like they were wild animals waiting to be fed. It freaked me out. I wasn't a monkey in a zoo. But there I was, in jail, hungover, and miserable.

What am I doing with my life? I thought. It was becoming a recurring question.

I sat there for two days realizing that I'd made too many mistakes and too many bad choices. I didn't want to admit it—certainly not then—but I *was* a loser. And I didn't want to be one anymore. I hadn't come to California to do the same things I did in Maryland. They say the definition of insanity is doing the same thing over and over and expecting a different result. If I wanted change, *I* needed to change. That was painfully clear.

I was released from jail and had to walk home because my car had been impounded. Our place was several miles away, which gave me time to start thinking about my plan. When I got home, I immediately looked in the Sunday classifieds for a job. I had a degree in economics, but I'd never really thought much about what to do with it when I graduated. Then I saw an ad for a position as a loan officer with a small regional mortgage company. I called first thing Monday morning and locked in an interview.

I got the job, although I wasn't sure I would be able to keep it. When I was hired, there were fifteen of us who started on the same day. Our manager said that if two of us lasted, it would be a success.

I was so nervous that I called my mom. She assured me that hard work and determination would pay off. So, that's what I set out to do. I would sit through the training sessions, get pumped over the ideas, and then walk out thinking, *What did they mean by that?* I felt lost and unsure. School had always been hard for me, and this was no exception. I didn't think I had what it took to make it. It seemed like everyone else in the room was nodding their heads, understanding everything, while I knew absolutely nothing. Worse, I'd had no idea that the job was strictly commission based: no one got paid unless they sold loans. Period. That's when it occurred to me that Bruce, my new boss, wasn't going to fire anyone. If we wanted out, we would have to quit. And I wasn't a quitter. I wanted to learn the business. I wanted to succeed. So, I asked him what to do.

"Take these business cards and go to these ten offices. Show up every day and ask if they need a loan. And don't stop asking until you get someone who does. Understand?" he said.

I was naive enough to do exactly what he told me to do.

I finally got interest from a landscaper who owned his own business. But he did a lot of transactions in cash, which meant he didn't necessarily report all his income to the IRS. Since his tax returns showed a lot less income than he actually made, it was difficult for him to qualify for a loan.

I went to Bruce and told him the situation. I explained that my client made enough money to qualify, but his tax returns didn't show that he did. Bruce assured me that there were ways to push a loan through.

What did I know? I was new to the business.

While I was working out the details on my first loan, I met a Realtor who asked if I wanted to sit in on her open house. She said it might be a good way for me to meet potential clients. She also asked if I might consider making some flyers to advertise the open house for her.

When I got to her open house, she suggested I meet her friend, another Realtor who was also holding an open house around the corner. I was eager to meet anyone I believed could bring in business, so of course I said yes.

When we got to his open house, her friend appeared very willing to help me. He mentioned two houses he was selling, both of which needed flyers. I said I'd be happy to make them, as long as I could also put my name, number, and loan rates on the flyer.

A few days later, I showed up at his office with the flyers in hand.

He took the flyers and said, "If I send you a five-hundred-thousand-dollar loan applicant, how much would you pay me?"

I thought about it for a minute and said, "I could pay you half a percent."

"Okay; I have business for you," he said.

I was really excited—so much so that I went back to my office and told my boss. When I mentioned that I had to pay the Realtor half a percent, he stopped me cold.

"You can't do that. Kickbacks are illegal in this industry," he said. "You tell him no!"

I didn't want to turn away the business. A half-million-dollar loan was a lot of money in 1988. I needed the deal. I didn't know what to do, so I went back and talked to the Realtor, who now wanted three-quarters of a point. When I told Bruce, he insisted I say no and reiterated that I would not be paying any commission.

I went back to the Realtor for a third time and explained to him that my boss wasn't going to let me do the deal if I had to pay him. To my surprise, he gave in, and we did the deal.

The family he referred to me had fled Iran during the revolution in 1978. They were somehow related to the Iranian royal family, and I thought they must be billionaires. I had never met people who were this rich before. At the time, I'd never even sat in a Mercedes-Benz. No doubt these were the wealthiest people I had ever talked to.

My contact was George Kortistani. He was buying two homes for his family, and to get the best rate, he insisted that both be listed as "owner-occupied." The problem was that an owner could occupy only one home, so the other would have to be listed as a non-owner property. But George claimed that he and his family would be living in both homes, and therefore both should be owner-occupied loans. I was too inexperienced to know how to pull this off. I ended up using some of my commission to buy down the rate on the second, non-owner property, getting it within one-eighth of a point of the owner-occupied rate. I was more than willing to give this client my blood, sweat, and tears. I wasn't worried about what I got out of it, as long as he was happy.

Every time George called me, my palms got sweaty and my heart began to race. I would look at the blinking light, take a deep breath, and finally pick up the line.

"Hello, Mr. Kortisani, how may I help you?" I'd say.

Each time, his secretary would be on the line and would say, "Please hold for Mr. Kortisani," and then she would place me on hold, always making me wait for the client to come to the phone. It wasn't unusual for five or ten minutes to pass. Once George finally did pick up, there was no small talk. He was all business, asking things like "Why is there a fifty-dollar credit-report fee charged to me? I'm not paying fifty dollars for that."

That was the fee for a credit report. Even so, I was anxious to close the loans, so I said, "No problem, sir. Let me look into that."

"Glenn, I want the best rate," he'd say.

"Of course you do. That's what I'm here for. Let me talk to the right people," I would respond.

A week later, it was the same dance. Palms sweating, heart racing, incessant holds, and my client demanding something else. I didn't know a lot about loans yet, so everything was about getting the answers. This was a difficult situation, especially when it came to actually closing the loans.

Just as the deal was being finalized, my phone rang. I was sure it would be Mr. Kortisani saying he was happy about a job well done. I was like a puppy who couldn't wait to be patted on the head for being a good boy. As usual, it was my client's secretary. When he finally picked up, I heard, "What the hell? My loan was supposed to be eight-point-five percent. Why is it at eight-point-six-two-five percent? And what ever happened to that credit report fee? You've done a terrible job!" he shouted.

I never expected that wrath. I'd been so happy to get the rate to where it was, especially because I'd reached into my own pocket to make it happen. As he was yelling at me, I started to interrupt him. When I got his attention, I said, "You know what, sir? I've finally figured something out. All the money in the world doesn't matter. It makes you an extremely unhappy man. I busted my butt for you, and this is the respect you give me back? No. No sir. That's not okay. So, I'll tell you what I'm going to do. Your other loan? I don't want it. I don't care how much money I'm giving up; it's not worth it. I could never have made you happy. I'm done. Good day, sir." And then I hung up.

No amount of money is worth giving up your dignity and self-respect. If you allow someone to push you around, they will always push you. They won't quit. *We are what we're willing to tolerate.* I've walked away from more deals than you can imagine because, in the end, it's not really about the money. It's about your self-worth.

No sooner had I gotten off the phone than it rang again.

It was my client.

I hesitated to reach for the receiver. I was sure he was about to let loose on me like I'd just done to him. Curiosity got the best of me, though, so I picked up. This time it was him, not his secretary. He said, "Glenn, I'm very sorry. Thank you for all you did. I really appreciate it. I want you to do the other loan. You *need* to do it, so calm down, and let's make this happen. I'm truly appreciative."

He was right about my needing the loan, but I didn't deserve to be disrespected. From that day forward, every time that client called me, if I was busy, I would put him on hold until I was ready to talk to him. I also told him I was charging him an extra point on the second loan because I'd earned it. He was happy to pay it, because he felt like he got a good deal. What I learned was that a good deal is a state of mind. It's about how you feel at the end of a transaction. It's not about winning or losing or being the best or the worst. It's about achieving the best results possible at that given time.

When I first started working at the mortgage company, I was also busing and waiting tables at Le Biarritz, a fancy French restaurant in Newport Beach. Since I'd just started out in the mortgage business working straight commission, I was flat broke. The only money I had coming in was from waiting tables.

The owner of the restaurant was from France. His name was Yvan, but the staff called him "Ivan the Terrible" because he was a crotchety old man. He grew up in Europe during World War II without a penny to his name, which made him very frugal. If someone ordered a rum and Coke, they'd get rum and half the can of Coke. If the can wasn't finished that night, the next day someone else would get flat Coke mixed with a fresh can in their drink. He wouldn't waste anything. Yvan was so cheap that he refused to pay anyone to do a job he could do, so he was the host, the bartender, and, when necessary, the chef.

One night I ran into the kitchen to put some plates in the dishwasher. As I was rushing back into the dining room, Yvan called out, "Come here, you motherfucker."

He was always cussing me out.

"What the fuck? What do you think this is? This butter patty cost me a nickel! You fucking throw that fucking butter patty away?"

I was sweating from rushing around trying to do my job, and now I was worried that Ivan the Terrible was going to fire me.

"I've got ten tables, man. I'm just trying to keep up," I said.

"Don't waste my fucking money!" he shouted, waving the butter at me.

And that was it.

I went back into the dining room thinking that Yvan was a jerk, but afterward, I thought about what he said. He was right. Every penny counts. In business, you have to watch every expense like it's one of those nickel pats of butter.

I also wondered about how his life and upbringing had made him that way. You don't just get to a point where you yell in someone's face and call them a motherfucker. Those things don't come naturally. They're learned. I discovered that, when

Yvan was a young boy, he hid in his bedroom thinking his house was about to be bombed at any moment. Because of the war, his family didn't have any money, so they had to scrounge for every tiny morsel of food. The more I thought about his history, the more empathy and understanding I had for him. I wasn't mad or hurt. I didn't enjoy his yelling at me, because I didn't believe that was an effective way to manage his team, but I never forgot the experience, either. Sometimes we learn as much from people about the way we *don't* want to behave as the way we *do*. And I was grateful for the job, because it kept me afloat while I was starting my career selling mortgages.

CHAPTER FIVE

WE ALL MAKE MISTAKES

---

*Life is never more fun than when you're
the underdog competing against the giants.*
—H. ROSS PEROT

ABOUT SEVEN MONTHS and twenty loans into my new career, I was still feeling lost. There was no real training. The only way I learned was through the school of hard knocks. I felt as if I'd been thrown into the ocean and had to figure out how to swim with the sharks or be eaten alive. One night, I broke into a cabinet in the office that housed all the loan files. I wanted to see how the other loan officers were putting their files together, how they explained credit, employment, and appraisal issues—all the magic it took to put a file together well. A lot of getting a loan approved is determined by how you present the file—it's about strengthening the weak points and highlighting the strong points. I was trying to learn how to be better at my job, but at the time I was extremely frustrated and oddly sad. I wasn't prone to depression, but I couldn't shake this feeling of emptiness.

I thought about my friends back in Maryland. There I was on a Friday night, alone in an office, rifling through files in the dark, while they were probably out laughing, drinking, and having a good time. I missed that. Sure, I was starting to make some decent money, but it wasn't making me happy.

With the extra cash I was making, I bought a used refrigerator for our house from Brady, one of my coworkers. On the side of the fridge, there was a magnet with the name and number of a psychiatrist. Brady had told me that he and his girlfriend, who later became his wife, had gone to see her. I thought, *Yeah, that's what I need—someone who can help me figure all this out.* So I called her and made an appointment.

"What's the problem?" she asked.

"I'm in the mortgage business. I'm making more money than I've ever made—more money than my dad ever made, too. Everything's going well, but I know it's going to end. I know something's going to blow this up. I never dreamed I could make this kind of money. I know it's going to go away, and I'm very anxious about it," I said in a desperate tone.

"Do me a favor: pay me for today and never come back," she said. "You're trying to find a way to sabotage yourself. Don't be afraid of your success. You've earned it. Now get out of here and go be successful."

I was a little surprised by her answer, though I was also grateful. I was wallowing in self-pity—over what? That was the first and last time that ever happened. She gave me a much-needed swift kick in the butt, and I've never looked back.

After that, it was all systems go. I wanted to succeed in the worst way, and I was willing to put myself out there to do whatever it took to make that happen. The only people I knew were those I worked with, so I started going to dinner with them. I thought it was a good idea to get to know them and believed it would give us a chance to network, too. We usually went to a local Mexican restaurant on Taco Tuesdays. I'd learned from my days waiting tables that building rapport and camaraderie among the people you work with has its benefits. When you have a strong team, everyone wins. Besides, you never know who you might meet along the way.

I spent the next two months canvassing new opportunities to write loans. I would go out and put flyers on the windshields of cars, meet builders who were selling small developments, prequalifying people any way I could. Every weekend I would check out new developments, looking for Realtors. At the time, those houses were being released in phases, and many wouldn't be ready for at least six months. In the interim, they would appreciate in value, so hundreds of buyers would show up to look at ten homes.

I would give Realtors a flyer with the name of the property, its address, and the listing price at the top, followed by comparisons of various loan rates and explanations of payments, interest, taxes, insurance, and what was needed to qualify. I did all the legwork. I made it so easy to close the deal. Occasionally they would even say, "These are great! I've got a buyer; why don't you come and do the loan?" That was exactly what I was looking for.

And whenever I could, I would plaster the neighborhoods with my flyers, too. Sometimes other lenders or builders would tell me to get off their property. One took to calling me "Flyer Boy." He'd shout out, "Hey, Flyer Boy, why don't you go play in the street back where you came from? Put your little flyers on *their* cars!" He even threatened to call my boss. What was he going to tell him? That someone named "Flyer Boy" was drumming up business? I had to laugh as I shouted over my shoulder, "Make sure to get my name right when you call!"

Sure enough, he did call my boss. When Bruce summoned me into his office, he said, "What are you doing going to private properties trying to get loans? Are you crazy?"

I just laughed.

"Keep it up," he said with a great big smile.

And so, I did. I got loans out of it. A lot of loans.

I was being so aggressive that one time another builder's agent called the police on me. Why? I had better rates than he did! Yeah, mortgages can be a rough business.

That agent called in a construction foreman as muscle. "Get off our private property!" he yelled while physically pushing me into the street.

I was so embarrassed about being pushed away that I started reverting to old habits. I was determined to stand my ground and fight back. Instead of throwing a punch, though, I shouted as loud as I could, "These people don't want you to do business with me because I have a better loan program and better rates than they do." There were several potential buyers around who could hear me. I kept saying, "Take my card!" and waving my business cards in the air.

A few days later, I received an unexpected call.

"Son, my name is Al Perez. I like your style. I met you the other day; you didn't give up. I want you to do my loan."

Naturally, I was excited for the opportunity. He explained that his daughter was getting married and the house he was buying was for her. By the time the home was ready and the loan was closed, however, the wedding was off, and Al was stuck with the new home.

"I've got this house," Al said. "I don't know what to do with it. It's such a good house."

We spoke about options, and I decided that I wanted to buy it. I convinced Greg, one of the guys I worked with, to come in on the deal. He would make the down payment, and I would pay the mortgage. He agreed—that is, until it was time to put up the money. He just didn't have it.

I felt bad for Al because I'd given him my word and didn't want to leave him hanging, but I couldn't afford to buy the house on my own. I reached out to Ron Harsini, a local Realtor I knew. I explained the situation to him, and then asked if he wanted to partner on the house.

He said no.

Instead, Ron suggested we open a mortgage business together. While my career in lending was taking off, the suggestion made no sense to me. No one would start their own mortgage company with as little experience as I had. And Ron was a Realtor—he didn't know anything about the mortgage business. I wasn't even sure if he'd ever sold a home. At least, I never saw him close a deal. So, I said yes to Ron.

I'd been in the mortgage business for only ten months. I wasn't the smartest guy in lending, and I surely had a lot to learn. But the prospect of moving on to something new and fresh where I could spread my wings and build my own business was very appealing.

What I knew for sure was that I absolutely had no idea what I was doing. I'd never run a mortgage company. All I understood was how to go out and get loans. What we needed was someone who knew all about the business side of opening and running a mortgage firm. That was Greg—yes, the same guy who hadn't come through on the house I wanted to buy. He didn't have a lot of money at the time, but he sure knew the business.

And so, in 1989, the three of us formed First Pacific Financial with a $100,000 loan we got from Ron's family. We were all going to be owners together once we paid back the money.

On our first day, Greg set the tone. He was spewing all sorts of terms and establishing expectations. He demanded everyone show up for work by 7:00 a.m. He said, "If you're on time, you're late." He spoke about commitment and dedication, and made it clear that anyone who wasn't at their desk on time shouldn't bother to come in. I thought, *This guy really knows what he's doing*. We had five new loan officers who had never been in the business before. These were all friends of Ron's or mine. The idea was to begin our training classes first thing in the morning. It didn't matter if one person or ten people were in the room. They needed to be at work by 7:00 a.m., ready to learn. We were pumped. I was so excited about our prospects.

The next day, everybody showed up for work at 7:00 a.m., as expected. Everyone, that is, except Greg. He was nowhere to be found.

I finally called him and asked what was up.

"I told Ron," he said. "I can't make it in." And then he hung up.

I was completely baffled. I had no idea what was happening, but I was certain it wasn't good. Greg finally rolled in around noon. He walked to his office, did a few things, and left. He never said a word to anyone.

Worried, I walked over to his desk and opened the drawers. There was nothing there. He had emptied everything.

I called him again.

"What's going on?" I asked.

"Bruce has made it impossible for me to leave. I'm sorry, I just can't do it."

Bruce, our former boss, wasn't taking kindly to our decision to start a competing company. In my case, he withheld $15,000 in commissions, and was obviously going to make it hard for me to take anyone else with me.

I was pissed about everything. I decided to fight and took Bruce to the labor board to collect the money he owed me. The day before the hearing, he called and said, "Meet me in the park."

"What is this, *Wall Street*? You want to meet me in the park, Gordon Gekko?" The film *Wall Street* had come out two years earlier, and in a now notorious scene at the end of the film, Michael Douglas meets Charlie Sheen in Central Park to confront him about turning him in to the Feds on insider trading charges.

"Meet me there. We'll figure this out," Bruce said again.

"Yeah, sure. Okay," I said, knowing damn well I wasn't going.

The next day, Bruce called and said, "You didn't meet me!"

"No, I didn't. I want my money. See you at the labor board." And I hung up.

The next day at the Labor Board hearing, Bruce's attorney twisted the story in such a way that it quickly became apparent it would take a lot more time, effort, and legal fees to collect my money.

Later that night, I called Bruce. I wanted to give him an out. I started to speak but he interrupted me, saying, "What did you think of my lawyer today? My attorney is on a fifty-thousand-dollar retainer. What's your lawyer on?" Bruce was full of bravado, and he was certain he had one over on me.

Not so fast. It's true that I didn't have a lawyer; what I did have, though, was determination.

"Why don't we just settle this thing?" I said.

"You're right, Glenn. Let's settle this. The settlement is zero." There was a long pause, and then Bruce continued: "One day we're going to have a beer and let bygones be bygones. But today, that's the settlement."

So, while I knew he had me, I let my old ways rear its ugly head one more time and explained that while I couldn't hurt him in his wallet, there was one thing I could do—and that was to sleep with his daughter.

Yeah, it's true—I was dating one of his daughters. He hadn't known that until our call. Looking back, this was a real-life David and Goliath moment for me.

I immediately picked up the phone and called his daughter to tell her what I did.

"Glenn, he's going to kill you!" she said.

From that day on, everywhere I went, I thought, *is this the day Bruce is going to murder me?* But I figured I might as well have some fun while I was being screwed.

She had, in fact, worked for the company. She was a beautiful and kind human being. It wasn't right that I put her in the middle of my dispute with her father. But when I told her, she got a chuckle out of it, just like I did.

Once I realized Greg wasn't coming back, I knew First Pacific Financial was in deep trouble. I didn't know how to get investor approval, how to process the loans, or what the heck went into all the file cabinets. I didn't know about business insurance, permits, licenses—nothing! We needed back-office support—fast—or we would go out of business.

By this time, Bruce's office manager had had quit. I called her, explained our predicament, and begged her for help.

"I'm in," she said. And thank God she was, because she knew exactly what to do.

She got us set up with Franklin Mortgage Group, the same company our prior employer used, so we could seamlessly begin delivering loans.

I was relieved for the first time in months.

In the end, her husband and his processor came to work for me too. Without all of them, I would never have gotten First Pacific off the ground. I needed every single one of those people to launch

I learned a lot about myself during those days. It was the first time in my career where I felt vulnerable and scared. I couldn't see how things were going to end. Yet a pattern was emerging by surrounding myself with good people who could and would make a difference in our success.

It is through these challenging experiences, that we have opportunities to learn and grow. Either way, we figure things out. There's no shame in owning the errors of our ways. Hell, my errors are what helped get me to where I am today. They say we learn more from our failures than we do our successes, and I believe that's true. It was becoming clearer with each passing day that what I really valued was loyalty and stability—two traits I wanted to earn by leading through example. And if I were going to do that, I had to make some adjustments to the way I moved through the world—as a businessman, a leader, a friend, and more. It was my time to grow up, be a man and take responsibility for my own life. In the end, Bruce was right. We eventually had that beer and laughed. As it turned out, he was more of a mentor to me than I could have imagined when I worked for him. To this day, we go to lunch together from time to time and he remains a good friend. Every relationship gets tested. But that doesn't mean you have to cut that person out of your life. I strongly believe in second chances and sometimes learning to forgive and forget.

CHAPTER SIX

RIGHT PLACE, RIGHT TIME

If somebody offers you an amazing opportunity but you are not sure you can do it, say yes—then learn how to do it later!
—SIR RICHARD BRANSON

ONCE I STARTED out as a broker in mortgage lending, it quickly occurred to me that the mortgage pie was much larger than just loan origination. There were credit, appraisal, escrow, title, and many other ancillary services that went into the buying or refinancing of a loan. So, when Ron and I started First Pacific Financial, I began looking at what other services we could provide to generate more income. For example, if we could do an escrow for every loan, we would easily add more profit to our bottom line. While companies that handle escrow are known to most of the rest of the country as title companies, in California they're called escrow companies—but they're essentially the same thing. They're neutral third parties, representing neither buyer nor seller, that hold funds and make sure loan documents are signed in a timely manner. In some states, title insurance and escrow settlements are done under the same roof, but in California, they're usually separate transactions.

Ron and I started Carriage Escrow in 1993 and five years later Carriage Abstract, which handled title insurance in non-escrow states. When we did that, I went out into the world of mortgage lenders and said, "I'm open for business."

We took in three deals during our first month at somewhere around $300 each, but that wasn't enough money to cover the rent, let alone the rest of our overhead. I started freaking out, thinking, *What have we done?* We needed this to work. So, I started to look at how we could make more deals.

I went to the Santa Ana office of the US Department of Housing and Urban Development, also known as HUD. At the time, HUD had dozens of satellite offices all over the country, and they were taking properties back from lenders who had foreclosed on them. Every month, they auctioned these properties off to the public in order to recoup their money, or at least some of it. I immediately saw a great opportunity. Maybe I could be the escrow/title company for those homes.

Jeannie Baker was the receptionist at HUD. I'd known Jeannie since I'd first become a mortgage broker. While most people might overlook someone like Jeannie because she was "just" a receptionist, I understood from the first time we met that she held the answers to a lot of my questions. I naively asked her how to become a mortgage banker. She said she wasn't sure, but she liked me, so she did the research and showed me what to do. She said I should get a line of credit that I could use as a funding source. HUD wasn't the right place to seek that advice, but I didn't know that at the time. Still, Jeannie taught me lots of things. A year later, I walked into her office and asked how I could get some of the escrow business from the sales of HUD properties. I told her I was screwed, that I had an escrow company that wasn't doing any business. We were failing miserably.

"You'll need a HUD contract, Glenn," Jeannie stated.

"What's a HUD contract?" I asked.

Once again, Jeannie helped me. She explained that each contract was bid on by escrow companies, and the lowest bid won the contract. "Fill out one of these forms," she said. "We sell HUD homes all across the country. Maybe you can do the escrow and title work."

That was music to my ears. I would love to do that!

A few weeks later, Jeannie called and said there was a contract coming up for an area in Southern California and that I should bid on it.

"I'm on it," I said. I wanted that soon-to-be available HUD contract—and to be frank, we needed it. To win that business, we'd have to come in lower than anyone else. Through several sources, I was able to find out the price the company that had previously held the contract was being paid: $150 per transaction. I had no idea if that was reasonable or fair. All I knew was that if someone else could figure out how to do it for that price, I could, too.

At the time, my office manager was a woman who'd started working only the month before, so I didn't know her well, but I was certain that she was resourceful. I promoted her to the new position of chief escrow manager. Thankfully, she had her act together and knew how to write the proposal. The document was what's referred to as an IFB, an invitation for bid. It's two pages long, and it essentially breaks down your price and that's it. An RFP, on the other hand, is a request for a proposal, and those documents can be many pages long and go into much greater detail.

To put in our bid, we flew to Denver, where the HUD contracting office was located. The bid opening was set for nine o'clock the next morning, so when we got to Colorado, we headed straight to our hotel. We had plenty of time to go over everything and make sure we had it all together.

Upon arriving at the hotel, we found that, without my knowing, my assistant had booked one suite for the two of us. I was immediately uncomfortable. I didn't mind sharing a room when I traveled with my business partner, Ron—you know, two guys saving money, keeping an eye on the bottom line. This was entirely different, though. There was no way I was staying in the same room as one of our female employees. I'd learned that lesson early on in my career, and I wasn't willing to risk my reputation or the existence of my company over a potential allegation.

Although my escrow manager insisted it would be fine if I slept on the couch, my conscience told me to get my own room. Instead of making a big deal out of it, I suggested we head out for some lunch. I left my bag by the door to the room and we left for some chicken wings. When we got to the restaurant, I privately called the hotel, arranged for another room, and had my bag moved.

Back at the table, I asked if she wanted something to drink. I was thinking more along the lines of a Coke or lemonade, not alcohol. Although she professed not to be much of a drinker, she ordered a glass of wine. That's when I said, "If you're having a glass of wine, I guess I'll have a beer."

The next thing I knew, hours had passed, and it was six o'clock. We shot a few games of pool with some guys at the bar, and all the while, my escrow manager was ordering glass after glass of wine. Maybe she was more of a drinker than she thought. She met a guy at the bar, and it was pretty clear that they were headed off together for the evening. Before they left, I took her aside and said, "I called and had my things moved to another room, so the suite is all yours." She smiled and left with her new friend.

One of the guys we'd been playing pool with suggested he and I stop off at a place called Shotgun Willie's, a local strip club. He turned to me and said, "You coming?"

"Why not?" I said.

When we got to the club, I walked up to the window to pay to get in. "There's two of us," I said. Just then, the guy I was with fell to the ground because he was so drunk. "Make that one, please."

I wanted no part of that, and besides, it was obvious that the bouncer wasn't going to let him into the club. I stayed for only a few minutes before realizing I would regret the decision the next day, especially since the meeting was so important to the survival of the company. Whenever I found myself in strip clubs, it was always because someone else wanted to go. I never suggested it or thought, *This is where I want to spend my evening.* I inherently understood that it was all transactional. Strippers are there for one reason—to take your money. They'll do and say anything to achieve that goal. The opportunity to stare at a naked woman until her song ended held no interest for me. I was far more curious about why these women ended up there. Sometimes I would ask the women to stay and talk with me for half an hour, offering them enough money to make it worth their while, with one condition: I just wanted to get to know them. And if, after our conversation, I could lean over to my buddies and say, "I know I can get that girl," it was enough for me. Sometimes I'd get a message from those women after I left the club, and they would ask what I was doing later that night. This, of course, gave me the opportunity to show my friends I could have closed the deal. Was it a game? Absolutely. This was my way of playing. But that night was different; I had work to do. It was time to go back to the hotel and get some sleep so I could be ready for our big day.

Around five o'clock the next morning, my phone rang. It was my coworker. She was frantically worried because she couldn't find me. I couldn't believe what I was hearing. "You were worried about *me*? You didn't seem that worried when you left the bar last night. I'm fine. I need the contract for HUD. We have to be there on time, and you're definitely going to be hungover." When I hung up the phone, I wasn't amused—I was pissed. I didn't appreciate her putting us in that position.

We met in the lobby of the hotel, and I asked to see the contract. When she pulled it out of her purse, it was crinkled and looked like she'd shoved it in there in a hurry. She'd started to smooth out the pages when I noticed there were coffee stains on them. I was horrified. There was so much riding on this. That's when it occurred to me that this woman, whom I'd thought had it all together, did not. She definitely wasn't the person I wanted running this end of our business. What had I done?

Before we'd gotten to Denver, I felt confident that the deal was ours to lose. But twenty hours later, I wasn't so cocky. I feared we might just lose it after all. There was no way I was going to submit the IFB in its current condition. Minutes before our meeting, I walked into the HUD office and asked if they could print another IFB document for me. Thankfully, they said yes. Next, I asked if they had a typewriter I could use. The receptionist pointed to a vacant machine off in the corner of their office, where I sat and typed out a new version, hunting and pecking with one finger from each hand. I finished just in time for the opening bids.

We were ushered into a room where a HUD official opened and read each bid to the public, only the public was just the two of us: me and a hungover non-drinker. We were the only people foolish enough to fly to Denver for this process. Truth be told, IFBs are the types of documents that are usually faxed, not hand-delivered, but I didn't know that. And it's really just a numbers game: Whoever comes in the lowest wins. It doesn't really matter if you're there or not. Since this was my first time bidding, I wanted to make sure nothing was overlooked. Maybe I was naive, but I also thought it would be a good idea to let the people from HUD see me, and it gave me a chance to meet all the contracting officers.

My bid was $149.50, fifty cents lower than the previous contract holder's price.

Did that make me the smartest guy in the room?

Not necessarily.

By now you know I didn't go to college and didn't start my business for the right reasons, but those experiences always led me to interesting places. I knew the price the last company had charged and, by design, I came in fifty cents lower, so yeah, I won the contract. It was the start of a beautiful relationship— sort of.

As a result of submitting the winning bid, we went from no business to hundreds of deals in a month, which was huge for a small escrow company like ours. Once we started rolling with those deals, though, someone on my staff figured out that between the time and the cost, we were losing around $150 for every transaction. You see, when I set our bid, I hadn't factored in cost. Regardless of the number of transactions I was doing, I could never make up that deficit. So, I went back to HUD and told them I had underbid the contract by grossly underestimating the costs.

One of the HUD contractors looked at me and said, "Glenn, I remember one time when I worked for another department and we put out a contract to paint the Statue of Liberty. One guy bid a dollar to get the job. We brought him in and said, 'You can't paint the Statue of Liberty for a dollar.' It just wasn't possible, right? The painter said that his grandfather had come through Ellis Island, and as a result gave his father and generations to come a wonderful life in America. He said, 'If I want to paint the Statue of Liberty for a dollar, that's my choice.' So, we awarded him the contract."

"Interesting story, sir, but what does that have to do with me?" I asked.

"You're painting the Statue of Liberty for a dollar. That's your bid, your price. You take it or you can give it back. If you do, we'll nullify your contract and you'll get an exclusion, which means you'll never get another government contract again."

That definitely wasn't the answer I'd been looking for. I was stuck, and I wasn't sure what I was going to do. How could I justify losing $150 per file? I had a lot of thinking to do.

Here's what I came up with.

At the time, California had some of the highest foreclosure rates in the country. If we did 150 loans a month, about 120 of those were for condominiums in Orange County that were in foreclosure. Lawyers tacked on $5,000 in fees to handle those foreclosures, because they knew the government would pay them. They also added on Homeowners Association (HOA) fees for a year and a half, because it took that long to go through the foreclosure process. My idea, which I thought might work for all parties, was to go back to HUD and say, "I can't make any money doing the transactions at the rate I bid. I screwed up." Then I would explain the lawyers' fees and how we, the taxpayers, had to pay that money. If the government added $300 per file on top of my existing contract, I would negotiate those foreclosure fees down by at least half, and in the process, my company would actually be saving the government $2,500 on every deal. That felt pretty fair to me.

HUD agreed. They added $300 to every deal.

I wrote a short letter to the attorneys who handled those deals that read "The federal government refuses to pay these types of egregious fees anymore" and sent it out with every transaction, wiping out the entire $5000 that didn't need to be spent and saving the government millions of dollars in the process.

It didn't take me long to realize that there were flaws in the HUD loan process almost every step of the way. I remember sitting in a meeting at HUD with all of my other escrow contractors. They were complaining that they were notarizing the HUD deeds without the signer being present. They said it was against the law to do that. Plus, they were getting paid only twenty dollars for every signature they notarized, which was the maximum amount they were legally allowed to charge. This created a quandary, one they needed to figure out. That's when I saw another opportunity to maximize our profits while solving a real problem for HUD.

After the meeting, I sought out the man who ran the home-ownership division for HUD and said, "Sir, I see you have an issue with notaries. Why don't I have my notary come here every day on her lunch hour and just notarize the deeds that you sign? That way, you'll be getting all of that done right here at HUD."

He loved the idea so much that he immediately put out a memo saying all deeds would have to come to HUD to be notarized. The other notaries were relieved, and my company notarized fifteen thousand deeds that year at twenty dollars each. Was I mining for scraps? Maybe, but it was like finding an extra $300,000 in the front pocket of my favorite pair of jeans. It was money we hadn't even realized was there for the taking. But once we discovered it, bam.

Our company started to do fairly well after that.

When you're building a business from the ground up, all revenue matters. Low-hanging fruit was easy pickings because no one else was going after it. They didn't even see it on the trees.

Before I sold the escrow company to First American Title Insurance Company, Ron and I were having issues. I felt like I was putting in all the work at the escrow company, and while he should have been pulling his weight at the mortgage company, it seemed as if I were doing the bulk of that work, too.

I began thinking it was time to get out of the mortgage business, or perhaps start my own firm without Ron or the liabilities we shared. I tabled that idea for the moment and focused on becoming the sole owner of the escrow company. In February, I made Ron an offer he couldn't refuse: I wanted to buy his half of the escrow business for $250,000. I told Ron I was putting in bids for large government contracts. If I got them, I was going to make a hell of a lot of money and wouldn't feel guilty about it. If I didn't, he would have gotten a great deal, because the escrow business wouldn't be worth what I offered him for his half. Intrigued, Ron took my offer to the accountants and evaluators, who told him to take the money and run. So, he sold his half of the business to me, thinking he'd made a great deal.

My connections with HUD continued to get stronger. I spent a lot of time cultivating relationships with the people who ran the offices and becoming friends with their support staff. Early on, I discovered the benefits of being nice to everyone, especially the gatekeepers, the people who answered the phones, the secretaries, the assistants, and so on. These are the first people you come into contact with, especially when you're new. Your future is in their hands. They decide whether you get invited to a meeting or if your phone message is entered into the call log. I was always making friends with the office staff. In general, contracting officers were supposed to remain neutral. I respected that, but I also believed it was important to treat people with kindness, respect, and dignity—and the best way to accomplish that was to do it in person.

THINGS AT HUD soon went from good to great. They expanded our territory, eventually allowing our company to pick up accounts all over the country. Inside sources told me that there were people who were jealous of me because of the way I broadened my business and grew my mortgage company through those HUD contracts. Whenever a company begins to be successful, there will be haters. I understood that. What I didn't expect was that some people would go so far as to protest HUD giving my company any further business. These were the same people who would say that they made my business. Maybe they did, maybe they didn't. I believe we're in charge of our own destiny. I tried to ignore the noise and continue doing my best to serve the accounts.

As our business grew, HUD began changing the way they did business, too. Instead of working with hundreds of settlement contractors, they wanted to streamline the number to one per state. In larger states like California and Texas, they thought three to five offices ought to be able to handle the business. HUD also went from having multiple centers around the country to having just four homeownership centers (or "HOCS," as they called them), located in Santa Ana, Denver, Atlanta, and Philadelphia. These centers were responsible for every deal made through HUD. The idea was to make the HUD contract process more efficient. Each center was run by someone different, so I had to reestablish myself and build a rapport with the new person if I wanted their business. Though I'd been doing business with HUD for several years, the people I'd built relationships with along the way were no longer going to be my contacts. It was almost like starting all over again. I would put together the required RFP, plus a detailed proposal, and I'd go in to make my pitch. Instead of just submitting the lowest bid like I usually did, I now had to create a one-hundred-page assessment of how we would work in each state, our method of reaching across that whole state, and how much we were going to charge. HUD wanted to know our past experience, prior performance, and expectations for future business. Small mom-and-pop escrow companies didn't stand a chance. Our company had a lot of experience with these deals, yet we still hired professional proposal writers, because keeping HUD's business was our top priority.

When these changes happened at HUD, I went to First American—the national title company I worked with— and immediately explained their potential financial upside of our relationship. They understood that there was title insurance behind every settlement we did, which was worth tens of millions of dollars in new income for them. That's when they offered to buy 49 percent of our company for $2 million. I was willing to make the deal, but not at that valuation. I was looking for $15 million, plus 15 percent of every title order I knew we would do. Typically, a title rep earned around 22 percent, so this was actually a better deal for them. And because I would act as the sole rep, there would be no need for outside reps on any HUD account. HUD insures and guarantees all bad titles, so there was no risk. The lenders required a title policy, and the government was willing to back it. There was no downside. Eighty-five percent of the fee was pure profit. It was a perfect plan.

There was a second reason the relationship made sense: It gave me an essential communication tool other vendors didn't have. First American had a thousand offices across the country. If we became partners, not only would I have an office in every state, I would have one in every corner of the state, where buyers could easily and conveniently sign loan documents.

They wouldn't have to travel long distances to get to one of the HUD offices to handle the paperwork. I would have a multitude of branches in each state, and we already had the capability to do the paperwork electronically. Now, that might not sound intriguing today, but back in the late nineties, being able to offer electronic documents was cutting-edge.

I negotiated with Craig DeRoy, who was the president of the title company; Parker Kennedy, the chairman and CEO of the parent company, First American Corporation; and all of First American's top executives.

"You can stretch us to fifteen percent, Glenn, but we can't go from two million to fifteen million." That was their response.

Were they playing hardball?

Perhaps, but I didn't agree.

Here's why: If I did a thousand orders a month, at $1,000 each for title insurance, that came out to $1 million a month. Escrow fees were now set at $450 per deal, which totaled $450,000. Even if the escrow deals paid for themselves, there was still $1 million in premiums coming in every month. If that number stayed steady for six or seven years, my ask of $15 million paid for itself in the first year and a half—so yes, they could easily do the deal I wanted.

My argument was hard to ignore. Besides, I was right; the deal was fair, and they knew it. There was one catch, though: My top title representative was the person who originally came to me about First American buying into the company. Although he was an independent rep, his wife worked for me as my assistant. I told him that if he brought me $15 million, I would give him 10 percent, or $1.5 million, when the deal closed.

I finally received the contract from First American, but there was an unexpected clause that stated there could be no kickbacks, for any reason. I wasn't allowed to pay anybody within First American. I had no choice but to go to my rep and tell him the situation.

"I've got a problem. Read this," I said as I handed him the thick legal document.

Naturally, he wasn't happy. And I completely understood. So, I told him I would go back to First American and say I couldn't do the deal if I couldn't pay him. I felt the need to be up front about it with everyone. With his blessing, I went back to First American and told them that not only was my sales rep important to my business, and someone who worked independently, he was also a friend. Thankfully, the decision-makers at First American understood and said *they* would pay his fee.

I was very pleased that First American stepped up. I couldn't wait to tell my sales rep the good news.

Unfortunately, a few weeks later, he came to me looking very upset. "They're not paying me," he said.

I assured him the company had agreed to pay, but he insisted that they weren't keeping their word. I promised I wouldn't pull the trigger until everything was good to go. As I spoke, though, I could tell his frustration was still growing. This was a tough decision for me as well, because our mortgage company really needed the money. We had a lot of cash going out, and not a lot coming in. The mortgage company was due to be audited for HUD in a few weeks—which was common; we were audited every year—but at that moment, I was upside down. By law, I was required to have at least $250,000 in assets in order to keep my HUD, Federal Housing Authority, Fannie Mae, and Freddie Mac approval. If they had audited me right then, they would have seen that I was $500,000 in the red. This meant I needed $750,000 if I were going to meet their requirements, a number that felt insurmountable. I thought my life with the mortgage company was over. I was sitting on a deal for $15 million, which would have solved a lot of my problems, and yet I was saying I wasn't going to go ahead unless my sales rep got paid. I couldn't live with myself if First American didn't honor my deal with my rep, because my word was my bond. What I'd promised to my rep was worth more than money. So once again, First American agreed to pay, and once again, my rep said he didn't think they were going to honor it. I needed the deal to close on or before September 30, the last day of my audit, so I approached them for a third time—only this time I wasn't being as nice as I'd been in the past. By this point, everyone was mad at me. My sales rep was upset that he wasn't being paid. First American was angry that I hadn't closed the deal yet. Everyone was frustrated, and tempers were running high.

I went to see Craig DeRoy and explained that I needed the deal to close right away. When I told him I was ready to move forward, I laid out two conditions: I needed my rep to be paid, and I needed a check that day so I could give it to my accountant for my audit. As collateral, I offered to sell DeRoy $2 million worth of judgments we held against people who owed my company money for the price of $1 million. Those judgments came from lawsuits First Pacific Financial had filed and won but hadn't yet collected. Craig likely knew they were basically worthless, but he agreed to make the deal anyway. He also gave me a check right then and there, with only a handshake binding the agreement between us. With the sale of those judgments, income went to my mortgage business, which greatly improved the audit taking place that same day. I could pay off all the debt. From that day forward, I never worried about payroll again—and that alone changed the way my company operated and grew.

CHAPTER SEVEN

QUITTING ISN'T AN OPTION

Failing is not the worst thing in the world; quitting is.
—EDWIN LOUIS COLE

I LOVED RON like a brother, but he had a difficult time when it came to making hard decisions. That's not a good trait in business. Making hard decisions is part of everyday practice. If we weren't careful, we were going to find ourselves in a situation we didn't want to be in. I could feel it coming, even if I didn't want to believe it. I was watching friends and competitors do things in business that made me uncomfortable. Some engaged in unscrupulous practices and ended up going down because of their actions. I didn't want to be like them.

While I had salvaged the escrow company, our mortgage company was upside down, deep in debt. My heart was really in the escrow business, which I'd already bought from Ron. I thought it made sense for the two of us to go our separate ways on the mortgage business, too, before the ship completely sank. So, I wrote down a number, slipped the piece of paper into my desk, and thought about it for a couple of weeks before presenting it to Ron.

A few weeks later, I cut my number in half. I just wanted out.

A couple of weeks after that, I cut the number in half again.

And then in August 1998, a banker from RFC Warehouse Lending came to see me. Warehouse lenders give lines of credit to mortgage bankers, which the bankers use to fund mortgages. Bankers then package the loans and sell them on the secondary market, thus returning funds and paying off the credit line. Without warehouse credit lines, a mortgage banker is out of business.

At the time, we were just a small company and had only one warehouse line. The man who came to see me shook my hand and said, "We've got a problem."

"What do you mean?" I asked as I motioned him into our conference room, where Ron was sitting.

"I'm pulling the credit line," the man said.

I was stunned. I had no idea why he was there, or why he was saying something so outrageous.

"I told Ron months ago that you needed to have more capital in this company to keep the line," he explained. "You haven't complied, so I'm pulling the line."

I turned to Ron in total shock.

"What do you want me to say? He needed more capital, and I said we'd put it in," Ron replied.

"You never told me. Not a word," I furiously shot back.

"I had to tell him something—"

I cut Ron off before he could utter another word. "You mean you had to bullshit this guy? Why didn't you tell me so we could work this out?"

I was completely blindsided. I was the outside guy bringing in new business, and Ron was the inside guy running the operation. He dealt with the warehouse line, investors, and banks. He was older and looked more mature than I did, so people had more confidence in him. I wanted people to feel that our company was strong and being run by someone who was wiser than I was. And because Ron was older, he looked the part—and yet he was always off playing poker or golf. He wasn't minding the store like I thought he was. He was spending his days bullshitting the very people who could take it all away.

"What do you want me to say, Glenn?" Ron asked again defensively.

"Nothing. I don't want you to say another word. You don't have to bullshit anyone. We've got to figure this out." I turned to the banker and said, "When are you pulling our line?"

"Next week," he replied.

"We'll be out of business, because we need a line to fund these existing loans. Can I have the evening to think this through and meet with you again tomorrow to show you what we have now and where we can go from here? I think I can convince you to give us another six months so that we can, at the very least, have time to get another line in place. I'll be transparent and show you everything that's happening in our company so you can present it to your boss, and then you can just wind the line down. But please, let me get another line of credit in place before you shut us down. Give me a shot." I was pleading my case. He agreed to give me twenty-four hours.

When he left, I didn't rip into Ron, though I wanted to. Instead, I got to work drafting a letter that showed all our business, where it came from, what we were doing—everything. As I pored over the paperwork, Ron announced that he was leaving promptly at three o'clock to play cards. He was the kind of guy who didn't ever want to think about the worst-case scenario. If he didn't acknowledge it, then it wasn't real. Well, sticking your head in the sand and pretending something isn't happening when it is never makes it go away. We were in a mess; it was one I believed I could get us out of, but it would take time. It would have been nice to have help, but I was in this all by myself.

As Ron left that afternoon, he turned to me and quietly said, "We should shut it down." He was giving up. But I believed that things were never over when you lost; they were over when you quit—and quitting was not an option for me.

"Let me work on this," I said, without lifting my eyes from the paper I was writing on.

I worked until five in the morning the following day and slept at my desk for a few hours before Ron got to the office. When I heard him come in, I went to see him. I was exhausted.

"Read this," I said and slipped the letter I'd written across his desk.

I needed to be in Pasadena to state our case by noon, so there wasn't much time to make changes. Ron took a quick look at it and said, "I have no problem with it." Even so, I knew there were a few things I could strengthen, so I went back to my office and worked until ten thirty, when I had to leave. I knocked on Ron's door one last time and said, "I'm taking off. What did you really think of the letter?"

"Good letter. Send it," he said.

He didn't even acknowledge that I was hand-delivering it in an hour.

It was right then and there that I knew I wasn't going to be this man's business partner anymore. Why? In the middle of the letter I'd written the word "fuck" three times in a row, just to see if he would actually read it. When I realized he hadn't, I knew he'd mentally checked out.

When I bought the escrow company, I knew I'd done all the work necessary to get it to where it was. I felt very confident in my decision to buy it. Now I realized that when it came to the mortgage company, I was pulling more weight than Ron was. It's always healthy when each partner feels like they're pulling more weight than the other, but because I knew Ron couldn't look me in the eye and say he was pulling his share in the company, I wanted out.

The sad thing is, I really loved that man, but it was clearly time to end our partnership. I drove to Pasadena and managed to buy us the time we needed to find another warehouse line. When I got back, I went straight to Ron's office and told him we needed to talk. We sat down, and I said, "Remember my offer to buy you out of the escrow company? Well, I've got another offer for you. This time it won't be the biggest number you've ever seen. It may actually be the smallest. I want you to buy me out of the mortgage company." Ron looked down at the paper. It read *$120,000. $10,000 a month.*

"Pay me ten thousand dollars a month, every month, until I have the one hundred twenty thousand; you assume all the liability and debts, and you can have the company," I said.

Ron looked at the piece of paper for a moment, then looked up at me and said, "I'll do the deal."

This time he didn't go to the accountants; he didn't even have to think about it. He was going to buy the company. But then he added one important condition: "You're going to sign a non-compete, right?"

"No, I won't. I intend to compete against you."

That's when Ron slid the paper back to me and said, "Okay, same deal, same terms, only I want you to buy me out. And I won't compete against you."

"Deal," I said.

I hadn't planned on buying the company that day. I wanted to sell it. But the timing was right to end things with Ron, for multiple reasons. First, I no longer felt aligned with Ron as a business partner. When any relationship loses trust, it's nearly impossible to get it back. It's also really difficult to feel as though you care more about the company than your business partner does.

Second, it was time to go our separate ways because I'd submitted all my new proposals for HUD in multiple states, and if I was granted those contracts, I would be doing thousands of deals a month.

For those of you who think you need to be perfectly aligned in your thoughts and have the best plan in place when starting a business, you don't. It is not how you get there so much as just getting there. Often times, people believe everything needs to fall perfectly into place to launch. That's not necessarily true. The mortgage company wasn't launched with great entrepreneurial spirit; it was started from a broken heart. You see, success can be born from the most unsuspecting circumstances.

After I bought Ron out, the mortgage company would need cash bad. A month later, bam! I was awarded fifteen states by HUD in one fell swoop. I got everything I asked for except the state of Texas. Although I really wanted Texas, they gave it to a group of lawyers. I went back to HUD and said I would give them back all fifteen states if they would give me Texas. Having Texas was the equivalent of all those other states combined, or more, in terms of transactions. Texas was the mother lode. I was concerned that I might fail if I tried to open fifteen states at once, but HUD said no to the trade. What's worse, they told me I had only forty-five days to open the states I got. That felt deliberate.

Okay—game on.

I went to First American and explained the task at hand, and we got down to business.

I found one person in each state who could lead each office, and one by one, we opened every state they gave me. Business took off, and we were doing well.

Unsurprisingly, the people in Texas failed. They had thousands of contracts that were ready to close, but they didn't have the manpower to make it all happen. If you can't close the contract, you can't transfer the property. People who thought they were going to be in their new homes within forty-five days were stuck extending their existing leases or living in hotels, or doing whatever else it took because they didn't have anywhere to go. It was a big mess. People were calling to yell at HUD because they just wanted to close their deals. HUD never wanted to be the reason someone couldn't close a home loan, so they turned around and put pressure on the contractors to get the deals done. It was a horrible cycle.

As a result of the massive delays, HUD ended up pulling the contract from the lawyers in Texas and asking if I would take it over.

You bet I took it, and when I did, my company managed to successfully catch up on all the backed-up loans. In the process, we became the rockstars of HUD. After that, we started helping them clean up other states, too.

By this time, First American had bought 49 percent of the escrow company for *sixty times* what I'd paid for it when I took it over from Ron six months earlier.

Even with all the business we had, there was one more state I really wanted: Maryland. Maryland was under the jurisdiction of the Philadelphia HOC. I wanted Maryland because it was my home state, and I wanted to have some business roots there. I already had my mortgage business set up, but I really wanted the title company there, too. Finally, in 1999, I got a call from HUD telling me the state was available and they wanted me to take over the contract.

"Absolutely. When do you want me to start?" I enthusiastically asked.

"In a week."

A week? I didn't have any title employees there, nor did I have enough office space. I needed at least a month to prepare.

"Why so fast?" I asked.

The representative from HUD explained that the last people who held the contract were being indicted for stealing proceeds from HUD. As a result, HUD had been holding back properties until they could get a new contractor in place. By doing this, they inflated the amount of inventory to sell, which meant that when I came on, there would be a tsunami of properties ready to close.

"Okay, we'll give you two weeks," the HUD rep said.

These were the moments I lived for—rising to meet a challenge that would crush the competition.

I immediately went to Maryland, rolled up my sleeves, and got to work. I visited my mortgage office, which was located in a two-story building with a parking lot on the second-floor level. The only solution I could come up with on such short notice was to cut the space my mortgage business occupied in half and dedicate one side to mortgage lending and the other side to the title company. I put in a big wall, added desks and computers, and then spread the word that we were hiring.

Despite the fact that we didn't officially have a contract with HUD yet, we immediately started working as if we did. Whenever HUD came to me with an opportunity, I would always say yes and then figure out how to do it later. I made sure to have the business before putting infrastructure in place. That way, I would never be left with overhead, employees, and office space I didn't need.

When we opened, HUD dropped five hundred deals on our desk. I was expecting 150 deals a month, not this many. At the time, I wasn't familiar with Maryland title law; I discovered that the abstract—the title—came from the courthouse, but court was open only until five o'clock Monday through Friday. There was no after-hours access, which meant we had to get the abstractors to pull the microfiche and take pictures of everything. Needless to say, it was a very old-school, time-consuming process. Once everything was set and ready for signing, we had to use a certified document signer, something that was peculiar to Maryland law. That limited the candidate pool to certified signers only. So here I was with five hundred deals at one time, trying to get five hundred title orders from the county recorder's office, which clogged their system and kept me from getting what I needed fast enough. All these deals were sixty-day escrows, which meant that in sixty days, people would expect to be able to move into their homes. I couldn't get it all done in sixty days. Instead of being in their new homes, people were living in their cars or in a hotel, waiting. It was quickly starting to look like the debacle in Texas. We were getting hundreds of calls from angry people who wanted their deals to close. It was an absolute nightmare.

I called HUD and told them I couldn't get the deals done in the allotted time frame. It was a setup for failure. Worse, the next month brought another five hundred purchase contracts. I was stuck. People quit, leaving me and our customers hanging.

Four months into the deal, we had hundreds of home-less customers. It was horrible. Everyone who remained at the company was pitching in to get the deals done. I had teams working all day long and throughout the night to meet the demand. At one point, I tried giving the deals away to other companies for free. I didn't want the money; I just wanted the customers to be taken care of. Our reputation and business practices have always been more important to me than how much money we made.

I was acutely aware that the wheels were officially off the bus. I was doing my best to manage things from my corporate headquarters in California, but given the amount of trouble this was causing, I decided I needed to be there in person. I flew back to Maryland to see what I could do to correct the course. On the day I arrived at the office, there were five people from the HUD office in Philadelphia working there, assisting our team. There were a handful of Realtors there, too. This was unheard-of!

As I walked past the receptionist, a young woman doing her best to juggle the nonstop phone calls, I overheard her say, "You're going to do what? You say you're going to firebomb our building?"

Anna Capelli, my contracting officer from HUD Philadelphia, was also standing there. She took the phone from the receptionist's hand. "Hello," she said. "I'm with the Department of Housing and Urban Development. What you've just said is a federal crime."

Sitting in my lobby were two men: one from the *Baltimore Sun* newspaper and another from the Department of Insurance.

"You Glenn Stearns?" the man from the Department of Insurance asked.

"Yes," I replied.

"I have information that you're operating your business without the proper insurance license. If this is true, we have a major problem," he said very matter-of-factly.

"Glenn Stearns? I'm with the *Baltimore Sun*, and I'm doing story about how you're making hundreds of people homeless," the reporter interjected.

It felt like the walls were closing in, and there was nothing I could do to stop it. Before I could answer either man, three local Realtors showed up on behalf of their clients. "I'm tired of waiting!" one of the men called out.

I'd hit my breaking point. I turned to everyone waiting in my lobby and screamed, "GET OUT! Get out of my building!" I was serious. I wanted them all out.

In the parking lot, the Realtor was still yelling at me about his deal. I did what came naturally to me: I calmly started to remove my jacket. One of the other Realtors asked, "What are you doing?"

"What am I doing? I'll tell you what I'm doing: I figure you and I are going to kick the shit out of each other. I'm as frustrated as you are! Do you want me to stop and entertain everyone who comes through our door? Do you want me to take every phone call from angry customers like you? Or do you want me to spend my time closing these deals? I've done everything I can to move the ball down the field for you. If you want to help me, why don't you go to your other title companies and ask if they'll take some of these files off our hands?"

Next, I turned to the reporter and said, "And you— why don't you do a story on why there's a bottleneck instead of why we're making people homeless? Tell people who think their deals will close in sixty days that it will be more like one hundred twenty days because HUD has a backup in inventory from the previous contractor—not me!"

And then I turned to the HUD representatives and said, "I don't want any more deals. I can't take them on. Do you want me to quit? Everyone else has. Tell me what to do."

The insurance representative seemed to take pity on me in that moment. He said, "Glenn, you seem to have bigger problems to deal with. How about if I investigate this on my own?"

No doubt the state insurance department had received complaints about us, and rightfully so. Still, we weren't doing anything wrong. We just had too much business.

I looked at the gathered crowd and said, "All of you people with all your frustrations—I get it. There's nothing for me to do unless we all learn to work together. So please be patient, put the word out that we need help, and in time, I promise I'll get this all figured out."

That was the kind of chaos we were dealing with every single day—until *that* day. The reporter *did* write a story on the bottleneck, just as I'd suggested. The insurance issue went away, too. Everyone stepped in to help get us back on track, something I'm extremely proud of. And the people who helped get us there were very pleased with their accomplishments, too. Within a month or two, we began humming along, and before I knew it, business was great.

Once I turned things around in Maryland, other title companies in the state started to protest because they didn't think I qualified as a small business and therefore didn't deserve the contract. Some of HUD's contracts were open to large business contractors, while others were open only to small businesses, and those definitions varied from contract to contract. Most of my contracts fell into HUD's "large contractor" category, which meant there were no limitations on the size of the companies that could win them. Maryland, however, was categorized as a small-business contract. Shortly thereafter, I received a formal letter saying other companies thought it was unfair that I had contracts all over the country because I wasn't a small-business contractor. People were protesting us *again*. And they were right: if you added my mortgage company to the mix, I didn't fit the criteria for a small business. HUD needed to pull the plug on our contract. They said they could drag their feet for eighteen months or so to allow me time to plan and get through the transition, but I was devastated.

My relationship with HUD was enormously important to me. Occasionally, I would fly to Washington, DC, to meet with Mel Martínez, who was the secretary of HUD at the time. We'd spend an hour together talking about things I thought HUD could do differently to improve the overall experience for everyone. He asked me a lot of questions, too. Finally, during one visit, Mel said, "I love all your ideas, Glenn, but there's just one problem. No one knows this yet, but I'm quitting next week. I want you to meet the new secretary of housing."

We walked to the office next to his, where Mel introduced me to Alphonso Jackson, the man who would take his place. He seemed like a solid guy, someone I thought I could have a good relationship with, especially because of my tenure working with HUD.

Jackson assumed his new position about a month after we met. The first change he made as Secretary of Housing and Urban Development was to declare HUD to be an organization for the little guy. It was going to be all about small-business contractors serving the underserved. While the sentiment was meaningful, there was one problem: all my existing contracts would no longer qualify under this new rule. I was the biggest HUD escrow/title provider in the country, and I was being cut out.

Around this same time, I was due for my annual HUD audit on my contracts. When the representatives from HUD Philadelphia arrived, I wanted to take them to dinner. I thought that, at the very least, I would try to show them a good time and express my gratitude for a long and, yes, prosperous relationship. None of them had been to California before, so I thought it would be fun to take them to Beverly Hills for dinner and then to see a show. Mr. Chow is a favorite Hollywood hot spot where I knew we'd probably see a celebrity or two. I asked my assistant to find out what the hottest play in Los Angeles was and to arrange tickets for all of us later that night. I didn't ask what show we were going to, only what time and where. When we arrived, I looked down at the tickets and realized we were seeing *The Vagina Monologues*. If you've never seen the show, it is, as the title suggests, all about the vagina. I was horrified, because I was with a group of people who were in their sixties and who, I assumed, might be on the conservative side. Throughout the show, I sank lower and lower in my seat, embarrassed for all of us. I could see how uncomfortable my guests were. It was one of the most awkward moments of my life. When the show was over, all I could think to say was, "Well, that's Hollywood for you!" I was hoping my levity would break the obvious tension.

Unfortunately, at the time, I didn't know I was doing anything wrong by taking the HUD reps out to dinner and the theater. I was just trying to be friendly and to express my gratitude for the relationship we had. It turned out that contractors can't pay for anything when it comes to a government agency, which HUD is. So, despite my intentions, each of my guests was required to pay for their dinner and the show. I felt awful.

When word got out that I was essentially through, there was an overwhelming surge of support for keeping me engaged. The people I knew in each office didn't want to lose me as a vendor. One of my friends in the Denver HUD office called and suggested that if I partnered with an Alaskan Native or a Native American, and did it correctly, I might still be allowed to bid on contracts, including "no bid" contracts, which meant that if I gave them a fair price, they wouldn't seek any other bidders and I would be awarded the contract.

In 1971, Congress passed the Alaska Native Claims

Settlement Act, which set aside forty-four million acres of land to be given to Alaskan Natives to provide economic opportunity. Instead of setting up reservations as in the lower forty-eight states, the government set up twelve regional corporations and more than two hundred village corporations, which allowed Alaskan Natives born before 1971 to become shareholders. As a part of that deal, these corporations could bid on government contracts under the no bid rule.

I flew to Nome, Alaska, where I met with one of the village corporations. Once we were able to come to terms, we began taking on contracts together.

For reasons I'll explain later, I found myself on *The Oprah Winfrey Show*. When Oprah asked how I made all my money, I gave her an answer I would later come to regret. I said, "I started working as a waiter, became a mortgage broker, a mortgage banker, and then I got into government contracting, and the rest is history."

The head contracting officer from the Denver HUD office happened to be a big fan of Oprah and caught the show. He was extremely angry with my admission that I made money from government contracting. Remember, HUD was now all about small business, and there I was, flaunting my wealth on *Oprah*. Looking back, I can see why he was upset. He immediately went to the powers that be at HUD and said, "We will no longer line Glenn Stearns's pockets. I won't give him any more contracts."

Some insiders at HUD Denver called to tell me this guy was furious. He thought I had to be stealing from HUD because of what I'd said on Oprah. This not only hurt me but also pissed me off. He was challenging my integrity. To protect my honor and dignity, I immediately called the Inspector General and demanded to be audited. As you can imagine, most people don't ask to be audited—quite the opposite. They usually ask not to be. I wanted them to come to my office and look at our company records. I said, "If I'm a criminal, you can have me thrown in jail. And if I'm not, I want a letter saying I'm clean, because I'm going to sue this guy at HUD for not awarding me contracts that we clearly had won."

And I meant it.

Perhaps this wasn't the brightest move on my part. Even so, the inspector general refused to investigate or audit me. There was no reason to.

One by one, I watched my contracts get awarded to other companies. It didn't matter whether they were charging more than I was—and most were. Cutting me out ultimately cost the government a lot of money, but the only thing I could do was protest. I went to war against this man from Denver, battling him in court and losing every step of the way. He kept shutting me down, which eventually ended my career in the title/escrow business.

In 2004, I sold my shares of the title company back to the people I was working with in Alaska and got out. I was done, over it, and ready to move on. It was time to focus strictly on my mortgage company.

Fast forward to 2017, when I attended the annual Horatio Alger Awards in Washington, DC. These awards honor outstanding Americans who exemplify dedication, purpose, and perseverance in their personal and professional lives. Recipients have often achieved success in the face of adversity. Each award recipient becomes a lifetime member of the Horatio Alger Association of Distinguished Americans. I was honored to receive a Horatio Alger Award in 2011, and was, at the time, one of the youngest members to be inducted into the association, but I'll tell you more about that later. At the 2017 ceremony, I was inducting new members into the Horatio Alger Association and voting to determine who would be inducted the following year. On the chartered bus that took us on a field trip to the Supreme Court, I sat down next to none other than Alphonso Jackson. He was hoping to be a member of the 2018 class of inductees.

When I realized who I was seated next to, I struck up a conversation and reminded him of when we first met. "Mr. Jackson, I don't know if you remember me, but I was the largest contractor at HUD until you decided to go with smaller businesses," I said in a kind yet direct tone.

"What are you saying?" he nervously responded.

I paused, took a deep breath, smiled, and said, "Don't worry. I'm voting for you. I want you to be a part of Horatio Alger. As a matter of fact, you did a fantastic job at HUD." And I left it at that.

By now, I understand that I can't go back in time to rewrite history. What's done is done. How we respond to it matters a lot more than what happened. I've since gotten to know Alphonso and his wife and today consider both to be friends. I also appreciate the time I spent working with HUD, but I'm genuinely grateful I was able to escape from all the drama. Without the HUD contracts, I was able to focus my attention on growing Stearns Lending. The relationship with HUD was significant, but it had run its course.

Not long after President Trump took office, I found myself back in Washington, DC, for another Horatio Alger event. Dr. Ben Carson had been named Secretary of Housing and Urban Development, and I knew Dr. Carson from Horatio Alger as well. To my surprise, while I was in DC for that event, Dr. Carson's office called and invited me to his home for breakfast. I'd been out very late the night before, but I couldn't turn him down. I arrived tired and unclear about why I was there. After some small talk, Dr. Carson turned to me and said, "I want you to run the homeownership centers. All of them," he said.

Without missing a beat, I responded, "Sir, out of respect, let me put it this way: not on your damn life."

Dr. Carson seemed surprised by my answer; I'm sure it wasn't what he was expecting or hoping to hear from me.

"Look, I would consider being your Undersecretary, because one day you'll move on and I can take over as Secretary. As you know, I'm more than qualified. I was the largest contractor and lender for HUD. I know I could execute on both policy and programs. It certainly would be a wonderful exclamation point on my résumé. It would allow me to give back to my country, and I do believe I would enjoy that." I meant what I said, though being a civil servant had never really crossed my mind before that moment.

Dr. Carson said, "I wish I'd had your name about a week ago, because I just nominated someone else to be Undersecretary. I didn't know the depth of your past."

The only reason to even remotely consider his offer to run the homeownership centers was that I would become the boss of the man from Denver who had shut me out. The mere thought was ironic and alluring.

"Play me a game of pool for the job," Dr. Carson said.

I was intrigued. I hadn't pegged Dr. Carson to be a gambling man.

"Okay, sure. I'll play you on one condition: win or lose, I'm not taking the job, but I'll play you for it anyway."

I don't regret anything that happened during my time working with HUD, and I don't regret turning down the offer from Dr. Carson. Having a job where my day-to-day responsibility was to oversee contractors didn't sound appealing to me, given all the other cool things I've gotten to do, but I'm not ruling out the prospect of someday stepping up to do what I can to help, when and if the time is right. What I know for sure is that you can't re-create the past, but you can re-create the feeling of pride you experience whenever you do something special. That's what fuels me to keep moving forward.

And by the way, I won the pool game.

CHAPTER EIGHT

EVERY CHOICE YOU MAKE, MAKES YOU

*Life is a matter of choices, and
every choice you make makes you.*
—JOHN C. MAXWELL

IN 1991, I met Amber, a woman who would change my life forever. Amber is the woman who would later become my wife and the mother of our three boys, Skyler, Colby, and Trevor. When we met, Amber was working the front desk at a local tanning salon. I'd been to the place only a couple of times at that point and hadn't seen her there before. When I walked in and gave her my name, she said, "I know who you are. You can go to booth number eight."

As I was undressing, I thought, *Hmm. She's pretty*. But how did she know who I was?

When I left that day, I saw her reading *Presumed Innocent*. "You like Scott Turow?" I asked.

"I love him," she said.

We began talking about Turow, and I promised I would bring her a copy of another one of his books. I thought I had one at my house but couldn't find it, so I bought the book and crinkled the pages to make it look like I'd read it before giving it to her.

"Want to go out for lunch?" I asked. I wanted to get to know this girl better.

She agreed to meet. Unfortunately, I was twenty minutes late, and Amber wasn't there. I went back to the tanning salon the next day to see her. I apologized for being late, thinking I could smooth things over.

Amber was reluctant to give me a second chance. "I'm not going to wait around," she said in kind of a rude way.

Up until then, getting girls to go out with me wasn't a problem. By this time in my life, I was doing well. I was twenty-five years old and had my own home, drove a Mercedes, and ran my own business. So yes, girls waited for me. But Amber didn't—and that got my attention. I asked her to meet me for lunch again. This time I was five minutes late, and—you guessed it—she had already left. I couldn't believe it! A few weeks passed before I saw her at the tanning salon again. I walked in and immediately said, "I get it. I'm an idiot. I want to try one more time. Would you consider going out with me again?"

She said she would.

I finally showed up on time, and we started dating.

We'd been together for one and a half months when I said I had two tickets to fly anywhere in the country. "Where do you want to go? Anywhere. I don't care." And I meant it. I wanted to take Amber on a great adventure, like my mom had done for me when I was a kid.

The farthest place I could think of from where we were was Bangor, Maine. Stephen King lived there. I told Amber we should find him and have him sign his new book, *Needful Things*, for us. She loved the idea.

We flew to Bangor without a plan. When we landed, we first went to find a copy of the book. I asked the clerk at the bookstore if he knew where Stephen King lived. He didn't. I pulled into Dunkin' Donuts to get a snack. On a whim, I asked the kid behind the counter if he knew where Stephen King lived. To my surprise, he did.

"He lives at the top of the hill," he said, pointing at the road leading to it.

Amber and I drove toward his house. When we arrived, the most incredible Gothic home stood before us. It was huge, and looked exactly like the house the Munsters lived in. There were gargoyles on the fence; wrought iron bats at the gate, which looked like a spider web; and four cars parked outside. I noticed several security cameras scattered around, too. I'd brought a small video camera to record our "meeting" with King, if we were able to get one. I told Amber to hop out of the car, take the book, and wave it in the air in front of the gate. I thought that if Stephen King saw this pretty girl with one of his books, he might come out to sign it. We were on a quest, and wouldn't give up until we got what we came all the way from California to get. Amber did her best, walking along the fence line, holding up the book, and trying to get his attention. I was videotaping it all and laughing hysterically, knowing we probably looked like two idiots. Unfortunately, our plan didn't work.

I looked around and noticed a black Chevy Suburban with darkened windows. I thought, *That has to be his vehicle*. If we waited long enough, we might be able to follow him.

Amber needed a restroom and asked if we could go back to the Dunkin' Donuts. By the time we returned to King's house, the Suburban was gone. It was as if he'd waited for us to leave before making his escape. But then I spotted a woman walking through the open gate. I shouted, "Hi, ma'am. Sorry to disturb you. We're on a quest. I bet this girl we could fly all the way here from California and get Mr. King to sign our book. Do you think he would do that for us?"

The woman was very friendly. She said King had gone to his office at the industrial park next to the airport. She gave us directions and sent us on our way. When we arrived, there was no black Suburban. We were so disappointed. Just as we began to back out of the lot, his Suburban pulled in, and there he was: Stephen King. I jumped out of the car as quickly as I could with the book in my hand and said, "Just the man we wanted to see. We've flown all the way from California just to say hi. Would you mind signing our book?"

And he did!

While he was signing, Stephen asked, "Why would you come all the way to Maine? It's boring as hell! You should go somewhere like Niagara Falls."

I was so stunned that he was talking to us, all I could say was, "Okay."

I had no idea how far away the falls were. When Amber and I looked on the map, Niagara Falls was two inches away. Well, you know how that goes. It was a ten-and-a-half-hour drive.

Somewhere in New Hampshire, I got pulled over. This was going to be a problem. You see, my license had been suspended because I'd gotten too many speeding tickets . . . again. I was able to rent a car because I had the physical license, but I knew that when the officer ran a check, he would come back and cuff me, which he did. He arrested me and took me to jail. On the way, I did my best to be nice. I knew that being difficult would only make things harder for me. I made small talk and didn't question why I was in the back of the car. The nearest jail was several miles away. Amber followed behind the patrol car in our rental. By the time we got there, the police officer had decided he would write me up and keep my license, but he wouldn't make me stay in jail. He turned out to be a really decent guy. While he was busy filling out the paperwork, Amber and I debated about who was taller. The officer told us to stand against the board where mug shots were taken and snapped a picture of us to settle the argument. I regret not getting a copy of that!

Amber and I left the station and continued on our great adventure. We made our way to upstate New York, where we'd planned to stop for the night. Having learned nothing from my previous arrest, I was driving. While we were trying to figure out where we wanted to stay, I noticed red-and-blue lights flashing in my rearview mirror. I was being pulled over again. This time Amber grabbed the video camera to capture the moment. Before the officer could approach the car, Amber flipped the camera on and said, "Hi, Glenn. How are you?"

"I'm okay," I said.

"What's going on?"

"Nothing."

"Oh, really? Why don't we show everybody what's happening here . . ." And then she panned around to where there were now five police cars surrounding our car.

"Yup. Just another day at the office," I said.

Just then, the first officer came up to my window. "Sir, can I see your license?"

I'm certain he knew I didn't have it. But just in case, I told him the truth. I explained that the police in New Hampshire had confiscated my license when they arrested me hours before. I admitted that my license was suspended right away.

The officer either took pity on me or appreciated my complete candor, because he wrote me a ticket and told me to keep it to sixty-five, or no more than eight miles over any speed limit. With that, all five cars left.

Amber and I finally made it to Niagara Falls. We stood on the edge of the American side and said, "Look, it's Niagara Falls," and then we left. We had a flight to catch back in Bangor. We should have just bought another ticket from Buffalo. But I loved the time Amber and I spent together, getting to know each other. Nothing seemed to bother her—not my "run-ins" or my suspended license. She was great.

Amber was still living with her parents when we met. About a month after our trip, she came to me and said she had missed her period. We bought a pregnancy test and went back to my house, where she took it. We sat on the steps and waited for the result. Amber was holding the stick in her hands. We could slowly see the plus sign emerging. She started to cry. I looked at her, grabbed her shoulders, and said, "This could be the worst moment of your life or the best moment of your life. It's all how you think about it."

Everything is about mindset.

Best moment or worst moment? We get to choose that.

Amber was sobbing. She wasn't ready to have a baby. Her first thought was to get an abortion. And I understood. It was her body, and her choice. I also told her I'd felt the same way when I was fourteen years old, except I didn't have a choice. Charlene's mom was having the baby. What came out of it was the most amazing daughter I never would have known had we gone through with the most convenient way of getting rid of the pregnancy.

Yet I assured Amber that she did have a choice, and I would support her decision. Even so, she could try to see this differently if she wanted to. Things could turn out great, and this could become the best thing that ever happened in her life.

"Absolutely not. There's no way. I'm too young. I won't do that," she insisted.

We sat quietly together, Amber in my arms. I turned to her and said, "Who's your best friend?"

"My mom."

"Why don't you talk to your mom and get her advice? You're making a big decision."

Amber asked if I would come with her, and of course I did.

When we got to her house, she suggested I wait in the car for ten minutes. When I walked into the house, Amber and her mom were sitting on Amber's bed. I could see the look of disappointment in both of their eyes. It crushed me. And then her mom said something I'll never forget:

"Whatever you two decide, this is going to affect you for the rest of your lives, no matter what you choose."

And she was right. We all make choices in life. But in the end, our choices make us.

I stood in front of Amber and her mom and vowed to be there for the child, and to support Amber in every way. She would never have to worry about anything when it came to that. I'd been down this road before, and had experienced both sides of this decision. I respect a woman's right to choose, and I felt a need to be the voice for our unborn potential.

I was supposed to leave on a business trip the next day. Before I did, Amber came to my house to tell me she and her mom had made an appointment to terminate the pregnancy the following day. She was going through with the abortion.

I made one last plea, assuring Amber that I would be there for her. I would help raise the child and would never let her down when it came to our baby. I wouldn't desert her. I wanted her to know that.

I decided to cancel my trip; I wanted to be the person standing by her side come morning. I would walk her into the clinic, hold her hand, and do whatever she needed me to do.

When we awoke the next morning, the first words out of Amber's mouth were, "Let's go." She was determined.

We got into the car and drove to the clinic in silence. By the time we reached the front door, Amber's legs were shaking. She started wobbling and fell to her knees, crying. I pulled her up, walked her back to the car, and drove off. We stopped in a McDonald's parking lot so we could talk.

"Let's do this. Let's get married and have the baby," she said. I was all in.

Amber showed tremendous courage and strength that day. Not only did she face her fears, but she also took a huge leap of faith, one that changed the course of both of our lives forever. Her decision to keep the baby was one of the strongest and most powerful decisions I'd ever witnessed.

We got married on February 14, 1992, at the Meridien hotel across from the John Wayne Airport. Our son Skyler was born in July. I will be forever grateful for the gift Amber gave us that day.

Amber and I barely knew each other when we married. We'd dated for only a few months. We were kids ourselves, and now we had a family. I was dedicated to keeping my word to her. At the same time, I was busy growing my company. My attention was unfairly divided.

We had two more children together, Colby and Trevor. What we discovered over time, though, was that we didn't have a lot in common. You could say we weren't evenly yoked, something I now believe is essential to making a relationship work.

Amber had taken some classes at community college, but then she became a full-time mom, which limited her ability to explore other interests and to meet a wide host of different people. In fairness, when we met, she hadn't kissed enough toads.

As my life grew bigger, I think Amber felt like she didn't belong anymore. As a result, our relationship slowly evaporated. We never spent time alone with each another. Neither of us was happy. There came a point when we had to ask ourselves, "Do I choose to merely exist, or to live?"

When Amber and I decided to divorce in 1998, I assured her that I would always be there for her, just as I had done when we had Skyler. I sat down and said, "The only thing I can promise you is that whatever the deal is—whether it's through a judge or us negotiating—whatever it is, I will do better than what's decided. When everything is said and done, I'll come back to you and up the ante. I just want you to know that if it comes to a win/lose scenario, in the end, you'll win."

I didn't want Amber to worry about the outcome of the divorce. I didn't want either of us to be concerned about winning or losing. I just wanted to do the right thing. So, every chance I had, I reiterated that message to her. Amber was the mother of my three sons. I loved her then, as I do now. I wasn't out for blood or victory. We simply grew apart. It happens. She didn't need to be punished for the loss any more than I did. Naturally, when you're in the middle of a breakup, even an amicable one, you don't have a lot of trust or confidence in your mate, because they're no longer your mate. They've left. You're divorcing. It can be difficult for a while, until it isn't.

Amber and I sat through countless meetings with forensic accountants and lawyers—hers and mine. They calculated my business to be worth this much, our home and assets that much. This was shortly before I bought Ron out of the company, so there wasn't a lot of money to divvy up.

On the final day of negotiations, I sat and listened as each person gave their opinion.

"Are you done?" I asked.

The bean counters at the table were stunned.

"Here's what I'm prepared to do. I'll give her the house. You say it's worth seven hundred thousand dollars. I happen to be in the business and know it's worth seven hundred fifty thousand, so you came in low. That's okay; I'm not going to trip over your lowballing everything. It doesn't matter. She can have the house. But if she takes the house, she inherits the four-hundred-thousand-dollar loan that goes with it. She can take the home, the loan, and the -three hundred fifty-thousand-dollar equity. In addition, she's getting money from the business and all our other assets, and I'll pay monthly alimony as agreed. That's my deal."

My lawyer tried to jump in to stop me, but it was too late. I'd put the offer on the table. Whenever your lawyer tries to intervene, it usually means you're about to make a mistake, at least in their eyes. I knew it was a good deal for Amber. Everyone in that room knew it, too.

"If you don't like this deal, I'm willing to offer you a new one. I'll give her everything—my company and every asset I own—and I'll walk away with nothing," I said, straight-faced, without so much as a blink.

The lawyers asked me to explain.

"I'll have to work my tail off over the next five years just to pay half of what I'm already giving her. So not only am I giving her assets, I'm committing to working harder over the next five years than ever before. If you think the business is worth more, then you can take everything and sell it. Sell the house. Do whatever you want to do. Your choice is simple: believe me or take everything. That's what I'm offering. There will be no negotiating. You think it over." Then I got up and left.

This wasn't about Amber being greedy. It was about lawyers trying to overreach and be unreasonable. Both sets of lawyers were posturing, playing a very expensive hand of poker with our future.

After I left, I drove down the freeway thinking I'd offered Amber a great deal. I wasn't trying to push something on her just to see if she would take it. My offer was genuine and sincere.

And then my cell phone rang.

"Where did you go?" It was my lawyer

"Where did I go? I left so I could go to work and pay your fricken' bill." I was pissed.

"You have to come back," he said.

I reluctantly turned around.

When I walked back into the conference room, her attorney quickly said, "We'll take deal number one. We'll take these assets, and you get to bust your ass for the next five years." He had a smirk on his face that I'll never forget. He was lucky I didn't smack it right off.

"Are we done?" I asked.

"Yes."

I turned to leave once more. But before I did, I swung back around and said, "I promised Amber one thing—that whatever deal we made, I'd make it better. So here's my new deal: Put the house in the kids' names, and I'll pay off the loan over time. She'll never have to worry about that obligation. Or if she wants the house in both of our names, she can have it. It's an asset that, in ten or twenty years, whenever we decide to sell it, we'll split fifty-fifty because I'll pay off the loan. She doesn't have to. What do you think about that?"

Her lawyers said, "We'll think it over."

Think it over? Wow. I thought I was doing the right thing, and that was their response?

Amber didn't take me up on the offer. She took deal number one. The day after we signed the paperwork and everything was final, she put the house on the market. It sold in one day. She got her money and thought she'd made the right decision.

Amber found another house a block away. She said she needed a place where she could have a fresh start. The house was inferior in every way, but it was hers. I couldn't stand seeing her live there. It didn't feel right. So, three years later, I bought a house in the neighborhood where I was living. I wanted Amber and the boys to be closer to me.

It had been several years since we'd finalized our divorce. I'm sure you're asking yourself, "What did he have to gain by doing this?"

The answer is nothing.

Amber didn't trust me that day in the lawyers' office. She made a bad choice. It happens. The reason I came back around was because I wanted to prove to her that my intentions were good and that I meant what I'd said before the proceedings began.

I bought the house and Amber moved in.

My intentions had always been to help Amber. I never wanted her to suffer. I wanted the best for her, and I wanted her to know that I'd been consistent whether we were married or not.

In life, everything is the result of the choices we make. I believe you can take the easy way out or you can fight your way through and do the right thing, regardless of the circumstances you face. Even when every part of your being is screaming, "Take the easy way!" you must realize there are consequences. Inaction is action. If you listen to the voice telling you to take the easy route, you'll lose every time. Why? You have to do the right thing every time. There's zero tolerance for anything less. There will never be a next time, because you'll always find an excuse for why next time isn't good. So, what do you do? Suck it up and do what you should do. You might lose money, time, or things along the way, but what you gain is immeasurable. You gain confidence in yourself and in life, because you did the right thing and kept your word. If you want a different result, make a different choice. It's really that simple

CHAPTER NINE

MINDERELLA

The real power of a man is in the size
of the smile of the woman sitting next to him.
—Unknown

IN THE EARLY 2000S, I became a partner in a television production company that worked on projects with people such as Brooke Burke and Art Mann from E! Entertainment. One of the projects we were involved with was *The Wildest Bachelorette Party*. The show was produced in conjunction with the L.A. radio station, 98.7 KISS FM, and was filmed in Las Vegas.

I didn't have my kids on the weekends, so I could usually be found there Fridays through Sundays. Oddly, when I was told about the *Wildest Bachelorette Party*, I wasn't that into it. As alluring as involvement with this kind of show might sound, I was at a point in my life when I didn't want to party like that anymore. Besides, I'd already been on the set for several other versions of this particular show, so I didn't think I'd be missing out on all that much. I was over it.

As it happened, my friend Parker, who'd come with me when I first drove to California in my twenties, called to say that he and his girlfriend were going to be in Las Vegas the same weekend we were supposed to shoot. He wanted to meet me there. I'd already told the production team I was out, so there was no way I was going back to Vegas, even to see Parker. When I told him no, he insisted that I come. I was resistant, but he kept pushing until I finally said, "Okay, if I can get on the last plane out, I'll be there." I thought it would be a long shot at best, but sure enough, there was room on the plane. I ran to the gate and barely made it on before they closed the cabin door.

When I landed, I met Parker and his girlfriend for dinner. I mentioned the *Bachelorette Party* event that was happening that night, and Parker's eyes lit up. "Are we going?" he asked.

"Okay, we can go, but I really don't want to stay," I said.

We did a flyby, and as I expected, it wasn't anything I wanted to be involved in. We left around midnight. Parker said he and his girlfriend were tired and wanted to go back to their room, but the night was young, and there were plenty of other places for us to go.

"Parker, I flew in to see you. You can't go to sleep now," I coaxed.

"Glenn, we're on East Coast time. It's three in the morning for us. We're exhausted. I'll see you tomorrow."

"Really? Tired? It's Las Vegas!" I rolled my eyes and left I went out by myself.

To blow off some steam, I went to play blackjack by myself at the Palms Hotel and Casino.

I was whooping it up and having the best time, high-fiving everyone at my table whenever I won a hand. I knew the pit bosses, and we were joking back and forth.

Suddenly, a woman from the next table yelled, "Hey, settle down over there. Don't be stealing our thunder. The party table is over here."

I looked up and thought, *Wow. She's pretty.* And then I said, "Well then, why don't I move my party over there?"

I picked up my chips and sat in the only open seat at her table. She told me her name was Mindy. I happened to be wearing dark sunglasses, which made me feel like a big swinging dick. Looking back, it was so lame. And Mindy saw right through it. She harassed me right away.

"Why are you wearing those cheesy sunglasses indoors? Take those off!" she said.

I loved it. I thought her boldness was very attractive.

We spent the rest of the night joking around and laughing with her friends. For whatever reason, we would break into song. And for no reason at all, we found ourselves singing, "Yo ho, yo ho, it's a pirate's life for me!" and kept egging each other on until sunrise.

When the sun came up, I called it a night—or a morning, because it was time for me to leave. Everyone said their good-byes. I waved and smiled, playing it cool, and then headed to the airport.

At the time, I had no problem dating. I was mostly seeing women I didn't care about, and I wasn't looking for anything serious. Just before that night in Vegas, I'd taken another girl there. She was beautiful and sexy, and I was the envy of every man at the pool that weekend. But sometimes things aren't what they appear to be. I felt empty. That girl represented everything I thought I wanted, and yet I also realized she was shallow. Being with her was so unfulfilling. Deep down, I realized I didn't want that anymore.

So, when I got into the cab the morning after meeting Mindy, I thought, *Hmm. She seemed different. She was fun and nice, and not like those other girls.* I left it at that. Besides, I hadn't gotten her number or her last name.

And then a few days later, I turned on my television to KTLA Morning News, and lo and behold, there she was. Mindy was dishing all the latest in entertainment on the local Los Angeles station. I stared at the TV. As she spoke, her name appeared across the bottom of my television screen:

Mindy Burbano.

Damn. She was as pretty as I remembered. My heart was racing with excitement.

Well, at least now I had her last name. All I had to do was reach out.

I decided to email her. I explained that we'd met at the blackjack tables and asked if I could take her out.

Mindy didn't respond. I was certain she was used to getting these types of "fan" emails and letters. Even so, I wasn't about to give up. This time I called the KTLA viewer voice mail and left a message for her. I said we'd met in Las Vegas and that I had tickets to a Jimmy Buffett concert and would love for her to be my guest.

MINDERELLA

This time, Mindy called me back. She said she'd never been to a Jimmy Buffett concert and thought, *Why not?* She asked if she could bring a friend, and, of course, I said yes. As it turned out, I had 150 tickets to the concert. If you've never seen a Jimmy Buffett show, they're like no other. Before the show, people love to tailgate. Everyone wears their "Cheeseburger in Paradise" hats, shark fins, and island wear while getting wasted on margaritas and beer. Every year, I hosted a party that got progressively bigger. That year, I brought in several RVs and parked them in a circle to create a wide-open space where my guests could dance and party. I even brought in semitrailer with a thirty-foot volcano on it that spewed smoke. There were orangutans, live parrots, and giant surfboards, too—and that's not all. I brought in dump trucks full of sand and created "Glenn Stearns Island." To be fair, I didn't plan this extravaganza myself; my party planners did. And they really went over the top. The police tried to shut me down because I didn't have a permit. I didn't care. I told them I had 150 tickets, which allotted me 150 parking spots. They couldn't argue with that, but they still insisted I needed a permit to have such a large gathering.

By the time Mindy got there, the place was so crowded that she couldn't find me. I was dealing with the police and the party. All she saw at first were half naked girls on surfboards, my orangutans being carted away by the police, and hundreds of guests having the best time. When she finally found me, she said, "Wow. Glenn Stearns Island?" I tried to blame my party planners, but I admitted the parrots and orangutans were all my idea. I handed her two tickets and told her to have a fun night. And that was the last I saw of her that evening.

The next day, Mindy called to thank me. She raved about how great the night was. She was blown away by how passionate Jimmy Buffett fans were. She said it was like the Grateful Dead meets the beach. And she was right.

I mentioned I had front-row seats to a Paul McCartney show later that week and asked if she wanted to go.

She said yes, but explained she had to work that night at ten thirty. She was concerned about missing work, so she called Hal Fishman, the beloved longtime news anchor on KTLA, and told him that she had a chance to see Paul McCartney. She asked Hal what he would do. Hal loved Mindy and treated her like a daughter. He said if it were him, he'd go to the concert. So, he sent a truck out to the Arrowhead Pond of Anaheim on the night of the event, making it possible for her to do a stand-up near the venue. Before the event, we went to dinner. We enjoyed ourselves so much that we missed half the concert. When it came time for Mindy to do her piece for KTLA, she ran outside, grabbed the mic, did her report and other entertainment news, and then came back inside for the end of the show.

We had a magical evening, and I knew then that I had met the love of my life.

I spent most of dinner that night telling Mindy all about my mom. I shared endless stories about all the fun times we'd had, and even told her about the last time I saw her before she died.

As I matured, my relationship with my mother deepened. Whenever I went back to Maryland for a visit, I would put together a large party of family and friends. Mom was always there. Everyone loved her, and she was usually the life of the party.

I especially enjoyed surprising my mom over the years. Once, she and her sister Joy, were planning to visit me in California. When I bought the tickets, I planned a deliberate layover in Las Vegas, knowing that the two of them would probably go outside to smoke before their next flight. When they did, they were greeted by a man in a dark suit holding a sign with their names on it.

"What's going on?" my mother asked.

"Ladies, please come with me," the driver said.

They got into a waiting limousine, where they were handed front-row tickets to see Tom Jones perform. My mother loved two singers: Tom Jones and Bette Midler. Someone I knew had connected me with Tom for the tickets. I'd asked if he would hand-deliver them. Bold, I know, but you don't get what you don't ask for, right? He was very gracious and said he would love to, except he also had family visiting. Instead, he offered me the two front-row tickets, which I knew would send Mom over the moon. I loved doing little things like that for her. It filled my bucket in ways I can't really explain.

The last time I saw my mom was in 2000, when she flew to Las Vegas to play in a pool tournament. When I was growing up, Mom could always be found at the local VFW or American Legion. Those were her favorite watering holes. When she remarried, she and her new husband, Dave, loved to play pool there. Mom was so excited when they won the local tournament and got to go to Vegas. Five thousand people would descend upon the city to play in the national tournament alongside her, but that didn't deter her one bit.

"I'll come out and cheer you on," I said.

At the time, I was in my first real relationship after my divorce from Amber, and let's just say it wasn't a healthy one. Those transitional relationships rarely are. A lot of it may have been my fault. Even so, I took her to Vegas to meet my mom.

Blackjack was my game of choice. The hotels and casinos treated me well because I went there a lot. But this trip wasn't about me; it was about Mom. Unfortunately, she lost early in the tournament. I could see she was disappointed, and that hurt my heart. Dave, Mom, the woman I was with, and I were walking through the casino, across the floor where all the slot machines were.

"I can't play slots. I'm such a loser at that game," Mom said.

I stopped cold in my tracks before turning toward her.

"Mom, don't ever call yourself a loser," I said. I didn't want her to feel that way. I handed her a hundred-dollar bill and said, "Go play."

She did, and she lost it all.

I handed her another hundred.

She hit the jackpot for $800. She was so happy that she jumped up and down with joy.

"You see? You're a winner. I told you!" I was thrilled for her.

But as suddenly as she'd gotten excited, she stopped. She turned to me and said, "You know, your mother isn't going to be around much longer . . ."

Before she could say another word, I grabbed the sides of her head with both hands and said, "Don't do that. Stop saying that."

Mom was just fifty-seven years old. I wasn't thinking about a world where she wouldn't be around. She had always been in the picture. I couldn't understand why she was saying this to me.

Mom reached up and held my face like she used to when I was a young boy. "I love you so much, son. I'm so proud of you. I love your sister, your dad, Dave; I've had such a good life. I have everything I could ever want. I'm just so perfectly set. I need you to know that when I go, I don't want you to be sad. I want you to throw me a party. I want you to dance at my grave! Promise me that."

In that moment, I knew she was saying goodbye. I felt it in my core. There was really nothing to say except "I love you, Mom. This is my official goodbye." I kissed her, and then she and Dave went their way while we went ours. As we walked in our separate directions, I stopped and turned. My mom had done the same. One last look. One last time.

"That's the last time I'll ever see my mom," I thought aloud.

"Stop it!" the woman I was with said.

But I knew it was true.

A week later, I received a phone call that my mom had been rushed to the hospital. Dave had also been hospitalized for a mass on his aortic valve, so he couldn't be with her.

Ironically, I was back in Las Vegas on business. I dropped

everything and headed straight to the airport. I wasn't sure there would be any flights that late in the day. When I arrived, I frantically begged for anything that would get me close to Baltimore. As luck would have it, there was a delayed flight they could get me on. I arrived in Maryland around three in the morning and went directly to Holy Cross Hospital, the same hospital where I was born. It was also the same hospital where my daughter Charlene was born. And now, it was where my mother was lying in a coma, brain-dead from an aneurysm.

When I walked into the room, she was on life support and breathing through a ventilator. I was able to spend two beautiful hours with her, sitting together, holding her hand. I knew she was gone, but I wasn't ready to let go.

By eight o'clock in the morning, a crowd had gathered in the waiting room. Amber had flown in from California; Charlene came; and my best friend, Shane, my sister Sue, and a few others were there, too, including a very flamboyant man I didn't know who appeared to be extremely upset. Midmorning, I met with the doctors to discuss Mom's prognosis. When they showed me her brain scans, I asked how often someone with something like that pulled through.

"Never," they said.

I wanted to be absolutely certain there was no chance she could recover.

"She won't make it, Mr. Stearns," the doctors reiterated.

"Then what are we waiting for? Let's pull the plug." I was very firm in my decision. I knew it was the right thing to do. The doctors all agreed.

MINDERELLA

A group of us gathered around my mom's bed to say our final goodbyes. The doctors turned off the ventilator and we watched her slowly fade away, until her heart stopped beating. I was oddly at peace, because I'd said goodbye to her in Las Vegas. I'd had closure a week earlier, and was able to say "I love you" to her.

Shane was in the corner of the room wailing, "That's just not right." Tears ran down his cheeks. I was happy he was able to show his emotions, but I wasn't feeling the same. She was ready to go. And she knew it was her time. I was at peace knowing we had said our goodbyes. How many times do we get the chance to tell our loved ones goodbye and that we love them, and then they go? It was the perfect way to say goodbye.

My sister and I went to the funeral home to make arrangements for the burial. The funeral director kept asking for my mom's wig. I didn't know anything about that, but Sue did, so I asked her to go back to Mom's house to get it. Sue was so upset that she couldn't think clearly, let alone find the wig. She was crying and frantically looking. I stopped her and said, "It's ok. We could buy Mom a new one."

When she calmed down, I asked her to look for it one last time, and sure enough, she found it. People fall apart—I get that—but I also know that the mind is very powerful. Once Sue knew we didn't *have* to find that wig, her mind was calmer, and she was able to focus.

While Sue was back at Mom's house, I went to pick the gravestone. On the way, I stopped at Roy Rogers to get a bite to eat. I was sitting by myself, deep in thought, when Terri

Lonon, the girl I took to the eighth-grade dance, walked in.

"Glenn?" she said.

I couldn't believe it. I hadn't seen her in forever. She sat down for a quick hello. We caught each other up on the past eighteen years. I told her I was back in Maryland because my mom had just died.

"How long are you staying?" she asked. I told her I wasn't sure.

When I was growing up, I always had a girlfriend. After eight months or so, when the butterflies in my stomach wore off, I'd want to move on. I always knew the luster would fade within a year. Things hadn't changed one bit for me as I got older, but seeing Terri that day made me realize that I wanted them to. I wanted someone in my life I was willing to stick with when the excitement of a new relationship died down. Someone I could be friends with. Someone who could help figure out how to stay together as a team when things got boring. Was I capable of that? I wasn't certain, but it sure sounded nice.

THE FUNERAL HOME was packed with people who came to the wake to pay their respects. The entire time I was there, I kept thinking about the fake diamond cross necklace my mom had had for years. It wasn't expensive, but she loved it and wore it all the time. At some point, I'd noticed the cross was worn out and several of the fake diamonds were missing, so I bought her a new one, only this time it was platinum with real diamonds. When I gave it to her, she cried and said, "I will never take this off."

After everyone left that day, I went back to my mom's coffin to retrieve the necklace. I slipped it into my pocket and took it with me to her funeral the next day.

When I gave her eulogy, it was a celebration of her life, just as she'd wanted. I wasn't sad. In a way, I was at peace. After we buried Mom, I walked over and stood next to my sister for a moment. I could see she was in terrible pain. I reached into my pocket and handed her Mom's cross and said, "I think Mom would want you to have this."

Sue dropped to her knees crying. She put the necklace on that day, and just like my mother, she has never taken it off.

THREE MONTHS LATER, I decided to fly back to Baltimore. I had one last promise to keep. I called Shane and asked him if he would go see my mom with me. Shane was always up for an adventure, and he's always there when I need a friend. He said of course he would go. This wasn't the first time I'd asked Shane to go to a cemetery with me. Once, when we were in high school, I asked him to go with me to Steve Stag's grave. Steve was a buddy of ours who was killed by a car in a hit-and-run. I fell asleep at his gravesite that night. Shane couldn't wake me to leave, so he just left me there.

I hadn't noticed how beautiful Mom's resting place was until that day. She was buried in a plot surrounded by woods. Shane stood back to give me a private moment. I thought about all the fun she and I had had over the years. I loved taking her out dancing and having such a wonderful time together. I thought about how my mom and her sister would twirl around the dance floor together until they fell down, their dresses flying up over their heads. They would lie on the floor, laughing so hard that they couldn't get up. It must've happened a hundred times, and it never got old. At least, not back then.

As I stood in the cemetery that day thinking about her, I began to dance. It was more of a jig, but it makes me smile to this day thinking about it.

Afterward, I realized I didn't have any videos of my mom. I really wished there were some family movies of her, but there weren't. I should have had something to show people who my mother really was, how she lived her life, and why she meant so much to me. At the very end of her life, she had lived with great passion. Fun followed her wherever she went.

I flew back to Baltimore again for the one-year anniversary of my mom's death. I had a layover in Las Vegas, which turned into an hour's delay. I decided to take a hundred dollars and play the slot machine in honor of my mom. I put a crisp one-hundred-dollar bill into the machine and hit an $800 jackpot, just like my mom had done the year before.

I just stood there smiling, remembering that time together, when all of a sudden someone came up behind me and said, "Congratulations. Eight-hundred dollars! Great job!" Then he looked at me and said, "You're Janet's son, aren't you?"

I didn't recognize the face at first. Then it clicked. He was the flamboyant man from the hospital who'd cried hysterically when she died. He introduced himself and explained that he'd been her hairdresser for years. We spoke about Mom for a few minutes before he said goodbye and I headed toward my gate.

Not long after my mom died, I knew I needed to end things with the woman I was seeing. I couldn't take the drama of our relationship anymore. It was so unpredictable and, frankly, exhausting. It wasn't going to be an easy relationship to get out of cleanly. I knew she was adopted, so I hired a private detective to find her biological parents. When he found them, I called her mom and said, "You don't know me, but I know your daughter. Would you like to meet her? She has a son— your grandson—who's an amazing baseball player. Would you like to meet him, too?"

She hung up on me.

Undeterred, I called her back. She said she'd been shocked and scared by my earlier call. I told her I understood and would love to give her and her daughter the opportunity to meet if she were open to it.

Once I met Mindy, I knew from our first date that she was someone I wanted to get to know better. I didn't want to screw things up with her. I was done with the intense relationship I'd been in and needed to let that woman know it was over for good. It wasn't all her fault, as I said before. We just brought out the worst in each other. When we'd met, I wasn't really ready to be in another relationship. Maybe I sabotaged it; I don't really know. But sometimes two people just aren't the best fit for each other, and that was definitely the case for this woman and me.

I told her I thought she was a wonderful person with a big heart, but I didn't feel the relationship was healthy for either of us anymore. I explained that I had a parting gift for her, because I wanted things to end on a good note, and handed her an envelope. Inside was information about her biological mom and dad. I looked at her in the eye and said, "Go find them. Get the love you need. You deserve to be happy." I didn't say another word. I didn't have to.

In a strange way, I felt like my mom that night in Vegas. She knew that was her last goodbye to me, and I knew this was my final farewell to this woman. There would be no turning back. At least, not in my mind. Something deep inside me knew Mindy was the one for me.

About two months later, my now ex-girlfriend unexpectedly showed up at my home. She called and said she was outside my gate and wanted to come in. She'd been drinking with some girlfriends and wanted to say hello. I knew it was a bad idea.

I stayed strong in my conviction and told her no, she should leave, and hung up.

A minute later, the phone rang again. I thought it was her again, so I answered abruptly, "Hello!"

"Glenn, it's Mindy. I'm about to go on the air—"

Before she could say another word, I blurted out, "I just want you to know that my ex-girlfriend came by tonight. She was drunk and was outside my gate begging to come in. I told her no."

Mindy said, "You're so good about things like that. It's

one of the traits I like about you." And then she hung up to do the news.

The next day, Mindy drove from Los Angeles to Newport Beach to meet me for lunch. We had a great conversation, but my ex-girlfriend never came up. If Mindy had told me an ex-boyfriend had drunkenly knocked on her door late at night, I would have called back to see what happened. Her nonchalance was making me a little curious, so I said to Mindy, "You never asked me if my ex-girlfriend came in last night."

"I trust you," she said.

I cocked my head and sat there quietly for a moment, just staring at the most beautiful woman in the world. Her answer was the complete opposite of what I'd been living with for so long with this other woman. In an instant, the weight of that relationship came off my shoulders, and I felt like a different man. Mindy didn't ask for details or feel the need to burden me with any of her insecurities, if she even had any. I knew right there and then that she was the woman I would marry. And I've never looked back.

If I have one disappointment, it's that Mindy never got the chance to know my mom—and that my mom never got the chance to know her. I would have loved it if Mindy's parents and our children got to know my mom, too. I deeply regret having nothing but old photos to share.

The more I got to know Mindy, the more I felt at peace. It was the happiest I'd ever been. I felt as though I were dancing on clouds. I kept thinking, *Damn, I'm one lucky guy. I've met the greatest girl.* I wanted to call my mom and tell her all about her, but I couldn't. That was the first time it really hit me that she was gone, and that's when I finally cried. It had been two years since my mom passed, but it wasn't until that day, when I longed for her and Mindy to meet, that I truly mourned her. In that stretch of time, I missed her every day. I still do.

ON OCTOBER 11, 2003, about a year after we met, Mindy and I were married. It was everything a fairy-tale wedding should be. Dr. Robert Schuller, from the famed Crystal Cathedral, officiated in the most romantic and unforgettable ceremony I'd ever seen. Okay, sure, maybe I'm a little biased, but so many people who attended our wedding told us they felt the same way.

Since her first appearance on *The Oprah Winfrey Show* (the crazy circumstances of which I promise to tell you about soon), Mindy had become one of Oprah's favorite guests. When the team at *Oprah* heard Mindy and I were getting married, they asked if we would share our wedding on her show. Of course we said yes—and it was during that appearance that I made the faux pas that cost me all my business with HUD.

If I've learned one thing about life, it's that the only constant is change. What you once thought was important will, at some point, no longer be. This was especially true when my best friend, Shane, got married to his wife, Debbie. There were so many times before then when I worried that Shane would die before he ever walked down the aisle. He went down the rabbit hole of addiction until he eventually hit rock bottom.

Things were so bad for my buddy that at one point, about a year or two after I married Mindy, I flew to Maryland to get him the help he needed. If I'd told Shane why I was there, he never would have agreed to it. He'd just been released from the psych ward, where he'd been held for seventy-two hours. He'd shaved off his eyebrows in a drunken stupor and looked really out of it. When I arrived, I suggested we hop into the car and get lost like my mom used to do with my sister and me when things were really hard at home. We drove to Gettysburg and spent the day exploring the historic city. I bought a CD and popped it in and hit play.

"Over the hill came Lee's men, battling from one field to the next . . ."

The CD dramatically explained the Battle of Gettysburg and we loved every minute of it.

At the end of the day, I drove Shane home. He was expecting me to drop him off and head out. Instead, I told him to go inside and pack his clothes. When he asked why, I said, "I'm taking you to rehab." We had a plane to catch in two hours. I put my hand on his shoulder and said, "Doing something amazing doesn't come easy, but it's always worth it. You have the chance to do something amazing, Shane, so let's do this." Much to my surprise, he didn't put up a fight. He must have realized it was time to make some changes and that his life was now in a different place—or at least he wanted it to be.

At Shane's house that night, I saw a VHS cassette on his credenza labeled "Wedding." I turned to Shane and asked if I could get a copy. I knew my mom would be included, and I was craving anything that might bring her back to me, even for a moment. My mom loved Shane like he was her own son. She was so proud when he got married.

Shane told me to take the cassette, and so I brought it home. When I watched it, there she was—my mom, having a wonderful time celebrating Shane and Debbie. The videographer captured her on the dance floor with me, whooping it up as usual. And then she fell—and, yes, her dress flew up over her head. Until I saw that on camera, I hadn't remembered feeling embarrassed by her, but then I thought back and realized that it was the first and only time that I did. I was over her getting falling-down drunk.

Watching the tape, I saw myself realize what had happened and walk over to help her get back up onto her feet. I'd wanted her off the dance floor, and perhaps to get some food into her. As I walked away to fetch a plate of chicken wings, she yelled out, "And bring me a beer!" I shook my head and said, "How about some water?"

I had never, not once, done that to my mom. I loved her dearly and had never judged her for her behavior.

I turned off the VCR and sat quietly on my sofa, wondering why God would have done this. Why would He have given me fifteen seconds of my mom falling down drunkenly as the sole captured memory?

It took me some time to realize that we all have a legacy we leave behind. There's great power in the fact that our actions will dictate how we're remembered. Don't get me wrong—I loved every minute of being young, doing dumb things, and having fun. I certainly had my share of drunken, idiotic moments, and I'd enjoyed the insanity of it all. But I was truly over it. Some people learn quickly; my journey was slow and painful. I didn't want to be that person anymore. It took me longer than the average guy to get there, but I did get there. And it wasn't easy. I had to shake a lot of alcoholics in my own family to maneuver past it. Thank God.

If my kids look back someday at footage of their dad, I want them to be proud of what they see. I don't want them to ever feel like I did while watching my mom that day. I want them to be proud of who I was and how I lived my life. It's the main reason I did shows like *Undercover Billionaire* and *Undercover Billionaire: Comeback City*. It was my way of investing in my legacy, because hopefully, way down the road, it will pay off.

Showing my family what grit, determination, integrity, kindness, and humor looks like paves the way to hopefully making them proud. That motivates me to set an example every single day. And whether I like to admit it or not, the day when they look for reminders of that example will come. I mean, I thought that day was closer than ever a few years back when I was diagnosed with cancer. Life is fleeting and could be gone tomorrow, so you'd better do the things you want to do today or it may be too late.

There's the old saying that "in this world nothing can be said to be certain, except death and taxes." Taxes never scared me, but death? Well, that's another story.

In late December 2020, I turned fifty-seven, the same age

my mom was when she died. It was the only birthday I'd ever dreaded. I don't know why, but I suppose I didn't want to meet the same fate she did during my fifty-seventh year. Unlike her, I wasn't ready to die. I knew I had so much life left to live. I've spent many years thinking about everything she missed, and I didn't want to lose out on any of that—especially not the chance to watch my younger kids grow up and someday become parents themselves.

I didn't tell anyone how I was feeling. As the big day approached, I just kept thinking to myself, *Fifty-seven, here it comes*. I'm the kind of guy who keeps himself busy as a way of not thinking about the things that might slow me down. It's an effective distraction that keeps me from going to a dark place. The busier I am, the better. It's easy to get lost in your thoughts if you allow yourself to. You have to trick your mind into being confident even when you're not, to be happy even when you're sad. I've always done that. It's a secret weapon that has helped me plow through the tough times.

And then one morning, I rolled over in bed and couldn't stop myself from telling Mindy. She loves to celebrate life events, especially birthdays, but I just wasn't feeling it. I explained that while I appreciated her excitement, I really wanted to keep things quiet that year.

Some people tend to wallow in miserable thoughts, allowing worst-case-scenario thinking to dominate their every waking moment. I don't choose to do that. I want to think about other things—about stuff that isn't scary, stuff that has nothing to do with dying. Whenever I feel a sense of doom seeping in, I go to Fiji in my mind, or any other place I consider fun, light, and not stressful. Or I think about building a new company. It takes discipline to be able to do that, because it's a lot easier to allow yourself to fall into a funk than it is to stay out of one. It's a lot like meditating, in that it's a hard habit to create, but the benefits are worth it.

Why?

Well, you learn not to take the weight of the world onto your shoulders. You manage expectations and don't allow pebbles to become boulders that hold you back from the bigger goals you're striving to reach.

My sister once said she thought it wasn't natural to be high on life the way I am. She said it was peculiar that I always seemed happy. "What are you hiding, Glenn?" she asked.

In a way, her question made me mad. "Sue, do you think there are people who enjoy staying in a dark place? People who like to wallow in their misery?"

"Yes, sure. I suppose so," she said.

"A lot of times that may be due to depression or a chemical imbalance. Something is keeping them low, right?"

"I totally agree."

"Well, have you ever considered that I might have a chemical imbalance, too—but one that keeps me *up*? I'll take that imbalance any day." And I really believe that could be true. Why not? Or it could be a trained mindset. Either way, I'll take it.

I admit to having my share of dark, brooding days when I can be withdrawn or maybe even lash out from time to time. My mom used to say that we hurt the ones we love, meaning we tend to hurt the people who are closest to us. Why? Because we know they won't leave. But no matter how many times I try to justify my short temper as a way of protecting the people I love from feeling the pressure I feel, it never works. All it does is make things worse, especially for Mindy, who takes that weight onto herself. I don't want that, so I do what I must to be sure my pressure doesn't become other people's pressure.

Negative thoughts are a lot like gravity. Their pull is strong. If they tug at you, you have to prepare to land on both feet when you fall, or at least to pick yourself up as quickly as you can.

I don't believe in the victim mentality. I actually think it's horrible.

Here's what I know for sure: Dark clouds don't follow people. Most of the time, we create our own clouds, and even then, the worst-case scenario rarely happens. I don't believe people are unlucky, and I certainly don't think they're *repeatedly* unlucky. I think people consistently make poor choices—decisions that can keep them in a dark place when, in fact, they have other options. We always have options. I know so many people who stay in terrible relationships because they're afraid to leave. I know even more people who live above their means and are consistently worried about how they'll pay next month's bills. And what about those who choose to stay in a job they know will never lead them to more responsibility, a bigger paycheck, or, better yet, a happier life?

Personally, it took a long time for me to believe I could stay in a relationship and be totally and completely open and honest about how I was feeling—to allow a relationship to go deep and flourish. Mindy understood my cadence from the very beginning. She's a really intuitive person, which is a gift. She's beautiful, too, so naturally other men are attracted to her, but she knew exactly what I needed to know about that, and what I *didn't* need to know. She had the sensitivity to protect me, and us, from anything that might hurt my manhood or our relationship. She saved me from getting inside my own head by turning the conversation whenever it was necessary. She got me from the start, and always made me feel like the king of our castle. She understood exactly what I needed. Before I met Mindy, I'm not sure I ever had that. It took me many years to understand what she needed, too, but I finally think I've figured that out. I became *vulnerable*. That's as real as a solid relationship gets.

I'm really proud and excited by how my feelings for my wife continue to deepen and grow with time. And this is perhaps the happiest surprise, because I love the way I feel. I now understand the meaning of unconditional love. You can't remain shallow in any relationship and think it's somehow going to become deep. You have to be willing to open yourself up to the possibility of pain, hurt, and disappointment to achieve greater love, lust, and passion.

CHAPTER TEN

THERE'S ALWAYS GOING TO BE A BIGGER BOAT

It's all right to be Goliath, but always act like David.
—PHIL KNIGHT

VERY EARLY in our relationship, I had a habit of asking Mindy questions as a way of planning special surprises for her. For as long as I can remember, I've loved giving people I care about unforgettable experiences. I feel like that means so much more than extravagant gifts. Whether it's for my children, my family members, my wife, my best friends, or even people I invite to a fundraiser, I like the emphasis to be on the encounter. If I leave you feeling good, cared for, and special, then I've accomplished what I set out to do.

So, when I asked Mindy "If you had the opportunity to travel anywhere you've never been before, where would that be?"

and her very quick response was "Fiji," I began planning. Two months later, we were off to that gorgeous country in the South Pacific. To me, their islands are the most beautiful in the world. We stayed at the Wakaya Club & Spa, because I'd heard that Bill Gates, Céline Dion, Michelle Pfeiffer, and their respective spouses had all spent their honeymoons there. If it was good enough for them, it would be good enough for Mindy and me. When Mindy's mom saw where we were headed, she said, "If this is where you're going on your first vacation together, how will you ever top it?"

The grounds of the resort were spectacular. While the club itself was amazing, the experience of staying in the owner's private residence was off the charts. Although it cost a lot more money than any other room, that's where I wanted us to stay.

We had an incredible time just being alone together and exploring the island of Wakaya. We were madly in love and had found a slice of paradise. We danced to "Somewhere over the Rainbow" by Israel Kamakawiwoʻole and "Bennie and the Jets" by Elton John. We laughed nonstop and made the most of every moment. A staff of four took care of our every need, serving us food and drinks while we relaxed to the music. It was perfect.

"So this is where Bill Gates spent his honeymoon!" I mused out loud.

One of the butlers said, "Oh no, sir. They didn't spend their honeymoon here. They spent it at a private residence around the corner."

My head turned so fast that you could have heard it

screeching. I was shocked. I thought I'd booked the same house. I was dying to see this other home, because I couldn't imagine a place that was nicer than where we were staying.

I asked if someone could take us over to see it. The owner of the residence hadn't been to the island in over a year. He and the owner of the resort where we were staying were in some type of fight, so he no longer wanted to come to Fiji.

We were told that the other home had been featured on the cover of *Architectural Digest*, which we took as a sign from my mother in heaven that we would have a connection to the place. As you'll recall, my dad used to work at the facility where that magazine was printed. The house was a beautiful open-air Balinese-style dwelling located on the tip of a peninsula over-looking the beautiful South Pacific. The butler explained that many other celebrities had stayed in the home, including Tom Cruise and Nicole Kidman, Ashton Kutcher and Demi Moore, and Jim Carrey.

Mindy and I fell in instantly love with it. And it was for sale.

A Canadian named David Gilmour owned the resort where all these homes were located. He founded the FIJI water company. He also owned substantial real estate in Chicago, including the Sears Tower (now called the Willis Tower.) Gilmour built the resort after his twenty-two-year-old daughter, Erin, was randomly murdered in her apartment in Toronto. He'd purchased the property before she died and had taken her there, promising to build a special place for her on the grounds. When she was killed, it wrecked him.

Corinna Gordon, the woman who built the house we were now touring, lived in Santa Barbara. When she was diagnosed with breast cancer, she sold it to a man who wasn't taking very good care of it. He let it get run down, which was a shame because it was such a beautiful place. When Mindy and I first saw the house, it was a diamond in the rough, a little gem waiting to be polished. There were only five other houses on the island, which meant everyone who owned property there got to know each other. Everyone, that is, except Mr. Gilmour.

On the long plane ride back to California, I had a lot to think about. At the top of my mind was my desire to buy the house in Fiji. When we arrived in Los Angeles, I received a call from Marcy Weinstein, my friend and longtime Realtor. She said it was the right time to make an offer on a house I'd been considering in Newport Coast, California. That home was owned by actress Tawny Kitaen and Anaheim Angels pitcher Chuck Finley. They built the house but never lived in it, as they were getting a divorce. Marcy told me they were in their settlement conference, which made the timing perfect. I put in what I considered a lowball offer. It ended up being one of the highest prices ever paid for a home in Newport Coast at the time. I then picked up the phone and called Doug Carlson, a representative for Mr. Gilmour who handled all business transactions on his behalf. I told him I wanted to make an offer on the home we saw in Fiji, but that it would be very low because there weren't a lot of buyers for a place on a tiny island in the middle of the ocean.

"All we can do is try," he said.

THERE'S ALWAYS GOING TO BE A BIGGER BOAT

I thought I would end up negotiating for one of the properties, and the other would fall away. Instead, both of my offers were accepted without negotiation or counteroffers. It was a classic case of be careful what you wish for!

The next two months were extremely stressful as I rearranged my finances to make both purchases happen. I don't regret a moment of it.

I signed the paperwork for the house in Fiji at John F. Kennedy International Airport while sitting in the Concorde Room. Mindy and I were taking one of the last Concorde flights to London so she could interview Brad Pitt. As the supersonic jet took off, it felt as though my life with Mindy was about to take flight, too.

Some of my best memories of Fiji include time spent with family there. I heard a legend about a man named Felix von Luckner, who was believed to be a pirate. There are many versions of this tale, but we had heard that he and a group of his cohorts raided boats around Fiji, took whatever was valuable and then burned the boats. The locals chased him to the small island of Wakaya, where he was eventually caught. Turned out, he was a German navy man who attacked Allied shipping during WWI. According to the legend, he stashed all his gold and treasure somewhere on the island. No one has ever found it. So, I thought it would be great to take my three boys on a treasure hunt—but first I had to bury some treasure.

Before leaving for Fiji, I bought a large wooden chest, which I intended to fill with thousands of coins, including two hundred silver dollars that I borrowed from my son-in-law.

Mindy's cousin is a cartoonist, so I asked him if he would help create a treasure map for us. We made the map look old and tattered, and then took everything to Fiji with us. I was worried the authorities would question our bringing so many loose coins through customs, so I made everyone stuff them into their pockets, luggage, bags—you name it. Somehow we managed to walk all those coins through without a fuss.

Wakaya is around three miles long and is made up of very lush, dense jungle. When it rains, the torrential downpours create waterfalls that cascade off the volcanic rock. There aren't a lot of places for the rain to go because the island is mostly made of rock, so the plant life grows thick wherever there's runoff from the mountains to the ocean.

The local villagers told us about a spot they thought would be perfect for our buried treasure. My dad, Mindy, her brother, and her parents came with me deep into the jungle to bury the "treasure chest." It took all of us to carry the loot.

When we got there, it started to rain. The water was flowing around the exact spot the villagers had told us about. All of us had shovels and began digging. The rocks and rain made it challenging, but eventually we dug deep enough to bury the treasure. Before we headed back to the house, we marked the location by arranging some rocks in the shape of the letter *X*.

Ten months later, just before another trip to Fiji, I took my three boys aside and said, "You're not going to believe this. Someone found the von Luckner treasure map in Fiji!"

Their eyes lit up like Christmas trees. They were so excited to search for the valuables.

I turned the hunt into a game, one I dragged out for days.

It was late at night and very dark when my boys and I walked into the village. We saw a local tribesman, and I told one of the boys to ask him if he knew where the treasure map was.

He said he didn't know.

We then found ourselves behind a church, where we bumped into another man, who was someone I'd planted as part of my plan.

When one of my boys asked him if he knew anyone who might have the von Luckner treasure map, he said, "I don't have the map, but the chief knows where it is. Let me take you to him." He led us toward a very small house.

"Who goes there?" a voice from inside demanded.

It was dark, so the boys couldn't see who was speaking.

"Come inside, sit down," the voice said.

It was the chief.

"We're here to seek the von Luckner treasure map," Colby politely said.

"You are not worthy of the map! You must be a man to see this map," the chief informed him.

I told the kids to ask him how they could become men.

"You must first drink the ceremonial kava. Sit down, boys." The chief directed them to an area where another man was waiting with a bowl in front of him. Kava is a root that's pounded and mixed with water to make a dark liquid, which is traditionally drunk from a halved coconut shell. It's so strong that it numbs your lips when you sip it, but it's known to be very calming.

The kids sat on the ground, nervous and excited at the same time.

"Boy, pass me the bowl of kava," the chief said to Trevor.

The ceremony took place with lots of fanfare as each boy took a drink. The chief then directed us to travel to the "great banyan tree" in the jungle, where we were to sleep for the night with lions and snakes to prove that the boys were now men. For some unknown reason, there was a small tent waiting for us when we got there. After we awoke the next morning, we found a leather scroll at our campsite. We unrolled it to find the map I had made of the island. The boys could hardly believe their eyes. We spent the rest of the day following the map's clues. It had been nearly a year since we buried the treasure and set rocks in the shape of an X on top of it, and in that time, the X became covered with moss and big leafy plants. I knew when we were in the general area, but we had to look a lot harder than I'd expected to find it. When we finally did, the boys were ecstatic.

Skyler, Colby, and Trevor took their shovels and began to dig. They must have been digging for twenty minutes before they finally hit the top of the chest. Skyler looked up at me and said, "Dad, this whole time I thought this was fake!"

The chest was so heavy that it took all of us to pull it out of the hole. It looked like it had been buried for a hundred years. When the boys opened it, they were amazed to see that it was filled to the brim with riches. The silver coins were on top, spread over the other coins and the faux jewelry. It appeared to be a very bountiful booty.

"Dad! We're rich!" they rejoiced. "Let's sell this!"

"Why don't we just split it up and keep it in the family?" I suggested.

"What a great idea! We'll sell it to you and then *we'll* be rich!"

I had to laugh. I appreciated their ingenuity!

A note to my boys: If you've gotten this far in my book, first let me say that I'm shocked; second, congratulations! It seems I did have something to do with the "von Luckner treasure." PS: There's no Tooth Fairy or Easter Bunny. They might have been me, too.

Nothing fills my emotional bucket quite as much as watching other people having the time of their lives. I suppose that's the best part of having means, but even when I didn't have a lot of money, I always knew how to provide and have a good time. That's one of the great secrets to happiness: *Always have fun!* When something stops being fun, it's time to move on. And that's what eventually happened in Fiji.

As hard as Mindy and I tried to befriend Mr. Gilmour, he wanted nothing to do with us. It wasn't unusual for someone from the resort to approach us to say that homeowners weren't allowed to be on a certain beach or buy food from the Wakaya Club anymore. All the privileges that were once extended to us ended. If we wanted to have a party, we were told we weren't allowed to have guests. If we wanted to talk to any of the Fijian villagers, we were informed that it wasn't allowed. It made no sense, and it took all the fun out of being there. The other homeowners were as fed up as we were, and we all decided to sue Mr. Gilmour.

One afternoon, he called and said, "Some of the home-owners have decided to sue me—"

Before he could finish his sentence, I cut him off and said, "I'm one of those homeowners, sir. I'm suing you for one reason: You told me I couldn't go to the beach. Let me ask you something. Is that your beach? As far as I know, you don't own that beach. You say I can't talk to the villagers. Do you own them, too? I would like to understand my rights here."

"Glenn, I have to treat you like I treat all the other homeowners," he said, trying his best to justify his inexcusable behavior.

"No, sir, you don't. I would like to be treated differently. Let me tell you why. You wanted revenue to fix the roads. They're dirt roads, but you say you need to maintain them. Okay, I get that. People come to your club because it's quiet and that makes it feel exclusive, but it's only twenty percent occupied at any given time. I brought other people to your club, which means I brought you revenue. My wife and I have rented out the entire resort at times, generating hundreds of thousands of dollars for you. You want us to commit to spending ten thousand dollars at the club each year, which we've done, and then some. So you see, we've made you a lot money. You've said to me on more than one occasion that 'even wealthy people can be assholes.' Yes, sir. I understand that. But not all wealthy people. I brought former vice president Dan Quayle to your club; General Charlie Duke, who walked on the moon; Reba McEntire; and John Elway, all of whom are high-profile people, wouldn't you say? None of them are assholes. You know who they are? They're people of influence who will leave your island and tell lots of other high-profile friends about their amazing stay at your wonderful resort. So, I think, as homeowners, we've done more than our fair share. And we've done it because we believe in peace. I want this to be my happy place, as it's been for the past ten years. Except now whenever I arrive, I'm told about some new rule you've laid down that I was previously unaware of. Is there a rule book, sir? If there is, I'd like a copy.

"And finally, when I brought my YPO group here, you suggested that we all come to your home to hear your story. Despite having the worst toothache that day, I sat there and respectfully listened to you talk. I was proud that my friends and colleagues got to hear you share your experiences—that is, until the end, when you asked the group, 'How does it feel to be staying at the Holiday Inn with *those* people?' meaning my wife and me. You insulted our beautiful home, and you insulted us. I've had it with you. So, no, sir, I'm not going to tiptoe around anymore. I don't want to live under the arbitrary rules you've set up. Just know that I plan on doing whatever I want to do while I'm on this island, as long as I'm abiding by the law. And that's all I have to say."

Although I understood that Mr. Gilmour had gone through some awful times, losing his daughter under such horrific circumstances, he made life on the island almost intolerable. I felt compassion for him, but he ultimately destroyed the magic of that place for Mindy and me.

As much as I loved Fiji, it was time for a new setting. Not long after that exchange, I decided to sell the house to Clare

Bronfman, the Seagram's heiress who later became a leader in NXIVM, the cult founded by Keith Raniere.

By this time, Mindy and I had been talking about purchasing a boat so we could sail around the world. It had been a dream of ours for years. "I'm going to buy you a boat, Mindy, and we'll call it the *Minderella*. We'll have a helicopter on board that we'll name the *Glass Slipper*," I would say.

I wasn't daydreaming when I said this to my wife. I was planning it for a long time.

Well, that day eventually came. We bought a Feadship yacht from Wendy McCaw, who had been married to Craig McCaw, the founder of McCaw Cellular. We wanted a few changes made to the boat before she would be ready to cross the Atlantic. The alterations were being done in Florida, so I would fly to Fort Lauderdale to check on the progress. Mindy and I were new members of the Monaco Yacht Club, so the first time we were set to board the boat, it was docked in Cannes. When we arrived in Monte Carlo, we were picked up at the dock, loaded into a tender, and led to our new two-hundred-foot baby. There were magnificent yachts all around us, each one prettier than the last. I was looking for the navy-blue hull of the *Minderella*, but I couldn't find it. Why? Our boat was tucked neatly between two massive yachts.

"Are you serious? Couldn't you have docked it down that way, where it would at least *look* like a big boat?" I asked the captain, half laughing and half serious. It wasn't good for my ego, which had been pretty full all day until this moment. Seeing the *Minderella* lodged between two monster ships was quite a blow and probably exactly what I needed.

Many years ago, Mindy and I attended a fundraising event at Chapman University, where my sons Skyler and Colby attended college. I was the winning bidder at the live auction for a four-person vacation aboard the *Queen Elizabeth 2*. The *QE2* was the flagship of the Cunard Line. It was top-tier, total luxury. I suggested that we take Mindy's parents with us. About a month before our trip, I decided to look into the suite that was being provided. It was a very small room with one queen-size Murphy bed that pulled down from the wall. Looking at the diagram, I couldn't tell how big or small the room was, but the idea of the four of us staying together in that limited space wasn't appealing. I needed to get another room, so I reached out to the cruise line and asked what they had available. I was told everything was sold out—except the presidential suite. I said I would take that suite so we could give Mindy's parents the other room.

When we boarded the ship, I was completely stunned by its size and grandeur. I'd been on a lot of ships, but I'd never seen anything like this. Our suite was a duplex, with a grand piano in the parlor, a spiral staircase leading up to the bedroom, and every luxurious amenity one could ask for.

Every night on the ship was black tie—tuxedos and gowns required. When you're dressed to the nines every single evening, people tend to be a little stuffy, so the overall fun factor was pretty low. We enjoyed ourselves, but I wouldn't say we had the time of our lives.

Two weeks after we returned from that trip, Mindy and I

had committed to going on another cruise my oldest daughter, Charlene, had planned for the whole family. The ship was scheduled to travel from San Diego to Cabo San Lucas, Mexico. Charlene's mom and stepdad would be there, along with her sister and brothers; my three sons and two young daughters, Brooke and Taylor; Mindy; and me. With such a big group of us I once again reserved the biggest cabin on the ship.

We got to our room expecting something fairly large, especially after our experience on the *QE2*. Instead, it was the smallest cabin I'd ever seen. There had obviously been a mistake. I took the three boys with me and went to reception, where I inquired about moving us to the right room.

"Sir, we're completely sold out," I was told.

I understood they were sold out, but the room I'd reserved wasn't the room we were given. I asked to speak to the manager, thinking the person I was talking to simply didn't have the authority to make things right. When the manager came out to see me, I explained the situation again and asked him to check my name and reservation.

"Dad, you're being so stuck-up," one of my children said.

"Are you being serious?" another asked in a humiliated tone.

After the manager checked the records, he came back out and said, "Sir, here's the map of the ship. You *are* in the largest room we have. Every other room is actually smaller."

I stood there frozen in shock, thinking, *Oh my God. I am stuck up!*

"C'mon, Dad. We'll figure it out," the kids said, pulling me away.

THERE'S ALWAYS GOING TO BE A BIGGER BOAT

As the week progressed, we all ended up having the best time. We spent our nights singing karaoke, and went to a hypnosis show and a comedy show. We had such a blast together. There were lots of laughs. Everything that happened that week surprised me, especially when I compared it to our experience on the *QE2*.

I learned something about myself on that trip, something that changed my perspective about everything. It's not the size of the boat you have or the ship you're on, because there's always going to be a bigger boat. It's not about the plane you fly on, because there's always going to be a nicer plane. In the end, it's about what you do with what you have in the moment. It's about who you're with, not where you're staying.

This was a wonderful lesson, one that wasn't wasted on any of us.

On our last night at sea, which happened to be my birthday, my phone rang. It was the casino telling me I had a credit, and if I didn't come and cash out that night, I wouldn't be able to when we were in port because the casino would be closed. I got dressed, went to the casino, and closed my account, and on the way back to my room, I stopped by the kids' center. I peeked my head in to see what was going on, and there must have been forty young people in there, huddled up with their arms around each other, singing together. It was great watching how much fun they were having. When the song ended, they all clapped and high-fived one another. In the middle was my son Colby, who struggles with social awkwardness. He was holding the mic, singing with everyone else around him. I smiled a great big smile and thought, *Happy birthday to me.* Seeing that was the best present I'd ever received. I went back to the room and told Mindy all about what I'd just witnessed. All those kids supporting Colby was truly unforgettable. I've always tried to make sure each of my children felt safe to beat to their own drum. Colby never liked crowds or being the center of attention. I was never sure whether that was because he was concerned that people might judge him. Seeing him find joy and confidence from the realization that he could do something well made my heart sing. I've always been proud that Colby carved his own path, albeit one that was different from mine. He stands firm in his beliefs and never feels the need to follow in my footsteps. I don't put that expectation on any of my children. I want them to do what makes them happy. And that night, it was clear Colby was doing just that.

That trip showed me that family is what you make it. My family life has always been unique. Having a daughter at such a young age was the start of my creating a different type of understanding when it came to family. Charlene's mom, Kathy, and I never took our relationship any further, but we always remained friends. We shared a daughter, and that was enough of a reason for me to always want to treat her with kindness and respect. The same can be said for Amber, the mother of my sons Skyler, Colby, and Trevor. When we divorced, our kids were young. We had a lifetime of sharing ahead of us. I never wanted things to be contentious. When I married Mindy, I knew she would play a large part in their lives, which meant Amber and Mindy would have to interact. They not only got along from the start, they became good friends. I think there was a deep appreciation from Amber for the way Mindy treated the boys. And, of course, when Mindy and I had Brooke and Taylor, Amber was equally kind in return. In fact, she's their godmother. Amber played such an important role in the children's life and education that when we eventually sailed around the world, she came with us. She was Brooke and Taylor's teacher, making sure they didn't fall behind academically. We couldn't have done it without her.

Our family may not be conventional, but it works for us and for our children. In the end, we all wanted the same thing—happy kids. The old saying that a parent is only as happy as their least happy child stands. There were a lot of years when I was more absent than I wanted to be, especially when Charlene and my three boys were younger. It wasn't until my divorce from Amber and after meeting Mindy that I realized the value of family time. Mindy helped me understand that life is a balance. You can't be all things to all people any more than you can be all work or all play. Something eventually breaks. I learned that in my marriage to Amber. I felt so guilty about breaking up that marriage, and I knew the kids felt very sad. I needed to be more present for them, especially if I was no longer living in the same house. Children should never have to pay the price for their parents' inability to work things out. On this we're all united. Once the kids saw the love among Amber, Mindy, and me, all their worries about our divorce just disappeared. Mindy is very inclusive, and she made it a priority to become close to Amber. I don't know how it happened, but

I'm so grateful it did. We put aside any anger and animosity that could have existed and put our attention on doing what was right for all involved. We wanted our children to see us as connected, not apart. In a world that often feels so disjointed, we owed it to our children to be the adults.

That's why whenever one of my children asks to do something with me, I jump at the chance. Whether it's traveling one-on-one or just going for a run, I never want to miss an opportunity to spend quality time together.

I used to love to go for long runs, an interest my son Skyler inherited from me. When he was sixteen years old, he ran cross-country for his school. Skyler had great stamina and he was fast. One morning, we all went to support Mindy who was hosting a local 5k run with Vanna White. While we were all there, Skyler turned to me and asked if I wanted to go for a run with him. I was wearing loafers and he was in his running shoes, but I wasn't about to let that stop me from saying yes.

We headed out the door and began with a slow jog. Man, I was out of shape, but I wasn't about to let Skyler know how hard I was huffing and puffing. We began talking and picking up the pace. I would lie down and die before ever throwing in the towel in front of one of my kids, so I did whatever I could to keep up with him. Although he could easily have left me in his dust, my boy stayed right by my side. As we reached the final turn back toward our house, we started sprinting as fast as we could. I felt as though I might've been able to take him in the short run home, but as we got closer, I grabbed his hand and said, "Let's get there together."

THERE'S ALWAYS GOING TO BE A BIGGER BOAT

There's no doubt he could've beaten me. I like that he knew it, too, yet chose not to. Of course, there's one rule in our home that must be followed: don't try to beat the old man. By the time I was old enough to beat my father, I realized I didn't want to. My sons have gotten to that point now too. It's called maturity.

CHAPTER ELEVEN

RUNNING INTO THE FIRE

With but few exceptions, it is always the underdog who wins through sheer willpower.
—Johnny Weissmuller

MANY YEARS AGO, I heard a story about a group of children who were offered marshmallows or other treats as part of a study. They could choose to eat the marshmallow immediately, or they could have a larger reward—most often two marshmallows—but in order to get the reward, they had to wait alone in the room with the single, available marshmallow for up to twenty minutes. Some of the kids couldn't wait. But those who had the ability and self-control to hold out, the study revealed, became more successful later in life than those who couldn't delay their gratification.

As First Pacific Financial grew, I did two things I'm extremely proud of. First, I committed to taking only a small draw instead of a salary and reinvested the bulk of my profits into growing the business. For twenty-five years, I delayed taking any significant money out of the company. I did this so we could ultimately have $2.5 billion in credit lines. In lending, your credit lines are based on your net worth, so the more worth the company built, the bigger the lines.

The second thing I did was to change the name to Stearns Lending in late 2004. At the time I thought First Pacific Financial was too long. I'd been looking at options to shorten the name—perhaps calling the company FPF—because one of the ways I intended to increase our brand awareness was by putting our name on the outside of our building. I also thought the name limited the public's perception of us because "Pacific" made it sound as if we were only a regional operation when we were, in fact, a national company.

In life and in business, you must be willing to plant the seeds today for what will grow tomorrow. About a year and a half after I started my mortgage company, I wanted to make the leap from mortgage broker to mortgage banker. We were doing a lot of business and making money. I went to my bank and told them I needed a $1 million line of credit, explaining that I wanted to fund loans with it. The banker I was dealing with knew me and understood our business. At least I thought he did, because he always praised me for how well we were doing whenever I saw him.

A week later, he came back to me and said, "I can't give you the line of credit."

I was shocked. He acknowledged that we made a lot of

money, but it appeared that we spent it on ourselves. When I asked what he meant, he said that the company had no retained earnings. I was so new to business that I'd never heard the term "retained earnings" before that day. If a corporation makes money and then takes it out, usually to give to its shareholders, it retains no earnings and therefore has no value. Ideally, you want to leave money in the company and let it appreciate to grow your worth and qualify for credit lines.

The banker was right. If you believe in your company, you leave the money in. So that's exactly what we did.

Over the following year, we retained our earnings and built the value of the company, and were then able to secure a $6 million line of credit. While many of our colleagues and competitors were buying fancy things, we kept our heads down and continued to save. As our company grew, we didn't touch the money, which meant our earnings and net worth grew bigger, too. Eventually, we were able to obtain billions in credit lines. Everyone said yes to us because we had such a large net worth.

But then, in 2007, the bottom fell out from under us— and from everyone else in lending.

Many presidents, from Franklin D. Roosevelt to Ronald Reagan to Bill Clinton to George W. Bush, set increased home-ownership as a priority. Before the 2007–8 global financial crisis, government policies had pressured the banking industry to allow more people to purchase homes. Around 2004, Fannie Mae and Freddie Mac purchased huge numbers of mortgage assets that included a high percentage of very risky mortgages known as subprime mortgages. They charged large fees and received high margins from these subprime mortgages and used them as collateral for obtaining private-label mortgage-based securities. Many foreign banks bought collateralized US debt obligations made up of bundled subprime mortgage loans. When people defaulted on their mortgages, American banks lost money on their loans, and so did those foreign banks. As a result, banks stopped lending to one another, and it became very difficult for consumers and businesses to get credit. It was the worst economic disaster since the Great Depression, and it quickly became a financial nightmare for our company.

The Reverend Dr. Robert Schuller and his wife were at my house with my attorney, Richard Watts, and his wife, as well as two other couples. He called us all together and said, "Let's pray for Glenn and Mindy right now."

Why?

Because by September 2007 my company had lost 85 percent of its revenue. The banks wanted me to buy back $100 million worth of loans that had gone bad. I was facing a slew of class action lawsuits. The California State Department of Corporations was asking me to go back through five years of loans and refund prepaid interest on every loan that wasn't disbursed within twenty-four hours. I also had thirty thousand square feet of office space when I needed only eight thousand.

Yeah, I could understand why the Reverend wanted to pray for us. From the outside, it surely appeared as if everything was working against me. But I didn't feel that way.

"Robert, I appreciate the prayers, but this is my time to shine," I said. I'd thought about it a lot and decided that I was grateful for the opportunity. How many times do you get the chance to work your way out of a situation that's put your back against the wall? My name was in big, bright letters on the side of one of the tallest buildings in Orange County. I used to worry about what would happen if the kingdom crumbled, and imagined if that happened, I'd just keep the sign up so the community wouldn't know I'd failed. I never wanted people to think there might be a crack in my foundation. I'd spent months worrying about how embarrassing it would be for me to lose it all. But now that worry was gone.

The night before, I'd lain in bed for hours. I was lost. I couldn't sleep or shake my depression, which was something I rarely felt. Whenever I'd experienced angst like that in the past, I simply closed my eyes and dreamt of our home in Fiji. At the time, it was my favorite place on the planet. I went there in my mind, and before I knew it, I would feel calm and totally at peace. When I tried this exercise that night, however, it didn't work. Not long before, a hurricane had blown the roof off our house in Wakaya, so there was nothing happy there that I could focus on. It was just another piece of the puzzle I would have to put back together. It felt as if there were nowhere I could go to escape the feeling of impending doom.

Despite every trick I tried to change my mindset, I was still restlessly tossing and turning in bed. I couldn't find a happy thought as my mind spiraled around all the negativity that was challenging me.

Mindy leaned over and whispered, "You can't sleep, can you?"

"Everywhere I look, it's dark," I said quietly. "Everyplace in my life where I used to find happiness, there's only blackness. I don't know if I'm going to be able to keep the lights on. I owe Lehman Brothers twenty million, Bear Stearns thirty million, and so on. The pressure is getting to me."

I squeezed my eyes so tight that all I could see were little white zingers darting across my eyelids. I wanted to focus on sunshine, not on the brooding clouds in front of me. I was so frustrated. But seeing those zingers helped me realize that there was sun behind those clouds. I just had to focus on the light and not on the darkness.

I'd studied many people who survived far worse challenges than losing money. People like Viktor Frankl, the Holocaust survivor who later wrote the book *Man's Search for Meaning*, and Nando Parrado, one of the Uruguayan rugby players who survived a plane crash in the Andes by eating the flesh of his dead teammates. If you consider how both men viewed time and purpose in their circumstances, you'll find ways to deal with your own troubles. When you put a timeline on something, you set an unrealistic expectation for results that are usually out of your control. When that timeline fails, you lose hope. And when you lose hope, it's game over. Countless studies have shown that the people who lost hope in concentration camps during WWII were far more likely to die than those who didn't—than those who believed, like Frankl, that someday they would get out of there. That mindset is the difference between life and death, whether literal or figurative. The stronger your mind, the more likely you are to continue the fight.

You'll get through this, I said to myself. I sat in silence for what seemed like several more hours. The whole time I kept my eyes closed and did my best to quiet the intrusive thoughts. And then, I felt the sun on my face and found myself saying the following words aloud: "*Be still and know that I am God.*"

Mindy sat up and asked, "Why did you just say that?"

"I don't know. It just came to me."

"I was going to tell you those exact same words," she said.

You see, John Lang, a friend of mine from Phoenix, had gone through a similarly challenging time four years earlier. He was going to lose everything and didn't know what to do. He opened his Bible to Psalms 46:10 and found his answer: "Be still and know that I am God." He tossed everything up to the Lord and accepted that whatever happened, happened. He didn't want his situation weighing on him anymore, so he released himself from the outcome. That same day he received a call from his next-door neighbor asking if he wanted to go into business. They opened Estancia Country Club, and it took off. When everything was settled in his life, he began to give his friends copper plaques that read "46:10." He'd given one to me, which I kept behind my desk for years. I'd forgotten what it meant until that morning.

That's when I knew I had to do what John did and accept whatever was to be. I could no longer attach my success or failure to losing my business. Losing my company? That wasn't going to kill me. Having my name come off the building? Well, that wouldn't kill me, either. No matter what challenges I was facing, I suddenly knew I would survive.

So, when Robert offered to pray for us, I told him with conviction that every great person I'd ever met came to a similar point in their life. Nobody had a perfect trajectory. They all almost lost what they had, or worse, and then came back stronger because they learned from the experience. I was fine with whatever would happen. I was ready to go headfirst into the storm.

The next day, I went to my office and gathered all the employees together. I told them what had happened to me the night before. I certainly wasn't trying to force my beliefs down anyone's throat. People are free to believe what they want to believe. I simply wanted to share my experience so that they, too, would know whatever was going to happen with the company was going to happen. It's nice when we can all come together in a common belief, especially one that is rooted in faith.

Malcolm Gladwell has written a lot about the advantages of disadvantages—and even the desirability of certain difficulties. In his book *David and Goliath: Underdogs, Misfits, and the Art of Battling Giants*, Gladwell opens with the biblical story of David and Goliath, in which one man takes on a daunting figure and succeeds against all odds. Gladwell then goes on to talk about the unusual number of successes the underdogs in our society have had in situations like that one. Looking back, I think the many personal challenges I faced when I was younger turned out to be advantages because they inspired me to fight my way out of any situation, to persevere and never give up. I had never been afraid of hard work. I was scared at times; there's no doubt about that. But I wasn't ever ready to lock the door and walk away. I still wasn't. Not yet. I knew we were a company made up of great people, and that we would have to fight hard to survive. It wouldn't be easy, but I knew that together we could figure it out. I thanked them for their support and assured them everything would be okay.

"We aren't going to die. Not today," I said.

I went back to my office, attached a blank piece of paper to a clipboard, and wrote down the names of all the banks I owed money to and the amounts:

Bear Stearns—$30 million

Morgan Stanley—$25 million

Lehman Brothers—$20 million

Next, I wrote down the cost of the thirty-thousand-square-foot office we were in.

Then I wrote down the details of the class action lawsuit that had been brought against us, which was based on the way stated income loans were done at the time.

Once I had a clear picture in front of me, I realized what I had to do. I got on a plane, flew to New York, and saw someone at each of the banks—which, by the way, were all having their own struggles. I wanted them to know I would work with them to get through the biggest financial crisis in recent history. I would do my best to survive and stay open. One by one, I detailed why I didn't believe I owed them money. I started at Lehman Brothers.

"Let me tell you why I think my balance should be zero . . ."

I explained that every loan we processed was a stated

income loan, meaning the customer stated their income without providing pay stubs or income tax returns. Lehman had accepted those loans, no questions asked. When the loans went into default, Lehman called the customers, who then claimed to make less money than they'd stated on their loan documents. That's fraud. How do I know this? Lehman set the parameters. If they had said we could do stated income loans but only with verification, that would have been different. If they had said we had to buy back any loans that went bad, that would also have been different. I pleaded my case to Lehman, suggesting that it was *their* responsibility, not mine. Then I offered to buy back the loans at five cents on the dollar. That's all I was willing to give them. Before they could answer, I made one other thing clear. I showed them a piece of paper on my clipboard and told them there were two columns: one for the banks that wanted to work with me, and one for the banks that were telling me to pound sand. I didn't care which they chose—I just needed to know where they stood.

"So, what do you want to do?" I asked, completely stone-faced and oddly calm given the circumstances.

I had the same conversation with every lender. Remarkably, they all said they would work with me.

Check. That was one big thing marked off my to-do list.

Next, I met with the class action attorney in Beverly Hills who was suing my company. Was that unorthodox? Yes, but it was necessary. I had yet to engage a defense attorney, so I wasn't legally represented at the time. I also didn't have the money to take on this lawsuit, and I'm sure he knew it.

I had just one question: "How bad are you going to stick it to me?"

I gave him the same "work with me or tell me to pound sand" speech. His response was a little different, though. He laughed at me.

"You've got some balls, dude. Here; call this guy." He handed me a business card with the name and number of another lawyer. "Talk to him, and we'll write you out of the lawsuit." And that's exactly what I did.

Check, check. That was now off my list, too.

Next, I went to see a contact at the Department of Corporations, which, as you'll recall, was demanding that we audit every loan we'd done in the last five years in order to repay borrowers for prepaid interest they said I owed. I pleaded with her, explaining that I didn't have the staff to pull this off. We'd lost over 85 percent of our revenue and our people. Besides, it had taken five years to do the loans; how could I possibly audit them in less time than that?

Their concern was over how much time passed between a loan being funded and the borrower getting to use those funds. As the funding source, we would wire money to the title company, and they would pay off the liens on behalf of the borrower. According to the Department of Corporations' rules, if the money sat for more than twenty-four hours, then any interest earned on those funds should go back to the borrower. Since we funded our loans immediately, all control went to the title company, and at that point we were out of the transaction. We made an agreement with each of our title companies specifying that if they failed to pay off the liens in twenty-four hours, they were responsible for paying the interest to the borrower. Every title company we worked with signed off on that demand. The problem was that it was almost impossible to find out when the title company paid off the liens. It would have taken more manpower than we ever had to go back and figure that out.

My contact's response? We were still responsible for the money and should still audit each file, but we could sue the title companies for every loan that was processed late in order to recoup the money from them. In other words, she was proposing that we start legal action over fees as small as forty-two dollars. It was absurd.

Because title companies are governed by the Department of Insurance, her department had no jurisdiction over them. She couldn't touch them. The only solution she had was for me to audit every loan and pay back each borrower one at a time. My contact knew I didn't have the millions of dollars that would be needed to pay back the money they were looking to collect. Even after I'd gone begging and pleading to her three times, she wouldn't budge. I was down to a staff of eighty people. I didn't want them to lose their jobs, but I was worried that was where things were headed.

The day after my final visit, she called and asked some further questions. Then she added, "Glenn, you need to get me this information, and you need to get it to me by tomorrow."

This new information took me by surprise. "If I didn't know any better, I'd say it's starting to sound like you're letting me off the hook," I replied hopefully.

"I'm not letting you off," she insisted.

"You know what? I want to come up there and give you a big, fat kiss!" I teased.

"You get me that damned information!" she said. And then she hung up. She wasn't relenting, but I just knew that when the call ended, she had a big smile on her face.

I took the documents she requested to her office the next day. Shortly thereafter, I received a letter in the mail from the Department of Corporations: "You have been found in violation of code this and code that, and you are being fined $382 for four loans. If this happens again, we'll go back and make you audit all your loans."

I had never written a check faster than I did that day.

She made us pay for the loans the Department of Corporations discovered had prepaid interest issues, but she didn't make us go back and review all the others, which was a lifesaver. It was very clear that if this ever happened again, however, we would have to conduct an audit going as far back as they wanted. I immediately instituted a new company policy: we would audit each loan going forward to make sure the title company did their job. Check, check, check.

Next on my list was my office landlord. Although we had a contract, I couldn't pay the rent. It was time for another "work with me or tell me to pound sand" conversation. When we met, I said they could enforce the lease, though I could no longer pay, or they could reduce my square footage to eight thousand and charge me for that. Several mortgage companies in their buildings had already gone out of business, so they understood what was happening. They said I could have the eight thousand feet of space, but I had to vacate the remaining twenty-two thousand square feet in two weeks. They would allow me to keep the corner offices and that was it. I had to be out at the end of those two weeks, or I was going to be charged for it all. If that happened, I was done.

"No problem," I said, with a sigh of relief.

Check, check, check, and check.

I'd recently purchased brand-new Herman Miller furnishings and cubicles for $200,000, so when we were clearing out the office space I reached out to everyone I knew to sell those items. I told them I would let it all go for $80,000. I thought someone would jump all over that opportunity, but I had no takers. So, I lowered the price to $70,000, then $60,000, $50,000, and $40,000. Still no takers. Time was ticking. If I didn't have that furniture removed by the end of the day, I was cooked. Finally, I found someone who said he would come haul it all away if I paid *him* $5,000! I took a deep breath and said, "Zero, and it's all yours if you can remove it today." He agreed, and miraculously made it happen.

One by one, other mortgage lenders were going under. Every day my assistant, Keely, would tell me about another company that closed. There used to be a website, mortgageimplode.com, that listed the failed companies. If you were about to go under, your company's name would appear there, which only hastened the death spiral. Employees would check daily to see if they still had jobs, hoping and praying they wouldn't find their employer's name on that site. If they did, they would run.

Everything around us was caving in.

As the guy was hauling away the last pieces of furniture, Keely came in to tell me that two of our biggest competitors had just collapsed. I asked her to get the head of one of those companies on the phone for me. At first he asked her if he could speak to me the following week. I insisted that would be too late. "I need to talk to him now," I told Keely. When he finally answered my call, he sounded terribly defeated.

"I'm done, man. I can't take it anymore," he said solemnly.

"I want to meet with you today," I responded in an urgent tone.

"It's been a bad day. Can this wait?"

"I'll buy you a beer."

"No. Not going to happen."

"How about tomorrow?"

"Ugh, fine. Where do you want to meet?"

"My office. I'm bringing my CFO and Katherine Le, our president."

Much of the success of Stearns Lending came about because of Katherine and the connection she had with all the hardworking people who helped build our company. She was no pushover. She'd fled Vietnam in the mid-1970s. Her first attempt to escape the country got her thrown in jail, but she eventually found her way onto a small boat that was rescued at sea by a cargo ship. She came to the United States without knowing English, but managed to get a college degree and then rose up through the ranks to run our company. I owed so much to Katherine, and I always listened when she spoke. She asked good questions, important ones that had helped us navigate all sorts of challenges over the years.

When I spoke with Katherine, she asked why I wanted to meet at the office. There was nothing to see but a vast, empty landscape. The only things resembling a proper workplace were the reception desk and the conference room.

I told Keely to find as many desks as she could for the offices lining the hallway, and to get monitors and chairs, too.

"Let me understand this, Glenn: we just had someone take all these desks and cubicles away, and now you're asking me to refurnish? By tomorrow?"

Yes, that was exactly what I was asking.

When my colleague arrived at nine o'clock the next morning, I was there to greet him at the elevator. We started the journey down the hall, walking and talking the entire time. We passed by empty desks, all set up and ready for business. When we got to my office, we sat down, and I began to explain why he was there. I wanted to hire all his people. Every single person was welcome to come work for me.

Curious, he asked why.

I told him that after what had happened, I felt loans would become more conventional again—the trend would return to Federal Housing Administration (FHA) and Veterans Administration (VA) loans. The underwriters were all my auditors at the time. If I switched my auditors back to underwriters, I'd be able to jump right in to the FHA and VA business. I thought I would be able to get everyone on board.

"Let me show you something," I said as I stood and

motioned for him to follow me. "See this area? This was my alternative document department. It's gone. I'll have your people sitting in those chairs Monday morning if you're on board. They won't miss a single day of work. I want them to fill this whole space." I opened my arms as wide as I possibly could, doing my best to convince him that this was the right thing to do. He wasn't as receptive as I had hoped. However, much to my surprise, on Monday morning he called and said, "Let's do the deal." I had his whole team in place by Wednesday of that same week.

To do that, I had to go back to the guy I'd given my desks and cubicles to. He said he'd be happy to sell them back to me—for $60,000. Yeah, that hurt, but I needed them, and fast. I told him it was a go, as long as he could have everything returned to me and set up in the next two days.

When my landlord stopped by and saw that everything was still in place, he turned to me and asked, "What's this? I told you everything had to be out of here by today."

"I changed my mind," I said. "I need the whole floor. I can't stop you from kicking me out, but I'm asking you not to. Please give me a shot to pay you. If you make me leave, I'll have to go somewhere else, and you'll never get your money. It's your call."

I was all in.

Katherine and the CFO of my company were worried I would lose everything. They were very supportive, but they didn't want me to jeopardize what I'd built for my family. I didn't want to do that, either. I knew this would end in one of two ways: the landlord would either have to throw me out and lock the door behind me or let me roll the dice on the biggest gamble of my career. It was an all-or-nothing situation. There was no middle ground. But I knew in my gut that this was the perfect opportunity to get the absolute best people working for me. If my competitors hadn't been dropping like flies, I never would have been able to bring their teams over. Up until this point, I was really a small company trying to compete against the larger lenders. This was the opportunity of a lifetime—one I wasn't willing to let pass.

Things were looking up, until one day I received a call from the head of the bank in New York that controlled all my credit lines. "Hey, the party's ending," he said.

"What do you mean?" I asked.

"We're done. We're out of this business. We've got ninety-three lines of credit out there and we're pulling all of them but a handful. It's 2008; the world is blowing up, and we want out."

The same thing that had happened to me with my former partner Ron in the late 1990s was happening all over again.

When I asked how long I had, he said one week. He knew I would be out of business if that happened, but he didn't seem to care. We were in the middle of the worst financial crisis to hit since 1929. From his perspective, there wasn't much I could do.

I asked him how he would respond if I sued him for putting a twenty-year-old company out of business.

"That'll be chump change compared to what we're dealing with," he said before hanging up.

The next morning at eight thirty Eastern time, I called him back.

"Hi. You mentioned something in our call yesterday that stuck with me. You said you were pulling out of warehouse lending and getting rid of all your relationships but a handful. I'd like to talk to you about that handful. But I want to look you in the eye to have that conversation."

"That's fine, Glenn," he said. "The only problem is that I'm in New York and you're in California."

"Actually, I'm in your lobby. I flew all night. Can I come up and see you?" I asked.

I knew how important being in front of him was that day. You have to make a personal connection, especially when you want something big. My being there in person was a game changer.

He ended up keeping two companies—Stearns Lending and Quicken.

Despite the stresses I was dealing with throughout 2007 and 2008, I remained active in my YPO group. It was actually a great comfort to have so many brilliant minds to tap into during the most difficult turn in my professional life. A member of YPO can stay part of the group until they turn fifty, at which point they graduate to YPO Gold. A good friend of mine was graduating, and we wanted to do something nice to commemorate his moment. We held his last meeting in my office. Mindy brought four bottles of champagne. We opened them and drank to his success and to the second half of his life. When the other members of our group left, I began cleaning up and noticed one of the bottles hadn't been opened.

I picked it up and thought, *Man, if I get out of this mess, I'm going to pop this bottle of champagne and celebrate.* I put it in the refrigerator I kept in my office. As each day passed, I would reach into the fridge to grab a bottle of water and see the champagne. "Not today," I would say to myself. That went on for over a year.

By March 2009, we had opened dozens of new offices and hired staff for each. For most lenders, the world was still crumbling. Many were having their worst year ever. We, on the other hand, were having our best year since 1989. I found myself on the CNBC show *Squawk on the Street*, talking with David Faber about our recovery and success. My segment followed AIG's CEO announcing their $61.7 billion fourth-quarter loss, the biggest single-quarter loss in the history of any company. Although I felt confident about how well we were doing and was proud to discuss how we overcame the odds, the bleak news about AIG overshadowed our segment. The same day I spoke about our turnaround on the show, the class action lawsuit I'd been written out of was set to be settled in court. The attorney who wrote me out of the suit happened to catch my interview. He was furious, and asked the judge to postpone the closing of the case. Luckily, the judge said they were too far down the road for that, and proceeded to settle it anyway.

Afterward, my CFO reminded me that that was the reason I should always keep my head down and not become a target. I couldn't argue his point.

BY 2011, we'd shot to the moon. And we did it by running *into* the fire—not away from it.

As business continued to get better, I would reach into the refrigerator for my water every day and still think, *Not yet.* I told myself I would open that champagne bottle when I sold the company and was done. That felt like the right time to celebrate. When that day did finally come, it should have been the happiest day of my career. But as I stood in front of my staff, I felt deep sadness. Was I really ready to leave it all behind? Would I truly be able to give up control? When I looked around the room, I didn't see employees—I saw family. I couldn't help but wonder whether I was doing the right thing.

I'd already cashed the check, so there was no turning back. Still, celebrating felt premature. Opening that bottle didn't feel right to me. It just wasn't a good day. Perhaps I'm a little superstitious, or maybe just overly practical, but I've witnessed friends and colleagues celebrate before it was time. Here's what I mean: I have a friend whose company was awarded a big contract. It was selected as one of four companies in the world to service a global account. He was so excited to share the big news with Mindy and me. We all went out to dinner, where the Dom Pérignon flowed endlessly in celebration of his big deal. I leaned over to my buddy and asked, "When do you start?"

He looked at me and said, "We just got the account. I'm not sure."

I shook my head and said, "I wouldn't be celebrating right now, but hey, that's just me." Not long after that dinner, I heard the company had gone through a big reorganization and no longer needed my friend's services. In the end, the company never got the contract. Here's what I know for sure: truth is circumstantial. What's true today might not be true tomorrow. Some people celebrate right away; others wait awhile.

It took some time, but I finally realized that there was never going to be a right day to open that champagne. I was never going to pop that bottle, because it didn't represent joy so much as an end, and I was nowhere near ready to call it quits. Someone once told me that life is really all about the chase, and I get that. Success isn't a line you cross but the journey you take. If that's true, then there is no finish line; you'll never pop the bottle.

CHAPTER TWELVE

BREAKING AWAY FROM THE HERD

We herd sheep, we drive cattle, we lead people.
Lead me, follow me, or get out of my way.
—GENERAL GEORGE S. PATTON

THE FIRST TIME I told Mindy "I love you," I said, "I'm telling you this because I know how vulnerable it makes me feel, and I love it. I love that you now know you could crush me—and though that might hurt, it doesn't scare me. Not one bit. I love it, and I love you."

Believe me, this was not an easy admission. But it was an important one.

When Mindy and I had our daughters, Brooke and Taylor, I felt even more vulnerable. I'd been a father four times before, but for whatever reason, having these two little girls changed me in ways I can hardly describe. I became softer and more present, and I wanted to be an important role model in their (and all my children's) lives.

Most people guard their life by building impenetrable walls around themselves. They never want to be seen as vulnerable, as some consider that weakness. I think it's the complete opposite. I believe it makes you strong—like Sampson.

I do my best to lead with vulnerability—not just by openly sharing what I've screwed up but by listening in such a way that it allows people to open up to me, too.

Why?

I want to go deep with those people. If I start off by telling as many screwup stories as I can, it demonstrates that I'm flawed. Imperfect. Human. And hopefully, others can relate.

Growing up, I hung around with a group of relative misfits. In some ways I was the least screwed-up of the bunch. I mean, I knew I was making mistakes, but for whatever reason, other people saw me as someone who would someday become a leader. The manager of the skating rink said it to me, as did many of my friends' parents. "Be more like Glenn," they'd say to their sons.

Honestly, I had to laugh whenever I heard those words, because I never felt like someone those guys should be emulating. I was doing bad things just like they were, and yet there were times when I knew I stood out in the crowd. Times when I made split-second decisions that kept a situation from becoming disastrous.

One day, two guys were wandering around our town tripping on acid. Another group of guys from the pinball arcade went outside and started to tease them. One of those guys was

Gary D. He wasn't a close friend, but I knew him from around town. Gary was known to be a scrappy fighter. We'd never fought each other, but I knew he was capable of inflicting great harm. I came out of the pinball joint and saw Gary beating up the two guys on acid. It wasn't my business, but I wasn't willing to walk away. The group from the arcade had gathered around, cheering Gary on and loving the action, as if they were watching a cockfight they'd wagered on.

"Get up!" Gary shouted at the two guys, over and over.

Those poor dudes kept standing up only to get pummeled to the ground again. The more they tried to fight, the louder the crowd chanted, "Beat him, beat him . . ." There was an awful herd mentality. It was as if somehow this was okay—acceptable, normal behavior. I could see the two guys were broken and battered, hanging on with their last ounces of breath. I made my way through the crowd, stepped up to Gary, put my hand hard against his chest, and said, "What more do you want? Stop it."

And he did.

I walked away, asking myself why no one else stepped in that night. Gary D. was going to beat another human being to his death; I was certain of that. And while I hated that no one else did anything, I kind of liked the feeling I got from putting an end to the brawl. Being a witness to that wasn't right. I spent the rest of the night asking myself, "What are you going to do to break away from the herd, Glenn?" I didn't want to be a loser. It's never hard to do the right thing. It may feel like it in the moment, but when you allow your conscience to guide you, your gut will always know what to do.

Someone once told me that you can't soar with the eagles if you swim with the ducks. A couple of years later, Gary and another friend of ours were skipping school. The other kid had a gun. He accidentally shot Gary in the head, killing him instantly.

I may have come from a world of dysfunction and pain, but when you connect the dots, it's clear that all my experiences made me who I am and informed the choices I made. I never look back with regret. And I wouldn't change a thing, because every experience helped shape me.

In general, life isn't as complicated as we tend to make it. And by now, you can see that I had a way of making things more difficult for myself than they needed to be. Sure, there are times when life can be challenging, stressful, or tricky, but it doesn't always have to be. It's a choice, a process of making either wise or poor decisions. As I matured, I discovered that I didn't especially like complicated circumstances. I much preferred my simple ways. Some people thrive on chaos and drama, but not me. Maybe that makes me unique, but living a less muddled life absolutely works better for me.

As I've gotten older, I've realized that it's not so great to live in a cave, frequenting dark bars and getting plastered every night. But the one thing I took away from all those times was that there are opportunities to learn wherever you are. I used to listen to the old guys sitting in those bars and telling the same stories, waiting to draw in some new sucker so they could have a laugh together. They must have told those stories a thousand times and howled at those same punch lines night after night, but they did it because they were always looking for someone new to connect with. After years of observing this, I realized that business is very much the same. These days I love to tell my stories almost as much as I enjoy hearing others share theirs.

Many years ago, I was a guest of T. Boone Pickens at his home in Texas. I had one question for him: "Sir, you were a billionaire, and you went flat broke. Then you became a billionaire again and lost it all a second time. And now you're a billionaire again. Why are you doing it all over?"

"Son, I just like being in the game," he said in his thick southern drawl.

I understood his answer. Perfectly.

I fully believe that when the student is ready, a teacher will appear. Here's the secret to making that leap: you have to be ready, willing, and able to receive guidance in order for it to make an impact. There's really nothing anyone can say that will change the way you think or act if you aren't ready to hear it.

As I grew in business, I wanted to learn from those who'd forged their own paths and graduated from their own schools of hard knocks. I made it a point to seek out a variety of mentors. I became a sponge, soaking up every droplet of wisdom from their experiences and expertise. It didn't matter what field they were in or how they created their success; if there were people I admired or wanted to get to know, I would ask for a meeting. Some were local businessmen in my community, while others were well-known entrepreneurs from all over the country. It also didn't matter how old they were. What I knew from my nights as a barfly was that the older guys were a lot more interested and eager to share their experiences and knowledge. I was always in awe when they began sharing their tales from the trenches, as it was quickly apparent that they'd forgotten more than I knew. Maybe they were so generous with their stories because not that many people were seeking them out anymore. These were the people I wanted to get to know and forge relationships with, because the amount of information I was able to glean over lunch or a cup of coffee was invaluable. It taught me how to build my business, become a smarter investor, and quite frankly how to be a better person. I learned so many critical lessons I never would have gotten from reading a book. There's simply no greater teacher than experience, and no better connection than eye-to-eye contact.

When I think of my greatest mentors in business, two men in particular come to mind: George Argyros and Chuck Martin. Both were very successful businessmen—one with a tremendous amount of street smarts and the other with an impressive education, having earned several college degrees. In the early 1980s George and Chuck went into business together, buying a huge stake in DST Systems. They created a hedge fund that would buy companies at one price and sell them when they attained a certain profit margin. George was the type of investor who tucked things away and never thought about them again. He rarely sold anything. Chuck's approach was different. Whenever he sold a company, it was for a very nice profit. While the money he made was great by anyone's standards, it wasn't what George's family eventually made when they cashed in his business. The difference was billions. George was a long-term thinker and investor, and I've always liked that method of investing. Fancy formulas, quick hits, and flipping for a profit work for some, but not really for me. I learned so much from both men. Chuck eventually became Stearns's first outside board member and was instrumental in setting up the remainder of the board.

When I was forty years old, I went on a hunting trip with Dr. Robert Schuller, who invited me to join him and some of his friends at a private ranch. First we flew to Portland, Oregon. When we landed, there was a row of private jets—each one nicer than the last. Robert pointed at each plane and said, "That guy will be at the ranch, and that guy, and that guy, too." I had some big-boy toys of my own because I felt the need to fit in with these business leaders, but at that moment, I didn't feel like I belonged there. Not at all.

I knew we would be in the company of some very successful people, but I didn't know exactly who. One of the guys was Foster Friess, a very gregarious American businessman, and philanthropist. I'd never met Foster, but I knew he was someone I wanted to get to know. Mike Ingram, a real estate developer from Arizona; former senator Al Simpson; and Jeff Taylor, the founder of Monster.com, were some of the others present. It's not often that I feel like the least accomplished guy in the room, but being in the company of those titans was rather intimidating.

At our first breakfast, Foster took control of the dialogue right away. Instead of everyone talking over one another, he turned to each of us and said, "Talk about your life for ten minutes."

I sat there hoping and praying he wouldn't call on me first. I knew a little bit about the other men in the room—that they were all successful—yet I wasn't sure how I could tell my story and properly fit in.

Most of the men were older than me. They surely had a lot more experience in the world and in business than I did. Thankfully, Foster started with the person to my left and kept going in that direction for the first few stories. Before it came around to my turn, Foster and Mike split us into groups and assigned us guides, and off we went to hunt. It quickly became obvious that Foster and Mike were running the weekend. They were definitely the bigwigs in the room.

When it came time for lunch, the routine was the same: we ate, a few of us spoke, and then we split up into groups again.

I was hoping by dinnertime that I would have the chance to jump in and share my story, but that never happened. It wasn't until breakfast the next day that my turn came.

And, thankfully, that was perfect. If I'd gone sooner, what a fool I would have made of myself. Instead, I got to sit and listen. What I realized was that these men were incredibly evolved human beings who weren't about their toys or possessions at all. They talked about giving back, making a difference. They were at places in their lives where what mattered to them was adding value to the world. It wasn't about how much money they had, how much liquor they could drink, or the women they could attract. All of that was irrelevant. What each one of those men spoke about were ways to leave an impact on the world and make it a better place—ways to explore and do things in life that make you proud.

So many people define themselves by their job titles. How many people do you know like this? It's such a mistake. You're not defined by your work any more than you're defined by where you live, the car you drive, or the college you attended. Sure, those things are parts of who you are, but they absolutely are not your identity.

At the time, I'd spent fifteen years of my life building Stearns Lending. I had more than one hundred offices all over the country with my name on the outside of each building and on the walls of the interiors. And yet that didn't define me. Integrity, grit, honesty, and kindness—those are the words I would like people to use when they describe me.

So, when they got to me, my original answer was out the door. I'd planned to talk about how well my company was doing, how much profit we were turning, how I had a big home in California, and so on. Instead, I spoke about how, at fourteen, I fathered a child who became a very dear part of my life. I told them how what I thought was the worst mistake of my life turned out to be the best thing that had ever happened to me. I explained that I had an ex-wife with whom I shared three sons. When that marriage ended, I thought that was the biggest failure of my life, and yet I was able to remain very good friends with my ex so we could raise our children together, teaching them that life isn't all about things going right but about what you do and how you react when things don't turn out as expected. Who are you when the world doesn't comply with your plan? *That's* the show of true character.

Making a lot of money doesn't make you great.

Giving a lot of money away to charity doesn't make you great, either.

What happens when the world turns on you and you feel as though you're losing everything? What happens when it tests your mettle? Who are you then?

Are you still a good person?

Are you still giving and caring?

As I spoke that morning, I began to cry in front of this room full of distinguished men I deeply respected and greatly admired. And because of my willingness to be authentic and the courage I showed by allowing myself to be vulnerable, I crossed a threshold I hadn't even known existed.

When breakfast was finished, Foster divvied up the room as usual, only this time he turned to me and said, "Glenn, why don't you come with Mike and me today." We spent the day hunting and getting to know one another, and from that day forward, they've been amazing mentors and great friends.

About a week after that life-changing trip, I received a letter from Al Simpson, a gentleman with a terrific sense of humor. In the letter, he wrote, "Glenn, I will never forget your story, son. Not until they throw me in the hole." And I believe he meant it, which meant a great deal to me then and still does now.

After that weekend, perhaps for the first time in my adult life, I recognized that I didn't want to be defined by wealth or other people's perceptions of who I am. I wanted to control that narrative.

I know so many people who think what table they sit at or

the level of giving they pledge at a charity event matters. They give to make sure everyone else knows about it. I don't want to be characterized by whether I'm sitting at the front table or in the back, whether I'm the host or a guest, and whether my picture is snapped and printed in some magazine. If you're driven toward only those types of goals, you'll eventually lose sight of the bigger picture—of what's truly important. Knowing you're comfortable in your own skin—that you like who you are—is what's truly valuable. It was then that I began to understand the significance of remaining humble and appreciative.

In 2001, a week after the attack on the World Trade Center, I had my three boys create a "Lemon-Aid for New York" stand to raise money for the families of the firefighters who lost their lives in that horrific attack. I told my boys that I would match whatever they raised.

I flew to Baltimore and then boarded the Acela Express, the high-speed train from Washington, DC, to New York City. I wanted to help in any way that I could, even if it meant lifting debris in search of missing people. When I got to the city, it quickly became apparent that no civilians were being allowed to help. The National Guard had been called in, and the entire area was fenced off and barricaded. I'll never forget the sight of the still-smoldering destruction, or the smell. It's hard to describe, but you could actually taste a combination of jet fuel and ash in the air you breathed.

I went to Battery Park to donate the gloves, hard hat, and other gear I'd brought with me. Since I couldn't be of much help at the scene, I decided to jump back on the train and return to DC.

I boarded and sat very close to the front of the train. There was one seat across the table from me, and another in the corner. A very pretty woman walked in and sat in the corner seat. At the time, I was single, and my initial thought was to ask her if she would like to join me at the table. Just as I was about to address her, she stood up and said, "I can't sit in the corner," and she was off to find another seat a few rows behind me. I was kicking myself for not speaking up sooner when an elderly couple boarded the train. I immediately said to myself, *Oh no. Please don't sit here. Keep moving.* Naturally, the wife sat in the corner and the husband took the seat across from me.

Just my luck, I thought. *Of course this happens to me.*

Then I noticed a giant ring on the man's finger. It looked like a championship ring, and I could read the word "basketball."

"I see you like basketball," I said, striking up a conversation.

"I guess you could say that," he replied. "I'm Abe Pollin, owner of the Washington Wizards and the Washington Capitals."

My eyes lit up, but I was shocked. Why was he traveling by train?

I began to ask him questions about his business philosophy—how he ran his company, how he treated his employees, and how he came to be so successful.

Mr. Pollin explained to me how important it was to treat your employees like family. He spoke about loyalty and staying humble, and about never cutting corners and always making sure you do every job the best you can. Quality matters. Whatever you build, build it to last. It's your legacy.

"Do you know the Irene?" he asked.

"Of course I do. It's a luxury apartment building in Chevy Chase, Maryland," I said.

"I built that building in the 1960s. To this day, it stands as one of the best apartment complexes around. Why? Because it's quality. We didn't cut corners. We built it to last. Do you want to know why I named it the Irene, son?" he asked.

I nodded.

"Hey, Irene, why don't you come up here and meet this kid," he said to his wife, who was sitting in the corner seat.

There I was, thinking I'd lost a great opportunity by not asking the pretty woman to sit with me, and instead I had an even greater opportunity. I would have paid thousands of dollars to sit with a guy like Abe Pollin for three hours and pick his brain—and there he was, sitting across from me, sharing knowledge for free. You never know when an opportunity is going to fall into your lap. So often, we focus on our losses and forget to see what we have right in front of us. This was a reminder that when one door closes, another door opens.

Mentorship comes in many forms. We can seek out formal arrangements or find them through strangers we meet on a train. The important thing to remember is that sometimes it's better to open your ears than to open your mouth. If I'd opened my mouth, the pretty woman would have been my company for the ride, and I never would have had that amazing experience with Mr. Pollin. Lesson learned.

CHAPTER THIRTEEN

THE ART OF FORGIVENESS

---

*It is not what you do for your children but what you
have taught them to do for themselves that will
make them successful human beings.*
—ANN LANDERS

AFTER MINDY entered my life, I felt as though old wounds
began to heal. She came from a completely different type of
family than mine. Hers was a big, very close-knit family. It
didn't take long for her to insist that I get to know her parents,
who still lived in Oregon. Despite the distance, we got into a
really good rhythm. We traveled together or visited each other
whenever our schedules allowed.

Life was great.

All the while, Mindy was advocating for my dad to come
visit. She kept reminding me that there was nothing more
important in life than good health and family. Even so, I was

reluctant to reconnect with my old man. I'd written him off years earlier and couldn't seem to find any good reasons to invite him back into my life. I was happy. I had a new family I was focused on. My dad is a quiet introvert, which made it even harder to engage with him. We just didn't seem to have a lot in common. Our conversations primarily revolved around hunting and fishing, and that was it. Once I left for college, I never circled back to him. My only memories of my dad were rooted in his miserable years, and those were what I clung to.

Mindy saw things through a completely different lens. She understood that everyone has their fractures, but those cracks don't necessarily make someone a bad person. And she was right. My dad had worked hard to turn his life around. He had successfully remained sober from the day my mom and sister walked out the door all those years ago, and I knew that couldn't have been easy. I respected it. My dad described his own father as a drunk and a miserable man, and swore he would never be like him—and yet he followed in every foot-step. Seeing my dad break that cycle while I was racing toward it made me realize that if he could break it, maybe I could, too. It wouldn't be easy, but nothing that important ever is.

With my wife's encouragement, we slowly started spending some time together. And as we did, I began to see what a great guy Dad really was. He was still quiet, but he was thoughtful and far more evolved than I'd ever realized. The more time we spent together, the more I got to know *this* man—the one I'm sure my mom fell in love with. We started to connect through common interests I never knew we had, whether it was diving, fishing, or love of motorcycles. He has a great sense of adventure and a willingness to try anything. Somewhere along the way, my dad embraced a world of *yes* when I had only known him as a *no* guy. This was not the same man I knew growing up. My dad was a wonderful human being, one I loved to spend time with. Finding this relationship with someone I'd dismissed years ago was one of the biggest surprises of my life. I never would've guessed that it had the potential to be one of the most important and poignant relationships of my life. This is the beauty of second chances.

One year, Mindy's dad suggested we all go to Las Vegas to ring in the New Year. Like me, her dad, Eric, loves to play blackjack. Mindy and her mom immediately put the kibosh on the idea. They wanted to keep the night simple, maybe go to the movies. Even so, they said if he and I wanted to go, they wouldn't stop us. So, we flew to Vegas. At the last minute, I asked my dad to join us, too.

When we arrived, Eric, my dad, and I headed to Caesars Palace, my favorite casino. We hit the blackjack tables right away. At around ten to midnight, I looked at my dad and said, "I think I'm done. Let's cash in and go outside to watch the fireworks." Eric decided to keep playing.

Vegas loves to put on a grand show for New Year's Eve. They stage the most elaborate pyrotechnics. Hundreds of thousands of people gather on the strip to wait for the stroke of midnight and watch the display. My dad and I walked outside and shimmied our way through the thick crowd. As the clock counted down and people began shouting "Happy New

Year!" I turned to my dad and said, "I love you, Dad." And he responded, "I love you, son." We hugged and kissed each other for the first time in many years.

As we stood there, it hit me that I was no longer angry with him. I leaned into his ear and said, "I want to get a picture," hoping he could hear me above the deafening noise of the jubilant celebration. I wanted to capture that moment and carry it with me forever. And I did. We took a selfie, which I immediately made the wallpaper on my phone. From then on, whenever I saw it, I would think, *I'm one lucky guy to have this man in my life.* And then one day many weeks later, I was flying somewhere—I can't really remember where—but I was looking closely at that photo and noticed, in the background, the Harrah's Hotel, the last place I saw my mom. I got chills when I discovered that little detail. I believe there are no accidents in life. I want to believe my mom was there with us in spirit that night, looking down, smiling with great joy. I want to believe she waited a lifetime to see my dad and me have that moment, and that she was proud of us for getting there.

Signs are all around us in life. They're there to show us things we need to see. Maybe it's a gentle tap on the shoulder or maybe it's a full-blown wake-up call; whatever the sign and whatever the purpose, I sure do love when things like that happen.

Several years ago, Mindy and I hosted an event on Necker Island called, "The Power of Forgiveness." We invited Kim Phuc to be a guest speaker. Kim was nine years old in 1972 when a South Vietnamese plane dropped napalm bombs on her village because North Vietnamese troops were hiding there. The image of her running down the road in tears, naked and severely burned, was captured by Vietnamese American Associated Press photographer Nick Ut, who won a Pulitzer Prize for the photo in 1973. We also brought in three other speakers: Jackie and Warren Hance, a couple who tragically lost their three children in a drunk-driving accident; and Amanda Lindhout, a journalist who was kidnapped, tortured, and raped by Islamist insurgents in southern Somalia in 2008. She was miraculously released fifteen months later, in November 2009.

Each of these remarkable people shared their stories. They talked about the horrific pain and suffering they endured, and incredibly, all of them spoke about the power of forgiveness—not just for their captors or abusers but for themselves. Each of these people ultimately developed the belief that the people who caused their pain were products of their environment. They were imperfect human beings acting out of desperation or under the influence of substances or people in power. I felt such deep empathy listening to their stories of survival and asked myself, "Would I be able to do that under the same dire circumstances?"

There's no doubt that forgiveness gives us perspective and a better understanding of who people really are, including ourselves.

One afternoon, an executive-level employee of our company suddenly quit. She gave no notice, nor did she give any warning signs that she wanted to leave. I asked my assistant, Keely, if she knew what happened, why she may have left.

"All I know is that a dozen roses were delivered to her today. When she got them, she quit." Then Keely added, "You should know that one of our executives goes to lunch with her three or four days a week." This implied the obvious—that this married executive was having an affair with her. We did a little more sleuthing and found that, apparently, everyone in our office knew about their relationship.

Now, ever since I first started in business in my early twenties, I've always been very careful about crossing the line with someone I work with. I learned some difficult lessons early in my career. They were painful, but necessary. As a result, once I started my own company, I never took a female employee into my office without someone else being present. When someone made a pass at me, I would instantly put a stop to it. If they rubbed my leg under the table, I would get up and move. I can hold my head up high knowing I've been extremely professional throughout the years.

While I knew there were some intraoffice shenanigans from time to time, I hadn't seen this coming. I wanted to get to the bottom of things, so I asked my executive what happened.

"Nothing happened," he said.

I wasn't buying it, so I asked again, "A bunch of roses are delivered to her, no one knows who they're from, and she quits? I mean, you take her to lunch several times a week, likely on my dime. Let me put it this way: if *nothing* happens again like that, I'll fire you."

Understand, he was a high-ranking executive at Stearns Lending whose alleged behavior was now messing with my family because he was destabilizing the security of my company. One thing I knew about this man was that he was proficient at shooting guns. I didn't want to anger the guy, but I needed him to understand that when it came to the well-being of my team members and my company, I'm as serious as a heart attack about following professional protocol.

About a year later, several people from my office asked to come see me about the same individual. Apparently, he had taken a liking to a young processor working at the company. His behavior made her uncomfortable, so she brought a complaint, complete with backup, to the head of HR. She had emails, messages on her cell phone, and other supporting evidence that she was being harassed. He even bought her a burner phone that he would use when he wanted to reach her.

I had no choice.

This time, though, I wasn't mad. I was in protective mode. His behavior was hurting our company and people I cared about. I wouldn't tolerate it for another minute.

I called him into my office and said, "Tell me what's going on with this processor."

"I don't know what you're talking about," he claimed.

I told him that I was about to bring HR into the office, and what they had to say might jar his memory. But before I did that, I asked him man-to-man if there was anything he wanted to tell me that he didn't want to say in front of HR.

Again, he insisted he had no idea what I was talking about.

I gave him one more chance before I called in our head of

HR. He didn't take it. When the head of HR arrived, I asked her the same question: "What's happening with the processor?"

"Well, Glenn, she's fearing for her job because she says she feels a lot of pressure from this man. She knows people in the office have seen his ongoing behavior and she's afraid of getting fired for coming forward."

I turned to the executive and asked, "Is this true?"

"No. She's a nice girl. I know her family. When I speak to her, it's about her family . . ."

I didn't let him go any further. I asked him to leave, pending a full investigation. I already had enough evidence to prove her allegations.

During our investigation, things went from bad to worse.

While on leave, this man's wife found out why he wasn't at work. When that happened, he became distraught. People called me to say they were afraid he might do something crazy. His job, his marriage, and his family were all at risk. I worried about his state of mind, and about his history with guns and shooting. I didn't want him to show up at the office and do something we'd all regret. I was so concerned that I called the sheriff and told her what was happening.

I hired full-time security guards to protect the safety of my employees. I felt it was necessary to do so. Every time I left the office, I slowly stepped outside, nervous that he might be waiting in the parking structure to shoot me. My heart would pound all the way to my car. I would sometimes bob or move my head so that if he shot at me, he might miss. I must have looked crazy, darting back and forth between parked cars. I was so concerned that I hired security for my home, too. My wife and children were afraid, and so was I. This was no way for any of us to be living.

A few months had gone by when I finally heard from him. My assistant, Keely, buzzed my office to say he was on line one.

Gulp. At first, I wasn't sure I wanted to take the call. But then I thought, *I may as well, or this will continue to haunt me.*

I picked up the receiver, but before I could speak, I heard him say, "Glenn, it's me. I want to apologize. I'm sorry I was such an idiot. It was all my fault. Everything I did."

I stopped him. I wanted him to hear me. "Say no more. You obviously caused some problems for the company. From what I understand, you've probably been through punishment enough by the reaction of your family and everything else. I'm sure any words I have to say will just pile on an already tall mountain. Consider this done."

I thought what I said would end things, put it all to rest.

I was wrong.

"No, Glenn. I want to look you in the eye and apologize," he told me.

This made me nervous—very nervous.

"No, it's okay. Really. We're all good," I assured him, hoping to thwart any further action.

Still, he insisted on seeing me.

I sat at my desk for a moment wondering if I wanted to keep walking around, dodging this guy everywhere I went, or if I just wanted to live in peace. When I looked at it through that lens, it was an easy decision. "Sure. When do you want to meet?"

"Today. Dinner," he said.

I agreed, hung up the phone, and looked for my gun.

When I got to the restaurant, he was standing outside waiting for me. My firearm was in the left pocket of my sport coat. I put it there because I knew he would want to shake hands, which we did with our right hands. Once we got inside, I excused myself to go to the bathroom, where I switched the gun from my left pocket to my right. I slowly walked back to the table, which was tucked away in the corner. I kept my right hand on the gun in my pocket, thinking, *I'm ready for this guy*. If his plan was to shoot me under the table, I could easily shoot him back. I was nervous all throughout dinner. I knew the shoe was going to drop, but I didn't know how or when. I expected him to say something like, "You know, Glenn, you didn't have to do what you did. You really caused me a lot of problems." I figured his plan wasn't just to shoot me. He wanted to tell me off first.

I could feel the tension building as we made idle chitchat and placed our orders.

And then he spoke.

My finger slowly closed around the trigger in my pocket as I leaned in to hear what he was about to say.

"I really fucked up my life," he confessed, tears filling his eyes. He was filled with remorse and begged for my forgiveness.

I realized then that his errors were old wounds. What he did certainly wasn't right, but he had wrestled with the fallout,

242

confronted his own actions, and come here to make amends. I gently let go of my gun, placed my napkin on the table, got up, and hugged the guy. I could feel the depth of his pain and anguish, and I wanted him to know I'd forgiven him. A few years later, I tried to offer him his job back, but he turned me down. He was probably right to do so, but I never stopped loving and caring for him. If he wanted to come back to work for me today, I would hire him.

Forgiveness can sometimes seem more complicated than it is. For instance, I'm often asked about the danger of loaning people money. It's a tricky thing to do. If somebody comes to me and says they're in a bind and they'll pay me back, my expectation is to be paid back. It's that simple. By now you know how powerful I believe one's word is. I think you should never make promises you don't intend to keep. There's just no upside.

If, however, I *give* someone money, I never expect to see it again. That's the difference between a loan and a gift. One comes with expectations; the other should not. And there is a distinction.

Several years ago, an old fraternity brother of mine came to me and asked if he could work for my mortgage company. I'd always known this guy was a big talker, but I thought he was harmless. He told me he was closing thirty loans a month at Citibank, where he was working at the time. I knew that couldn't possibly be accurate, and I didn't really want him to come to work for me, but I thought if by chance he *was* doing all that business, then why not?

When I offered him the opportunity, he promptly informed me he'd need a $5,000 signing bonus to come onboard. I told him if he closed fifteen loans in his first three months, he could have the bonus at the end of that time. It was a good deal for him, so of course he said yes.

Shortly after he started working for my company, this old friend went behind my back while I was away in Baltimore. He approached my head of production, Dave Loyst. Dave and I worked together at my first job in loans. We reconnected again and he had been working for me for about a year. My fraternity friend told him I said he could have $5,000 as a signing bonus and asked Dave for the money. Dave didn't think anything of it, so he cut my friend the check he wasn't supposed to get until he'd put in the fifteen loans. When I came back to the office and heard about what had happened, I immediately confronted the guy. He knew the deal. What was he doing?

"I need the money, and I feel I'm good for it," he said without even flinching.

I was pissed. I called him out on the spot for bullshitting Dave. It wasn't right to put him in that position, let alone me. As it turned out, by the end of three months, he had put in only two loans, so he quit. He never gave me back the money, and never spoke to me again.

A few years later, I wandered into Mutt Lynch's, a local pub in Newport Beach, for brunch. This was the kind of place that was already raging by ten o'clock in the morning. It's always loads of fun, and a real hot spot on the weekends. I was at a table with two women I knew, laughing and having a great time, when I noticed a familiar face in the crowd. It was my old fraternity brother. There was no avoiding each other. He finally made his way over to our table and said hello.

"How ya doing, Glenn?"

"How am I doing? I'll tell you how I'm doing. Why don't you and I walk outside and let me punch you in the fucking face? That's how I'm doing. How's that?" I was livid, and I didn't stop there. "I want to take a five-thousand-dollar punch in your fucking face. How'd you like that? You want to spend three years not talking to me because you dodged me and ripped me off? You're a fucking loser."

I want to be clear: It wasn't the money that upset me. It was his tuck and run act. It's happened so many times over my life, especially during my early years in business, and it never ended well.

It's taken me a long time and a lot of personal losses to come around to the understanding that loaning friends and colleagues money isn't a great idea. When people ask me for money now, I simply tell them I don't do that anymore. It's a clean and easy answer they can't argue with. There's a responsibility that comes with taking money from someone, and I've lost so many friends in this way, because when they fail to keep their word, they disappear. And that really hurts me, because their friendship always meant more to me than the money.

It takes time and maturity to find your way when you've made certain choices that, in retrospect, weren't the right calls. It doesn't always happen, but occasionally someone will own their mistake and do what it takes to make things right. Here's what I mean: After my fraternity friend quit working for me, he began a career in real estate. He went to work for two very close friends of mine. They knew that we were old fraternity brothers, so they asked me about him. I confirmed that I knew him but said we hadn't spoken in a long time, for private reasons. When they pressed for more information, I just told them it was between two old friends and left it at that. I don't believe in throwing people under the bus. I wanted my friend to do well. What had happened between us was over. There was no reason to dredge up the past. And the two women he was working for were important to me, too. I didn't want our bad experience to taint their opinion, so I kept quiet.

Shortly after our run in, I received a heartfelt apology letter and a check for $5,000 in the mail. The letter was hand-written and sincere. He said he regretted putting money over friendship and took total responsibility for jeopardizing the one thing that mattered. No amount of money in the world was worth losing our friendship and missing out on weddings, funerals, and everything in between. Getting that letter meant so much to me. I called him up and told him I loved him, and that we were done being on the outs. It was time to move forward. And with that, our beef was over.

There's great salvation in forgiveness. You don't realize how much anger weighs you down until it's suddenly gone. When you forgive someone, you're the one who's healed. It's equally important to forgive yourself, too. I'm certain my friend felt like a giant weight was lifted off his chest when we were able to put our differences behind us. Self-forgiveness is necessary when we've wronged somebody or committed a deep or personal hurt. It's common to suffer because of something we did, even by accident, and it's especially difficult if we view our actions as unforgivable—whether those actions involve cheating, stealing, lying, breaking trust, or causing physical or emotional harm. It's important to acknowledge our mistakes, but it's also critical to be able to move on from our worst actions.

The greatest value of forgiveness, whether of oneself or another person, is that it allows you to proceed with your life free from anger, resentment, and bitterness. Acknowledging that what happened was wrong can help heal the pain. The sooner you own your mistakes, the better. But here's something to remember: Forgiveness isn't always a two-way street. You won't always get the apology you're seeking. That's a bummer, but it doesn't have to stop you from forgiving the person anyway. I know it's hard to imagine, especially when you've been deeply hurt, but forgiveness is very liberating. It doesn't require a response, just an action on your part. If your forgiveness requires an apology, then all the power is in someone else's hands. You give them control over the outcome of the situation. You're always in control of how you respond, so you can choose to hold on to harsh feelings or you can decide to let them go. And letting go doesn't mean forgetting; it's really all about acceptance—accepting the situation for what it is. Nothing more, nothing less. It's a healing process that often takes time.

CHAPTER FOURTEEN

DON'T TAKE ABUNDANCE FOR GRANTED

Abundance is not something we acquire.
It is something we tune into.
—WAYNE DYER

WHEN I WAS twelve years old, I developed a passion for collecting old beer cans. It wasn't really a stretch for me, since my dad and his buddies were always drinking beer and leaving their cans around. I liked the different brand logos and thought it would be cool to see how many I could accumulate. Everywhere I went, I looked for old cans. The better their condition, the more interested I was in keeping them. There was something comfortably familiar about the smell of stale beer. If the cans had a tiny bit left in the bottom, I would tip them over, pour out the dregs, and shove them into my coat pocket or backpack. I even started going into other people's yards and wriggling like a rat into the crawl spaces under their houses or sheds, looking in the dirt for older cans left behind from when the places were built. Railroad tracks and ditches were bountiful hunting grounds for me, too. By the time I was sixteen years old, I'd amassed an impressive collection.

A buddy and I went to Pittsburgh with his family. We were walking along an old country road looking for cans. We'd been walking for miles, just talking and searching for our treasure, when we spotted some woods.

"Let's check that out," I said, pointing to the thick lot of trees in the distance.

We trudged through the field between the dirt road and the forest ahead, walked into an opening that ran parallel to the road, and, before I knew it, were very deep into the woods. It was then that I spotted a heap of what I thought were old, rusted oilcans. Someone must have put them there years before. It looked like a junkyard in the woods.

Out of curiosity, I started digging through the massive pile and came across a can that read "Old Export."

These weren't oilcans.

They were cone-top beer cans. They didn't make those anymore and hadn't for many years. The cans were made of steel and looked more like Pepsi bottles. You had to take the top off to drink from them.

I'd found the Holy Grail of beer cans!

I began furiously digging deeper in the pile.

"Stearns, did you find anything yet?" my friend called out.

"No. Nothing," I replied.

I kept digging and digging until I was standing in a hole so deep that I could barely see my way out.

I got a charley horse in my leg and had stopped to let it pass when my friend peered down to check on me. I was lying in this pit of cans, in terrible pain.

"Holy crap! Are you serious? Look at all those cans," he said.

All I could do was laugh, because he had no idea what I'd stumbled upon.

He jumped into the hole and started digging for cans, too. We needed something to put them in, so we searched the woods and found two old, tattered trash bags. By the time we finished, the garbage bags were bulging. We carried the sacks over our shoulders like Santa Claus.

As we walked down the road, every now and then a can would fall out through a hole in one or the other of the bags. When that happened, I would turn to my friend, look at him, and then step on the can and crush it.

"Can you believe it?" I said. "I would've died to find this can, and now I'm going to crush it. Why? Because I can!"

Crunch.

And then I would laugh.

I was ecstatic. I couldn't believe my luck. I crushed five cans that day, thinking I was the coolest guy ever.

When we got home, I decided to take two cans down to a local store that sold vintage collectables and skateboards. I know, weird combination, but the owner shared my passion for old beer cans. When I showed him the two cans, his eyes lit up.

"I'll trade you those two cone tops for this skateboard." He picked up a Banzai board, with X-Calibur trucks and Road Rider wheels. It was the baddest skateboard I'd ever seen. And by bad, I mean badass.

And then it occurred to me: he was willing to trade that skateboard for *two* of my cans?

I was quiet for a moment.

"Why?" I asked. I wanted to understand the catch.

But there was no catch. He understood the value of those cans a heck of a lot better than I did.

And on that day I learned a very valuable lesson, one I've never forgotten. Just because I had abundance, it wasn't okay to waste it. Why would I ruin something that was thirty years old and in beautiful condition just because I had a lot of it?

Today, those beer cans would sell for over one hundred dollars a can. I don't know the exact value they were back then, and it doesn't really matter; what I do know is that I'd been such a jerk. You should always appreciate whatever you have. It doesn't matter how much you have or how little—it's about gratitude and respect.

That lesson has served me well throughout my life. You come to realize there will be times that aren't always full of abundance. Being grateful in those moments is even more important than it is when your cup runneth over.

When my son Skyler was in high school, he asked if he could take a class trip to Washington, DC. He explained that the tour cost $2,500. I told him he could go, but I would pay for only half the trip.

"Half? How am I supposed to pay for the rest, Dad?" he asked, in what could only be described as a tone of shock and disbelief.

I explained to Skyler that this might be an ideal time for him to go get a job somewhere. When I was his age, I had a baby, worked at the local movie theater, and went to school. (To be fair, though, no kid wants to hear anything that starts with "When I was your age" from one of their parents.)

We began looking in the newspaper and around town for openings he could apply for. I wanted him to try to figure it out on his own. I mentioned mowing the lawn as a possibility. I told him to find out how much I paid the gardener, and I would pay him the same fee. Skyler came back and said I paid fifty dollars every time they cut the grass.

"Okay, deal," I said, and we shook on it.

Of course, now I had to go out and buy a lawn mower, because no one in our neighborhood had one I could borrow.

The first time he cut the grass, Skyler called to say he'd finished.

"Great! Don't move. I'll be right there." I was eager to see how he'd done, so I dropped everything and raced home.

I walked around inspecting his work. I strolled every inch of the yard, pointing out the various spots he missed. "Son, if you're going to do a job, do it right. Take pride in your work. Go get the lawn mower and redo it," I said firmly.

I could see the disappointment in Skyler's eyes. I wasn't trying to break him down; I wanted him to understand the importance of doing the job right.

"One more thing," I added. "Next time, I'm going to deduct ten dollars from your pay, and then twenty, and eventually, if you can't do the job to my expectations, you'll end up owing me money, because I'll have to rehire the gardener."

Four days later, I received another call from Skyler. "Dad, I cut the grass . . ."

Once again, I dropped everything and ran home to see his handiwork. I walked the yard just as I had done a few days prior; this time, however, I liked what I saw. "Congratulations. Well done, son," I said, and shook his hand.

After that, he not only understood how to cut the grass but why it's important to take pride in your work.

Months passed. It was close to the time when Skyler was supposed to go on his school trip. He'd earned enough money to pay his half, plus an additional $500. I was very proud of his accomplishment. At the time, the only caveat I'd added was that he kept at least one hundred dollars in his savings account, regardless of how much extra money he made. Skyler agreed. The day before the trip, he decided to buy himself a Sony PlayStation for $400. I didn't have any issue with that purchase, as long as he kept to our deal and the one hundred dollars in savings we'd agreed upon was in the bank. The problem was, he'd forgotten about sales tax, which meant he was now twenty-nine dollars short of our agreement.

Skyler came to me to explain why he had a deficit. He was truthful about it, which I admired. Unfortunately, he didn't meet the criteria for the trip.

"I'm sorry, son, but you can't go. We had a deal. We shook on it. A deal is a deal."

In our family, when you shake hands, it's a deal. Your handshake is your word, your bond. And we don't break our bond. All my children learned this at a very early age.

Skyler was devastated. But then he thought about it and asked if he could cut the grass one last time.

"Sure. Go for it. But you better get started, because it's late in the day," I said.

A few hours later, Skyler came into my bedroom and said, "Dad, it's too dark out. I couldn't finish the yard."

"Then I'm sorry, son. If you don't finish the job, you won't get paid," I replied.

Skyler left the bedroom deflated and defeated.

Charlene and Mindy were in the room when Skyler came to tell us he was giving up. I turned to Charlene and said, "You owe me an apology."

"You're right, Dad. I'm sorry," she said.

"What's this all about?" Mindy asked.

"Ten years ago, I was with Dad in Los Angeles. We were talking, and I began to cry, because I thought the boys would never have to work for anything—that they would never have it as rough as I did. I believed he was going to spoil them rotten. I never got any of that," she said.

It's true. When Charlene was a little girl, I was just a kid myself. I couldn't afford to give her the things I could provide to my three boys, and there were times when she resented that. Even so, I did my best not to spoil them. I wanted all my children to be able to stand on their own two feet.

I got up, walked downstairs, rummaged through the junk drawer in our kitchen, and found a flashlight. I turned to Skyler, who was sitting on the couch moping, and said, "Come with me." We walked the yard for the next forty-five minutes. I held the flashlight, and he mowed the lawn.

When he finished, I turned to him and said, "Congratulations. Well done."

By the end of that night, he was packing for his trip.

When Skyler and his class returned, they were asked to write an essay about the experience. One of the prompts for the essay asked them to write about what they were most proud of. Skyler wrote that he was most proud that he'd paid his own way.

As a parent, and especially a parent of means, it's so easy to give our children everything they want. But what's easy today becomes hard tomorrow. My job as a dad isn't to be my children's friend, it's to teach them to go out into the world and become the best version of themselves. I want them to be kind and caring, and to do something that makes a difference in their lives and the lives of others.

I don't believe children are entitled to an inheritance just because their parents have earned money. In many ways, I think that becomes a hindrance more than a help. That's not to say I don't give my kids assistance from time to time, but that usually comes in the form of a life lesson, like the one I taught Skyler, more than it does in the form of monetary support.

It has always been incredibly important to me to raise kids who have resilience and, yes, grit. It's really the only way

I know how to live. I expect and want my children to understand that the value of having both traits is far greater than any amount of money.

In early 2007, I was asked to appear on the CNBC show *Untold Wealth: The Rise of the Super Rich*. It was hosted by David Faber, whom I knew from my appearances on another one of his shows. He explained that this show was going to focus on new wealth. I believe one of his guests had gone to Europe to buy a fully customized car. Another, who owned a Bugatti, talked about how it cost $25,000 just to change the oil! It felt like the height of decadence. Given where the economy would soon end up, flaunting one's wealth didn't feel like a good thing to do.

I politely called David and declined his invitation. After all, I'd learned my lesson when I appeared on *Oprah*, discussed how I made my fortune, and promptly lost my HUD contracts. David was surprised by my response, but I'd seen too many people talk about wealth that had been built on a house of cards I knew would collapse, and I didn't want to be one of those guys who thought I was something special just because the economy was inflated.

A few weeks later, David called me back and said they were going to include a segment focusing on what some people were planning to do when it came to their children and inheritance.

"Sign me up for that!" I said. I made my kids work to earn money. There were no free lunches in our house. So, that segment felt much more aligned with what I thought, believed, and practiced.

I wasn't told beforehand who would be featured in the special, so I had no idea what they might say. As it happened, everyone else focused on how well they'd done and the things they were able to purchase because of their wealth. I focused instead on the lessons I'd taught my kids. Despite their family's affluence, they still had to work for everything they wanted. I thought back to my hunting weekend with Foster Friess and Mike Ingram. I understood that he who dies with the most toys does not win. It's about legacy, and what better way to convey that message than to declare, "Our kids are getting nothing. I don't want them to sit around and live this grand life like they've earned it. They have to work for every penny. I worked for every penny, and I'm giving all my money to charity."

At the time, we lived in an exclusive enclave of Orange County, California, full of obscene wealth and decadence. My biggest worry was ruining our children, so as a result, every decision I made as their dad was driven by what I thought and believed was right for them.

As they get older, I want to pass along opportunities for them to create and do the things they're passionate about, but it'll always be in the form of a loan, never a gift. We established a family bank where they can borrow money to do good things and invest in business ventures, but they'll have to support their requests for loans just like they would at any other bank. The validity of each loan is assessed in the same way. I want my kids to understand that they have what it takes to make it on their own. It's by far the most valuable gift I can give them.

After the show aired, word got out that Mindy and I

planned to donate all our money to charity. Not long after that, we were being honored by the Starkey Hearing Foundation in front of three thousand people. Everyone from Bill Clinton, Garth Brooks, and Whoopi Goldberg to Steve Martin and Chevy Chase was there that night. When it came time for the live auction, Billy Crystal and Robin Williams started off the bidding with Glenn Frey's guitar. Robin Williams urged the crowd to go as high as they could, saying, "C'mon, folks—you've got to give, and give big. The money is going to the Stearns' kids, because apparently they're not getting shit!"

CHAPTER FIFTEEN

HORATIO ALGER

*In adversity there is opportunity. Show me
someone who has done something worthwhile,
and I'll show you someone who has overcome adversity.*
—LOU HOLTZ

WHEN I FIRST arrived in California, I couldn't help but notice that a lot of people had their names at the top of office buildings. Who were these people? What did they do, and how did they get their names on buildings? I figured they must be pillars of the community, and, no doubt, phenomenally successful.

As my career began to take off, I started meeting a lot of these amazing business and community leaders. One of those people was Dr. Robert Schuller, the well-known pastor from the *Hour of Power* television show. I got to know him through the church I attended, and he eventually officiated my and Mindy's wedding.

One day, Dr. Schuller asked if Mindy and I wanted to attend a party in Palm Springs with him. How could we say no?

The party was hosted by Phyllis and Dennis Washington, dear friends of the Schullers'. When we arrived at the restaurant where the event was being held, expensive French champagne was being served in tall crystal flutes and trays of beluga caviar were being devoured by the spoonful.

"Who are these people?" I asked.

Dr. Schuller explained that they had been his close friends for many years. He said that although Dennis was a wealthy industrialist, he was a Horatio Alger Award recipient, just like George Argyros, Ron Simon, Harry Rinker, and even Dr. Schuller's own father. He named several other people I considered to be icons in Orange County, people whom I either knew personally or wanted to know.

I had never heard of the Horatio Alger Association of Distinguished Americans, but was intrigued, so I asked Dr. Schuller to tell me more. He explained that every year, around ten Americans receive the distinct honor of being inducted into the Horatio Alger Association. The organization looks for people who bootstrapped their way up in life, overcame challenges, and worked their way to the top despite the obstacles they faced. Each has done well in their respective fields. These men and women, in turn, help mentor and provide scholarships to thousands of high school students who are about to attend college. These students have also overcome great difficulties to pursue their dreams of higher education. People such as Oprah Winfrey, Ronald Reagan, Condoleezza Rice, Hank Aaron, Buzz Aldrin, and Maya Angelou, among many others, were all a part of Horatio Alger, too. I was hooked, and wanted to know how one could become a recipient of the Horatio Alger Award.

"You're on the right path," Dr. Schuller said.

Apparently, my humble background made me an ideal candidate, as did my increasing success. I was very intrigued, especially because so many people I respected and admired were part of this organization. They'd built amazingly successful companies, given back to their communities, created unforgettable legacies—they were doers and great leaders.

I filled out an application to be nominated and sent it in, but didn't hear anything back. I've never been the type of guy who takes no for an answer, especially when it comes to something I really want. I wasn't willing to this give up, so I kept at it. I wanted to be included in the same category as those esteemed men and women who'd been honored before. Looking back, I can see that I really wasn't ready for it then. They probably knew that more than I did.

As time passed, I began to think less about the Horatio Alger Association and more about getting to know these people better, and I was so grateful to be welcomed into their social circles. Mindy and I would travel with many of these new friends, or sometimes I would go with them on my own. This exposed us to a new community of philanthropists and change makers. And through this experience, we began to refine our own legacy.

In 2008, when the mortgage industry fell on its face and I lost nearly everything I'd built, my two mentors—Robert Day, founder of Trust Company of the West, and George

Argyros—came to me and said, "We want to buy half your company." They knew I was struggling and wasn't sure how I was going to get myself out of the financial mess I was in.

I was thrilled about the prospect, and flattered. I wanted to be in business with both of them. To be certain, they were throwing me a lifeline, and it felt incredible to know they believed in me and my ability to be a big lender again. It was good timing, because I needed help. For a brief moment I wasn't sure I would be able to find a way out. It was a desperate period in my life, no doubt about it.

Robert and George told me to name my price for half of Stearns Lending. I thought seriously about it, and as appealing as the idea was, I ultimately came to the conclusion that my friendship with them was worth more than all the money in the world. I wanted—and, frankly, badly needed—their support, but I didn't want to lose the camaraderie or relationships we'd developed. They were more important to me. So, as hard as it was, I thanked them and said I needed to figure something else out on my own.

There are some things that are more valuable than money. Even when circumstances are as bad as they were then, integrity and respect will always outweigh the dollar amount someone offers, as tempting as it may be. I'm certain Robert and George understood my situation, and I'm equally sure they appreciated my decision. It's not easy to say no when you want—*need*—to say yes. But it's always best to follow your north star.

A year later, after I'd bailed out my sinking ship one cup of water at a time, George came back to see me. This time he said he wanted me to be in Horatio Alger. George and Harry Rinker, George's mentor, nominated me.

I was honored and full of gratitude. I told them I would be thrilled.

"Glenn, this is a slow process. It can take five or six years to get approved, so stay patient. We want this to happen," they told me.

In 2010, Harry reached out to me after the vote. He said, "We just came out of the meeting. You garnered enough votes to be inducted, but since it was your first round and you're still so young, the board felt it would be better for you to wait a year."

I was excited that I was in, and understood their position and the reasons for the delay.

A few months later, I received a call from the association informing me that I would be accepted in 2011.

I did it.

Of all the awards I've received throughout my life, this one has meant the most to me. To be part of such a wonderful organization alongside so many inspirational men and women is what all my hard work and perseverance has been about.

At the time I was inducted, I was the youngest person to receive the Horatio Alger Award—but then Leonardo DiCaprio was added to my class, making *him* the youngest inductee. Still, it was such an honor.

On the night of the ceremony, my loved ones filled five tables. All my friends from Maryland and my entire family were there, not to mention Leonardo DiCaprio, Michael Bloomberg, Jim Rohr, Byron Trott, Harry Patten, Frederic Malek, and

Anousheh Ansari, some of the other distinguished inductees from the Horatio Alger class of 2011. I was deeply privileged to be in that group of people.

I had to give the Horatio Alger Association a copy of my speech in advance so they could review it and have it ready on the teleprompter for me. I'm not the greatest public speaker, and because of my dyslexia, I have a hard time reading from a device like that. I didn't want to let anyone down, though, so I memorized my speech. I spent hours going over it until I knew it cold.

The night before the ceremony, David Foster, another Horatio Alger Award recipient and a great composer, gave a wonderful presentation to the group in which he shared his life through story and song. He'd been married four times, and told a story about an ex-wife while he played a specific song, and then he would say something like, "She's a wealthy woman today, thanks to this song." The audience loved every moment.

When it was time to give my speech, I had a little something up my sleeve, too. You see, I had some special guests in the audience. When I got up to the podium, I said I wanted to thank my wife, Mindy; my ex-wife, Amber; and Kathy, the mother of my oldest daughter, all of whom were there. And then I said, "David Foster, eat your heart out." It was a great way to lead into my story.

The induction ceremony is performed in the Supreme Court. From what I understand, it's the only nonjudicial act allowed there. Supreme Court Justice Clarence Thomas, who is also a member of Horatio Alger, places the medal around the neck of each new inductee. It's said that this is the closest thing to being knighted in the United States.

I became a board member of Horatio Alger in 2012. Since then, Mindy and I have had the privilege of hosting leadership gatherings of influential trailblazers many times on behalf of the organization. These events have taken place all over the world. It's something we're quite proud of. The first event we hosted, called Surviving and Thriving, was for business leaders from throughout the United States. It took place on Necker Island, Sir Richard Branson's private island in the Caribbean.

We invited speakers who'd been through harrowing adversity in life to share their stories of hope. Each spoke about how they grew and thrived in the face of their challenges. Sir Richard provided the venue, and we secured the speakers. Although they were usually paid a significant sum to appear at events, each speaker understood that there would be no payment in this case. We would cover their travel costs, but the purpose of our event was to raise money for the Horatio Alger Association, which supported young people who sought to overcome difficult obstacles themselves. Everyone who attended as a guest paid a fee to be part of this small, exclusive gathering for four days. Six Horatio Alger students were also invited to participate.

Each morning, a speaker gave a presentation about a specific topic, and then two of the students shared their stories. From noon on, it was playtime. Sometimes in life, we can forget the value of allowing ourselves to cut loose, relax, and have a good time. Fun is a necessary component of success, and Sir Richard Branson personifies that philosophy. He loves to live life on the edge, which is a trait I greatly admire in him. He also enjoys good old-fashioned competition. Whether it's a game of backgammon or a sailboat race around the island, the rules are simple: *there are no rules*. Whoever circumnavigates Necker first wins. Every time I went up against Sir Richard in a sailboat race, he would pick all the ladies to be on his boat, while I would get stuck with the dudes. Sir Richard knew the island so well that he would be soaking in the hot tub with all the women by the time we finished the race.

In the early evenings, a band would play as everyone gathered for drinks, dinner, and dancing. The next morning, we started all over again. One morning Sir Richard was our guest speaker. He talked about his hot-air balloon adventures, including his failed attempts to circle the globe in one. Former fighter pilot Captain Charlie Plumb, another guest speaker, talked about his six-year ordeal as a prisoner of war in Vietnam, one of the longest stints of any serviceman in that war. Dr. Beck Weathers, who had been left for dead on Mt. Everest in 1996, also agreed to speak. He hadn't shared his story with the public in over five years, so I was shocked when he said yes. Eight climbers died on that trip in a terrifying blizzard near the summit. When he spoke, you could feel the cold and pain he described. He was one of the most mesmerizing speakers I'd ever heard.

I also asked another climber, Joe Simpson, to address our attendees. He and his friend Simon Yates set out to climb the West Face of Siula Grande in the Peruvian Andes. The feat had been attempted in the past, but had never been achieved. Joe and Simon tried to scale the mountain in one long push, hoping to reach the peak within three days of leaving base camp. The two men made it to the summit; on the way back down, however, Joe fell and broke his leg. Despite his injury, the friends continued to descend the mountain. Joe was harnessed to a rope that Simon let out for approximately 148 feet before descending to join him. The conditions were horrible. Strong winds and blinding snow hampered their vision and movement. At one point, Joe slid and found himself dangling precariously from an overhang, with no way to climb back up. Simon tried his best to pull him to safety, but he didn't have the necessary strength. He could feel himself being pulled by the weight of his friend, so he made the gut-wrenching decision to cut the rope. Joe fell into a crevasse. Simon assumed the fall had killed him and made his way back to base camp. Unbeknownst to Simon, Joe had survived the fall, and four days later, he miraculously found his way back to camp.

As humble as we all felt after hearing these accounts, we were especially moved and inspired by what the Horatio Alger students shared with us. One of the girls had a twitch in her eye, or so I thought. I asked her if there was something in it and if she needed something to flush whatever it was out. She told me her mother's boyfriend had stabbed her in the eye with a hypodermic needle. My heart sank to the bottom of my stomach. I couldn't imagine such a thing, and yet all the students had equally heartbreaking stories to share. Remarkably, none of them spoke as if they were victims. They were grateful for their education and the opportunities they'd been given through Horatio Alger. It helped them get to a place where they could be on their own. They all had extraordinarily positive outlooks on life. Their bravery and tenacity were truly admirable. Their optimism was astonishing, especially considering how dark the world around them had been at times. They reminded me again that everything is a choice. Adversity can be a wonderful teacher, or it can kill us. It's all about harnessing that experience and using it for good.

The British are known to have stiff upper lips, but I could tell Richard was moved by the weekend as well. We all were. Joe Simpson was so inspired that he proposed to his girlfriend on the spot, sharing that very tender and private moment with all of us. Thankfully, she said yes!

CHAPTER SIXTEEN

GETTING IN YOUR OWN WAY

*In any moment of decision, the best thing you can do
is the right thing, the next best thing is the wrong thing,
and the worst thing you can do is nothing.*
—THEODORE ROOSEVELT

I ONCE HEARD someone describe worry as an addiction. There are some people who can't seem to get past the "what ifs" in life, even though they're just the mind's false and idle chatter. These worriers just can't turn off their negative thoughts, even when those thoughts hold them back from living up to their full potential.

I'm not one of those people.

Okay, so maybe I'm a world-class compartmentalizer. I can admit to that.

No matter how bad things got in my life, I never chose to make room for negativity. That's not to say I didn't have some

271

tough times; of course I did. I just had a way of looking at whatever difficulties life threw my way as, well, nothing more than challenges. They're a series of "How am I going to get out of this?" puzzles waiting to be solved. So far, nothing has stopped me from getting where I want to go.

Growing up, I used to drink alcohol as fast as I could. I would gulp everything down until I blacked out. I must have wet the bed a hundred times in my teenage years. (My friends would say this number is low.) When I passed out, I was O-U-T.

When I was a freshman at Salisbury State College, one of my professors announced that our class was going to take a field trip to the local jail. "Who would like to go?" he asked.

I was all in.

The idea was to expose us to what life was like for the prisoners. It wasn't pretty, that's for sure—and it was very different from the one or two times I spent the night in the clink for traffic violations. As we made our way around the jail, I heard one guy yelling, "Why am I in here? What happened? Did I black out? I don't remember anything."

The officer giving us the tour that day asked our group, "Does anyone know what a blackout is?"

I thought about it and guessed I'd had at least a hundred blackouts between the ages of fourteen and twenty. There were countless nights when my buddies would have to drag me home, where I'd wake up with absolutely no recollection of how I got there.

Most people think a blackout is only when you drink until you pass out. Not necessarily. You can still be functioning, doing everything you normally do, but you don't remember a damn thing the next day. You wake up wondering where you parked the car or how you got home.

When I got older, these occurrences lessened as I became much more focused on my family and career. But every now and then I would let it rip. And when I did, it became painfully obvious that my body could no longer keep up with the abuse I inflicted on it. I would have awful panic attacks from dehydration and lack of sleep. I would beg myself to just get through the horrible anxiety I was feeling, swearing I would never do it again—until the next time.

The last time this happened, I woke up in a hotel room where my friend Michael Johns, an early star of *American Idol*, was staying. That show produced a lot of talent. Many of the winning contestants went on to do great things and become household names, but quite a few of the nonwinning, fan-favorite contestants also went on to have successful careers. Michael was one of those favorites. We met at a charity fundraiser Mindy and I were involved in called Life Changing Lives. While planning the event, Mindy and I watched the finale of *American Idol*. We were mesmerized by both Carly Smithson and Michael Johns. I turned to Mindy and said, "Wow, if we could get those two to come to our event, that would be amazing!" Two days later they were in our backyard working out the details. Two weeks after that, they were performing for the five hundred guests at the event. That night, Michael caught the eye of Jimmy Walker, the celebrity charity-event organizer.

Six months after Michael performed for Life Changing Lives, Jimmy asked him to be a part of Celebrity Fight Night. Many big names would be attending to honor Muhammad Ali and to raise money for the Muhammad Ali Parkinson Center at the Barrow Neurological Institute in Phoenix. There were several performers that evening, but Michael quickly impressed Grammy Award–winning composer David Foster. Jimmy introduced the two of them, and David ultimately took Michael under his wing.

On the first night of the weekend-long event, there was a reception for the original founders. By the end of the evening, Michael and I found ourselves sitting in his room at our shared hotel, talking into the wee hours about life and solving the world's problems.

Around 6:00 a.m. the next morning, Mindy called looking for me.

"Michael, do you know where Glenn is? He never came home," she said.

"Yeah, he looks like a bum. He's on my couch passed out," he told her in his thick Australian accent.

I woke up when I heard Michael talking to my wife. *Man, I'm not feeling good*, I thought. I could feel the panic setting in, so I headed straight to my room.

By this point, Mindy was all too familiar with my routine. If I'd worn myself down and then partied like a rockstar, all of a sudden I would panic and think I was dying. She would always sweat it out with me and help me get through the terrifying angst, but this time she was over it. "Shut up, Glenn. You're not dying." She was so mad at me. And she should have been. My body was telling me to stop, that I was done, and I had to start listening to it or I might just cash in my cards for good.

Throughout the inevitable pangs of anxiety I felt that day, I kept repeating my usual mantra, "All you have to do is get through it and you'll be fine." But later that day, as Mindy and I were getting ready for the big event, another attack snuck up on me. By this time, two thousand people were already in the ballroom, and I couldn't get my tuxedo on.

"Mindy, help me. I'm dying," I gasped, pleading with her.

"You're not dying, Glenn. Just breathe," she said calmly.

"No, this time is different. I swear to you, this time I'm really dying," I insisted. "You don't believe me? I'm getting into a cab and going to the hospital. *I'M DYING!*" I yelled.

Mindy wasn't buying it. "Okay, well, I'm going to the party," she said, and then walked out the door.

I called a cab and went to the hospital by myself. This wasn't the first time I'd done that. When the car pulled up to the emergency room entrance, I got out, flew through the revolving doors, and dramatically proclaimed, "I'm dying. Help me!"

That got the attention of the hospital staff!

A nurse immediately put me in a wheelchair and took me to an examination room. After checking everything out, the doctor said, "Mr. Stearns, it appears you're very dehydrated. You aren't dying. You need to drink water."

"Are you sure?" I asked.

"Very sure, sir."

Someone handed me a tall plastic cup of water and said I could go. By the time I returned to the hotel, Mindy was nowhere to be found. I changed into my tux and headed to the ballroom. The first person I saw was Michael, standing at the bar, drinking, laughing, and having a great time.

"How does he do it?" I asked myself. It took every ounce of energy I had just to stand. I couldn't comprehend how Michael had the stamina he did, or how he kept his body so strong with all his drinking, but it got me thinking about how important health is, both mental and physical. Strong body, strong mind. If I made stupid decisions that compromised either, I would only have myself to blame for the outcome.

Shortly afterward, it was Michael's turn to perform. I walked toward the stage and found myself standing next to Glen Campbell. I'd always admired Glen, though we didn't actually meet that night so much as just nod hello. At some point in the evening, David Foster introduced me to Celtic singer Keith Harkin, who was also a huge fan of Glen Campbell. Keith and I hit it off right away. Glen had donated a few original art pieces he'd created to help raise money, which I ended up bidding on and winning. Despite my earlier fears that I was dying, it turned out to be a very nice night. And, as luck would have it, as I flew to New York on business the next day, who sat next to me but Keith Harkin. We spent the entire flight talking and getting to know each other. He was headed to New York to play a gig, and he invited me to come. I explained I was meeting with some investment bankers and asked if I could bring them along. He said sure. We ended up having a great night, and it was the start of a wonderful friendship.

Mindy and I were very proud to be associated with Muhammad Ali and this annual event. A year or two later, we were the honorees. Sitting at our table was Jane Seymour. We'd never met, but we immediately loved her. Mindy and I invited her to go to Necker Island on our boat many times, and have hosted her at our home in Jackson Hole. Ironically, Jane and her former husband, James Keach, produced *I'll Be Me*, a documentary about Glen Campbell. Jane ended up hosting an event for her Open Hearts Foundation after Glen Campbell died, to which she invited Glen's wife, Kim, and daughter Ashley as her guests. Keith Harkin, whom we'd introduced to Jane and who became a close friend of hers, was also in attendance that night. Keith and I got into a bidding war over Glen's guitar. I kept telling him to stop bidding, but he kept right on throwing his hand up. Finally, I bid more than I knew he wanted to spend, just to shut him down. I walked onstage to get the guitar from Ashley. Everyone congratulated me. I turned toward the crowd, grabbed the microphone from its stand, and said, "Hey, everyone—I bought this guitar on one condition. I'm going to give it to this man if he'll come up here right now and play a Glen Campbell song for all of us—Keith, this one's for you." I held up the guitar and motioned him to the stage.

I love connecting people, especially those I deeply care about. It really fills my bucket to see those relationships grow. A zest for life and a common desire to give back is the glue that binds us.

Another time, I planned a YPO event in Japan with Joe

Ueberroth, the son of Peter Ueberroth. I'd been voted chairman of our chapter, a role I'd resisted playing for quite a while. I knew it would be very time consuming, and besides, it's never easy to wrangle a group of Type A chargers. When I finally agreed, though, I took the position very seriously.

Forty guys were slated to travel to Japan with us, but just before the event, the country was hit with a massive earthquake. There was so much damage and potential danger that we weren't permitted to go. So, we decided to move to plan B—only there was no plan B. That's when I thought, *Hmm. Cabo has a B in it—let's take the group to Cabo San Lucas.*

Within a week we'd rearranged the entire event to take place in Mexico. It was a Herculean task, but somehow we pulled it off. I asked Michael Johns if he would come and play for the group. I told him I already had a band for one of the nights and thought they would be willing to play with him if he agreed to perform. He said he could get some of his friends to come and set up his own band. That sounded great, and it would save our group a lot of money.

We had a fantastic couple of days, jet skiing, racing sailboats, and enjoying time in the sun. Michael and his buddies settled on the beach one night and began to jam. Everyone gathered around them, singing along and having a great time. I didn't want to break up the spontaneous party, but we had an early morning the next day, as we were set to meet the mayor of Cabo.

Everyone there was a business owner and very successful in their fields. They were also the quintessential work-hard, play-hard group. I did my best to be responsible and to serve as a voice of reason before the group headed out for the evening. I let everyone know there would be no late-night craziness. I actually stood in front of them and, like a parent, reminded each of them of what was on the agenda for the next morning. I wanted all of them in suits and ready to go bright and early.

"Do I have your attention? Do you understand that you need to be fresh and on time? So please, don't stay out late," I said.

As soon as I finished, they all bolted.

Mission failed.

The next morning, we all met in the lobby. Everyone was dressed in a suit and tie, except Michael. He was nowhere to be found. He must have gone out the night before. I'd seen that movie, and knew how it was going to end. Unfortunately, we couldn't find him anywhere. We were on a tight schedule, and time was getting away from us. We had a meet and greet with the mayor, and were then expected to depart for California.

When we couldn't find Michael, I made the decision to leave without him. On the way to our meeting, I received a message informing me that the mayor had to cancel. I announced that there had been a change of plans. "Might as well head home," I said to the group.

On the way to the airport I received another call. Michael had been found. Naturally, he'd partied hard all night and had passed out in his hotel room. I told him to pack and get to the airport ASAP.

We'd flown down on several private jets belonging to members of the group. When Michael arrived, we boarded our planes and took off for California. When we landed, there was a lot of confusion. You see, what I hadn't told the group was that although our meeting with the mayor had been canceled, another meeting had been arranged in its place. I'd wanted to keep it a surprise. When we landed, everyone asked, "Where are we? What's happening?"

There were two buses waiting for us on the tarmac. When we deplaned, I told everyone to get on the buses and just go with it. A short ride later, we arrived outside an ornate private gate, which opened right away. We pulled up to a massive, majestic home, where we were greeted by El Presidente Vicente Fox, the president of Mexico.

"Welcome to my home, please come in," he said as he opened his arms wide.

I'd faked everyone out with that bit about a meeting with the mayor; I'd never actually planned for that to happen. The meeting was intended to be with the president all along. One of our members had helped arrange this private get-together.

The president and his wife graciously welcomed us into their home with a traditional shot of tequila.

I spoke on behalf of the group and thanked the president and his wife for having us as their guests, and proceeded to explain that we had with us a true *American Idol* who, with the president's permission, would like to sing for everyone.

I knew Michael was terribly hungover. He could barely talk, let alone sing, because he'd been yelling over loud music and crowds the night before—but I wasn't letting him off the hook.

"C'mon up here, Michael," I said with a big grin on my face.

Michael walked past me and muttered, "Fuck you very much," under his breath. He didn't care if the president heard him or not. He grabbed the waiting guitar and began to sing. His voice was cracking and gravelly. It was, by far, the worst performance of his life.

You play, you pay.

And pay he did. Not long after that trip, I hosted another event with Sir Richard Branson on Necker Island to benefit his charity, Virgin Unite, and Horatio Alger. While we were there, Michael fell while playing tennis. When he hit the ground, he started convulsing. One of the guests began to treat him. While this guest had "Dr." in his title, he wasn't a physician, but he was able to help anyway. It turned out that Michael had had a seizure. Once it passed, he was fine—sort of.

Later that day, Michael said to me, "Wow, having one of the world's top heart surgeons here today saved my life. He said that if I continued drinking, I would die. I need to stop drinking."

I didn't have the heart to tell Michael that the gentleman wasn't a medical doctor, but it didn't really matter; if Michael kept drinking, I knew he was indeed going to die. If hearing this from someone else was what it took would take to get him to stop, I wholeheartedly supported it.

Michael's drinking had become a problem. A month before that trip, I'd discussed taking Michael to rehab. He'd asked to have dinner alone with me.

"I need help," he said. "My drinking is out of control."

"Absolutely. Let's get you the help you need," I quickly responded.

A week later, I called to tell him I'd gotten him set up at a facility, but he said, "I think I've got it, mate," and refused to go.

Sadly, Michael never stopped partying. He got to a place where his drinking wasn't fun to be around anymore. He'd become kind of miserable, and that made me really sad. While I was on a fishing trip in British Columbia, I heard Michael tripped and fell while drunk. As a result of that fall, a blood clot developed in his leg and traveled to his heart, which was already damaged and diseased. Michael texted me a photo of his leg. It looked awful. The next day, he dropped dead at the age of thirty-six.

Losing him was tough. Looking back, I wish I'd taken him to rehab like I did Shane. I should have forced him to get help. When you drink like Michael, your body builds up a tolerance from years of abuse. It's like climbing Mt. Everest. Once you get to the top—once you hit your peak—the only way from there is down. And once you start heading in that direction, the pace of the decline accelerates. I grew up watching my dad and even my mom struggle with that. It's why, later in life, I wouldn't allow myself to go there.

I spoke at Michael's funeral. His mom, sisters, and fifty of his closest friends were there. They were all so mad at him. He was such an amazing guy. But he was hardheaded and wouldn't listen to anyone. Usually people are sad at a funeral, but at this one, it appeared that everyone was just angry, because he didn't have to go that way.

As for me, I sometimes think I could have done more. *Should* have done more. But in the end, Michael didn't want to do more for himself, and that's the saddest part of the story. He was such an incredibly talented guy. He had a future as bright as Sirius. I believed in him, perhaps more than he believed in himself.

We all get to places in life where we have to make difficult decisions, especially about ingrained habits. What makes these types of choices so challenging is that they usually require turning the lens inward and looking at ourselves. That can be really scary for some people. Facing down our demons, our past, or the things that hold us back is never easy, but it's important to do so if we want to break free from the chains that bind us. And we all have them.

I did.

When Michael passed, it was a wake-up call for me. While I didn't do it frequently anymore, there were still nights when I abused my body or did things that could cast me in a negative light. But now it felt like I'd finally shed the last layer of my past and grown up. I found no joy in doing things that were unhealthy, especially just for the sake of keeping up. I could now see life was precious, valuable. I could still achieve the same feelings, experiences, and levels of depth, connectivity, fun, and excitement without having to drown myself in alcohol. As with those old beer cans, I didn't have an endless supply of time. Time isn't infinite; it's a valuable commodity that shouldn't be taken for granted. I no longer had an abundance of time but a scarcity of it. Every day counted.

If you want a different result in life, you have to change your habits and choices. They're things you control, decisions you get to make. It's really that simple. How you manage difficult choices as they arise determines the outcome.

You have to love yourself enough to want the best—not just the best things in life but *the very best life*—one where you're surrounded by people who love and care for you. And you need to trust your instincts. Listen to that inner voice telling you "This is right" or "This is wrong." You know better than anyone what's best for you. I can't tell you that. Making hard decisions that require difficult changes is about learning to respect and honor your future self.

I heard a story about an ancient Hebrew philosopher who met with a man who wanted to convert to Judaism. The man requested that the philosopher explain the entire Torah to him in the amount of time he could stand on one foot. The philosopher easily met the challenge. He said, "That which is hateful to you, do not do unto your neighbor. That is the whole Torah. The rest is commentary. Go and study it."

To me, the single word that stands out in his answer is "hateful." I think he was suggesting that when it comes to our actions, decisions, and choices—how we move through the world—our first thought shouldn't be *How does this serve me?* but rather *How will this impact someone else?* By putting ourselves in others' shoes and asking ourselves how what we do will affect the people we care about most, we're better able to see the repercussions of our actions.

Throughout my life, especially when it comes to business, I've never focused on the things I can't control, including the actions of others. It wouldn't have done any good. Yes, it was painful watching Stearns Lending go down after the sale to Blackstone. Very painful. But that's what happened. It certainly didn't turn out the way I thought it would, but it didn't fail in my hands. Management stopped listening, and people started getting upset. Some left while others stuck it out, but the culture was forever changed. No amount of money was going to bring back the atmosphere I'd built over the course of twenty-five years. The damage was done by corporate bureaucrats who didn't care enough about the impact of their decisions on the people who worked there. After acknowledging this, I didn't spend a lot of time thinking about why it happened. What was the point? Instead, I put my attention on something I did have control over: launching Kind Lending. I felt like I owed it to my team and to myself to do it one more time.

I've always tried to come from a place of kindness, compassion, and empathy. I understood that the people who went down with Stearns were being hurt; their families were being impacted, and the customers they serviced for years might take their business somewhere else. That part mattered to me *a lot*. So, when I was assessing the prospect of getting back into the lending business, you bet I took that into consideration. That philosophy had served our company well. I always made it possible for people who left to come back. With few exceptions, I treated every employee exactly the same, whether they still worked for me or not. It didn't matter if they'd gone to a competitor; that didn't change a thing about how I felt. Whenever I went out with our team at night, I was the last man there, making sure everyone else got home safely. I celebrated our receptionists, and made sure to know their names and what was going on in their lives. I attended weddings, funerals, christenings, and bar mitzvahs. I listened, made myself accessible, and never tried to put myself above the rest of the team. I acknowledged that their contributions helped make our company successful. It was a smart way to motivate, but I never did it to be manipulative. I really wanted people to feel valued, empowered, and able to make a difference. That drove every tough decision I ever made.

In the end, change is always about commitment. How hard are you willing to work to create that change? What are you willing to sacrifice in your life to get to where you want to go? What arc you willing to give up if you stay exactly where you are right now? Are you who you want to be yet? These are questions I ask myself often. Why? Because we're always changing and evolving.

When you commit to one path over another, put your whole self behind that choice; when you do, you open yourself up to a world of possibility.

CHAPTER SEVENTEEN

YOU'RE NOT THAT SPECIAL

Expect the unexpected.

—BEAR BRYANT

IT'S ALWAYS SEEMED that throughout my life, whenever I began to take things for granted—whether it was my success, my health, or even my wealth—God clobbered me over the head really hard and said, "Not so fast. You're not that special." Sure, it was a shock every time, but it was also a calling to rise to whatever challenge I was facing.

Things happen in life that change the trajectory of our journey. We don't always see them coming, and rarely can we understand the impact or purpose in the moment. But every moment, every challenge, every glitch, every bend in the road has purpose and meaning. And rarely, if ever, is it the end of the world. Even if it feels like it in that moment, the reality is that it's probably not. Sometimes it's even a new beginning.

In 2013 as my fiftieth birthday approached, I noticed I wasn't feeling my usual energetic self. For two months I was feeling—well, *off*. Then I noticed a swollen lymph node in my neck. I thought I might have contracted mono because I was so run-down. I knew *something* was wrong, I just didn't know *what*. Reluctantly, I saw a doctor in Jackson Hole and had a CT scan. I kept minimizing my symptoms, thinking that if it wasn't mono, maybe it was Lyme disease. One thing was for sure: I wasn't about to slow down for a sore throat, so I plowed through. My schedule was jam-packed, and there was no time to be sick.

Mindy and I headed to Washington, DC, for the annual Horatio Alger Awards. Attending the ceremony each year was extremely important to me, and I wouldn't miss it.

The night after the awards ceremony, Mindy and I had dinner with Liz, Lynn, and Dick Cheney at their home. Dick was talking about his new heart and how good he was feeling. "Glenn, I can breathe, walk, go up a flight of stairs." He was beaming.

"Dick," I said, "I feel like shit." And I meant it. It wasn't like me to make such a revealing and personal statement, certainly not to someone like Dick Cheney. Deep down, I knew something big was going on. Everything inside me was screaming, "Something isn't right!"

Mindy jumped into the conversation and said, "And he's going to Fiji in four days with his friends. I don't want him to go because I think he's going to drop dead, or that something bad will happen while he's so far away."

"Let me call my doctor and we'll get her to look you over—if you don't mind." Dick paused and added, "She's also Hillary's doctor."

"Well, good. Then we've got both sides covered!" I shot back with a hearty laugh.

I was full of gratitude for his insistence and sense of urgency. There's nothing quite like a former vice president paving the way for your physical. Let's just say that it gets you through the front, back, and side doors.

The next day and several tests later, the doctor said, "You've got a swollen lymph node."

I explained that I'd taken an antibiotic, but it didn't seem to help. So, she sent me to the ENT across the hall for more tests.

"I want to do a needle biopsy," he told me.

After poking around my throat, he said, "You know, I'd like to put you under and have a closer look. How's tomorrow?"

I was amenable to that. I hadn't mentioned to anyone other than my wife and Dick how I was really feeling. If we looked into things further, at least I would know what I was dealing with.

I didn't want to make a big deal out of the biopsy or the exploratory surgery. My plan was to quietly have the second procedure and head off to Fiji the next day. Purposely downplaying everything, I told Mindy to take our daughters and fly home to Jackson Hole. Reluctantly, she agreed, and left DC that afternoon.

While waiting for surgery, I was on the phone with a literary agent who was trying to convince me to write a book. I was lying on the gurney with a needle in the back of my right hand and tubes taped to my arm. When the nurse came to take me to the operating room, I asked the agent if I could call her back in an hour to two, explaining that I had this "thing" I had to do. Just then, the doctor came into my room, looked at me, and said, "Yup. Just as I thought. Squamous cell carcinoma." I guess he knew that from the biopsy.

All I heard was "carcinoma." I knew that was a bad word. My brain was spinning, moving a million miles an hour.

"Yes, Glenn, cancer."

All of a sudden, I saw myself in a dark tunnel. It was black, with no sound. It was exactly the way I felt at fourteen when Kathy told me she was pregnant.

The doctor kept talking, and I caught only every third word—that is, until I heard him say, "It could be completely curable, but it's a fifty-fifty probability."

Fifty-fifty? Like a coin toss?

The wide gap at the end of the dark tunnel was suddenly the small end of a long hose.

Throat cancer?

I'd never smoked in my life. How could this have happened?

Then the doctor said, "If the cancer is tied to HPV, there's an eighty-five percent survival rate."

"*YES!* Can I have that one, please?" I asked.

"Okay, Glenn, ready to do this?" the doctor said.

As the gurney rolled down the long, cold hallway, it felt like they were taking me to my execution.

I closed my eyes and thought back to two nights earlier. I pictured my youngest daughters, Brooke and Taylor, in their pretty dresses at the Horatio Alger after-party. They were too young to go to the actual award ceremony, but they were at the hotel waiting to join us later. They were so beautiful, swaying and dancing to the music the band played for the guests as we arrived.

"Daddy, will you dance with me?" Taylor asked.

I took Taylor's hands and we spun all around the floor. Now here I was, lying on a gurney, about to have surgery on my . . . cancer. My last thought before I went under that day was, *I'm not leaving these girls.*

In that moment, it was perfectly clear what was most important in my life—my wife, my children, and my grandchildren. In a strange and unexpected way, I was grateful for the reminder. We're tested all the time. Sometimes we know it, and other times we don't. When I heard the word "cancer," it stung, but that reaction didn't last long. I've been a scrappy fighter my whole life, and now cancer was my opponent. Whenever I've found myself in a situation where I'm being tested, I've always prided myself on fighting my way through. Some people cave and hide in a corner. Not me. I have grit—an attitude that's been earned the hard way.

I didn't care about going under that day, only about coming out of the surgery. I had a lot of life left to live. This wasn't how it would end. No way.

When I awoke, I was alone in my hospital room. Because Mindy was on a plane to Wyoming, I couldn't call her. So, I called the agent back. You know, business as usual. She wanted to put a writer on the phone.

"I might have to postpone this a bit," I said.

"What do you mean?" she asked.

"They just told me I have cancer."

Whoa. It was weird to say those three words.

I.

Have.

Cancer.

The reality of what that meant certainly hadn't sunk in.

"Glenn, this is going to be the *best* chapter in your book!" the agent shrieked.

I hadn't really thought of it that way, at least not yet. I guess I'll let you be the judge of whether that's true. I didn't want to die. I wasn't ready to leave my wife, my family, my six children, and my two grandchildren. I was numb from head to toe. One thing I was certain of, though, was that I didn't want to be defined by my cancer. I hoped it would be a small blip on the screen, a brief moment in time—not the way I would be remembered.

The instant Mindy landed and heard the news, she turned around and flew right back to DC with the girls to be with me. That's my wife. She's devoted in every way. When she arrived at the hospital, she told the doctors all the bad habits and physical challenges I had. She shared my trouble sleeping, so they immediately ordered a sleep study to be done the next day. Yeah, you read that right: immediately after finding out I had cancer, I was being tested for sleep apnea. That seemed to be a good time to check that out—said no one ever.

All I could think was, *How can I possibly sleep? I'm dying! I could be dead in a month!* That was what my brain was screaming inside my head. Meanwhile, I was lying in bed saying to the nurses and doctors, "Wow, what a great hospital this is."

I'd suffered from sleep apnea for as long as I could remember. I would wake up thrashing and gasping for air. My family made jokes about it because they could hear me from the other room. My poor wife had to endure my grunts and, worse, my actual loss of breath more times than I can remember. Whenever I stopped breathing, I would fight my way out of it—meaning I would punch the bed. I didn't mean to. I was suffocating in my sleep. She would have to wake me up and help me breathe again. Mindy often worried that I would have a heart attack in the middle of the night if I didn't get this under control—so yeah, she told the doctors. She wanted them to have a thorough medical history so we could make some very important decisions.

At the time, I still believed I was going to Fiji the next day. I figured I would already have had the surgery, and now I was having the sleep study test, so off I would go.

Not so fast.

The ENT who did the biopsy explained that I had a tumor located at the base of my tongue; a challenging location, but not impossible to get to. That same day, he set me up with an oncologist and a different surgeon. After reviewing my case, they concluded I would need surgery to remove the tumor.

They wanted to schedule it two to three weeks from then. I wasn't willing to wait that long. I wanted the tumor gone, right then and there. Somehow, I got them to agree to schedule it for the following Monday, there in Washington, DC.

When the doctors left the room, I began to wonder if acting so fast was the right decision. There was no doubt I was in great hands at a top-notch hospital, but I wasn't sure these doctors were the very best for my type of cancer. When it comes to health, sometimes you have to take matters into your own hands and act as your own best advocate, even if it's just to confirm that you're doing all the right things.

I had so many different tubes in my arms that it was hard to reach for my iPad. I wanted to google "best hospitals for head and neck cancers." Without revealing why, I asked Mindy to hand me the iPad, and I began researching. MD Anderson Cancer Center in Houston, Texas, kept showing up in my search results as one of the premier cancer centers in the world. I'm a big believer in seeking the best, especially when it comes to matters of health. I wracked my brain for the names of anyone I knew with ties to MD Anderson. If ever there were a time to call in a favor, this was it.

Former Texas governor Rick Perry is a good friend of mine. I've supported him throughout his political career. I got to know him well over the years, even spending a night in the governor's mansion. I figured he would know the right people. When I reached him, he was happy to make some calls on my behalf.

I also thought about reaching out to Julia and George

Argyros, two of the most connected people I knew, so I gave them a call, too. Julia answered right away.

"Julia, I've got a problem," I said, and explained my condition. I told her that MD Anderson kept appearing in my search results as the best hospital for my cancer. Julia said she knew someone there—and, in fact, she said I'd had dinner with him at the Horatio Alger ceremony two nights before.

"Call Mel Klein," she said.

I'd had no idea he was also the Chairman of the Board of Trustees of MD Anderson. Julia sent me his information right away.

When I called Mel, he was as gracious and kind as anyone could be.

"Mel, I've got cancer," I said.

"Get your butt down here *now*," he replied.

"Okay, I will."

"No, I mean now. When are you coming?" I could hear the steadfast determination in his voice.

"I can be there tomorrow."

"Okay, be at the hospital at 10:00 a.m. I'll meet you at the front doors." With that, we hung up, and I knew I was in the very best hands. Every team needs a quarterback, someone calling the plays and executing them with great precision, and Mel was mine, at least in the beginning. I knew he would put together the right team of professionals to get me through whatever this journey had in store for me. There was a great sense of relief in knowing that the people surrounding me were the best of the best.

When I arrived the next day, Mel and Dr. Ron DePinho, the president of MD Anderson, greeted me at the entrance as promised. My kids, who were with me, noticed the waiting room full of people that we breezed through without stopping. Brooke said, "Dad, do you think it's fair that you're getting this sort of attention, having the president and the chairman of the hospital meet you, when most people don't get that sort of welcome?"

Admittedly, there was a part of me that felt like I was taking advantage of the connections I had. And perhaps that was true. I felt guilty about it, because I think everyone should have the same opportunity to receive the best medical care. Unfortunately, that isn't how our system is set up. I recognize that my ability to easily navigate the complicated area of health care without worrying about bills or insurance is a blessing. I know that isn't the case for everyone.

I turned to Brooke, bent down to look her in the eye, and said, "Yes, it is fair. Very fair. I'll tell you why. There are hundreds of people in the hospital right now who can't afford to be here. They need help, better care, updated machinery. Do I think the chairman and the president are walking me in for free? No, they're not. They're expecting me to pay, and to provide money for all those people who can't afford to be here, Brooke. Nothing is free in this world. I know that. The people walking me through the door aren't doing it because they like me. They want something from me, and I want something from them. That's called 'quid pro quo.' There's always a price to pay. I can choose whether I want to ante up or not. They want to show me the best of MD Anderson so I'll want to support the hospital and help all these people. That's how it works."

I was being brutally honest, because here's the thing: there's no such thing as a free ride. Ever. And that's okay. There isn't supposed to be. I'm fortunate to be able to help. Don't get me wrong—I didn't want to be there, and no one in that waiting room wanted to be there. But if I had to be, at the very least, I wanted to help those who were struggling to pay for their treatment or to fund a study that would advance medical knowledge.

Cancer sucks. It really does.

Here's what I know: Mindset is everything. You can't go into battle already defeated. So it never bothered me when the hospital's chief development officer showed up and mentioned MD Anderson's newest project. I understood I was in for the long haul. As long as they took care of me, I would take care of them.

I've said it before and I'll say it again: The main currency we have in life is our health. That's it. Forget about money or possessions; when you're forced to face down a life-threatening disease or any potentially fatal challenge, you have to come at it with the knowledge that those other things aren't important. Without your health, you really have nothing.

CHAPTER EIGHTEEN

IF YOU'RE GOING THROUGH HELL

If you're going through hell, keep going.
—WINSTON CHURCHILL

THE DAY AFTER my assessment at MD Anderson, I found myself lying on a cold steel table awaiting the first of many targeted proton radiation treatments. Everything was happening so fast that I didn't understand what was going on. The team of doctors in charge of my case pointed me in a direction, and I dutifully showed up. I have an uncanny ability to just go with the flow. When it came to this journey, I knew I would have to be unflappable every step of the way.

What happened on my first day of treatment was unexpected. Two friendly nurses approached the table with a dripping-wet mesh cloth. I have no idea whether it was water or some other substance. It looked like a small fishing net that they'd just scooped out of the ocean. I watched but didn't speak as they gently laid it across my face. It felt cold and soggy. I could feel droplets of liquid dripping down my neck and into my ears until the mesh hardened. I remained still, acting as if it didn't bother me a bit.

Clunk, clunk. That was the sound of them stapling the hardened mask to the metal table. When they fastened it my head and neck were now tightly secured.

Inside the mask was a mouthpiece that I was told to bite down on. As I did, the mesh continued to tighten over my face. My eyelashes popped through the tiny holes in the fabric. I could feel the tension increasing, and I felt terribly claustrophobic. I couldn't move. I began to panic, reaching my hands into the air, grasping for someone, something. My heart was pounding so hard that I thought I might die. I tried to speak, but all I could do was groan. I'll admit, I was completely freaked out. The nurses could tell I was anxious. They came over and began stroking my head, calming me and assuring me that if I wasn't ready, we could stop. The only form of communication I had was through my eyes, which were filled with fear. But I couldn't do anything about it. If I let fear get the best of me, it would be awful. All I could do was surrender to the situation.

I tried to close my eyes, but my lashes were stuck in the hard netting. Even so, I saw myself dancing with my daughter again in my head. *I've got to do this for my children*, I thought, over and over. I had to do whatever was necessary to get rid of the cancer. I could do this. All I had to do was focus on the reasons my fight had to be stronger than my fear.

Fifteen minutes later, it was over.

"Next time we'll give you something to calm you down before we start," one of the nurses said. "Take it forty-five minutes before your appointment, and this will feel a lot easier for you."

"Okay, great! When is my next appointment?" I asked with zealous enthusiasm.

"Tomorrow at ten o'clock."

Okay; I planned to take the pill at 9:00 a.m. and I would be good to go, or so I thought. The next morning, I received a call from the hospital at 8:45. "Mr. Stearns, we have an opening at nine and would like to move your appointment. Can you be here in fifteen minutes?" the nurse asked.

Mindy and I raced from our hotel room to the hospital. When we arrived, I realized I hadn't taken my pill yet. I reached into my pocket, grabbed the pill, pushed it into my mouth, and swallowed. No water, no saliva to help slip it down my throat.

I climbed onto the cold, steel table and repeated the routine from the day before. Unfortunately, the pill never kicked in. There simply wasn't enough time before I was once again stapled down and unable to move. It didn't take long for me to realize that enduring this treatment was going to be a mind game, one I would have to battle daily. Popping a sedative wasn't the answer. I needed to find another way to create calm amid the chaos.

At someone's suggestion, I created a playlist on my phone to help get me through. Music has wonderful healing properties. It can be both soothing and inspiring. What I needed was encouraging songs to keep me motivated—songs that supported my "I got this" attitude. My favorite song during treatment was Rodney Atkins's "If You're Going Through Hell." Whenever I played that song before the procedure, I didn't need to take a pill to calm myself down.

I spent the next three months at MD Anderson going through rigorous chemotherapy and radiation treatments. It was hell. Worse, insurance didn't pay for a thing. I would have sold everything I had to have my health back. I was more than willing to start all over if I had to, especially if I was given a second chance at life. I was fiercely determined to beat the disease.

I'm not going to sugar-coat it: my treatment was a rough go. I was tired and frustrated, and felt like the enemy was beating the crap out of me. There were private moments when I would sob—wishing, hoping, praying that this would all be behind me soon. I hated for Mindy to see me in such a weakened state, and I hated feeling that way, too. I'd been a fighter my entire life. Sometimes I would win, and sometimes I would lose. Many of those battle scars helped me get to where I am, and I wear each of them proudly. I may have lost some battles, but I always found a way to emerge victorious in the war, because I never lost sight of why I was fighting in the first place.

I couldn't lose this war. No way. I had to dig deeper, try harder, search for different answers. I would do whatever my doctors told me to do. While I believe Western medicine is proven, I was willing to try Eastern medicine as well: acupuncture, reiki, making a pilgrimage to Mecca, spinning around on one foot—I was willing to do anything. You name it, I considered it. I didn't care; I just wanted my mind and body to be strong and healthy.

While many patients with the same diagnosis get a feeding tube, I chose not to have one—at least not in the beginning. There were times I wish I had—really awful days and nights when I coughed so much and so hard that I vomited. It felt like my entire insides were coming out. I couldn't keep anything down. Even the meal replacement shakes I drank for nourishment became tough to swallow. My throat was painfully burned from the radiation. Some days, my wife found me curled up in a ball, just trying to get comfortable. I was losing weight, my voice was changing, and I was in a constant state of dehydration. Mindy pleaded with me to get the feeding tube, but I wouldn't do it. Whenever she mentioned it, I would get mad because I didn't feel as though she was on my side, helping me get stronger. I equated the words "feeding tube" with giving in. I wasn't going to do that. Cancer wouldn't beat me. I didn't want Mindy or anyone telling me to cave. The mere suggestion really made me angry.

Boy, did I have that all wrong. I was so caught up in my ego and pride that I got stuck. But none of that mattered to Mindy. She was more concerned about my getting enough nutrients to sustain my health and strength. The harsh reality was that I'd lost forty-five pounds—weight I didn't have to lose. I was emaciated. I didn't see it as a problem, but it was. Mindy thought I was being stubborn—and that was true. I wasn't getting enough food. The body needs nourishment to survive and to fight. Mindy kept saying that if I agreed to a feeding tube, I would get enough of what my body required to help me heal faster. She wasn't wrong. And at the time, I thought I wasn't, either. We just saw things differently. I would later understand how frustrated she was by my resistance.

The thing is, I was on morphine for six months and wasn't thinking clearly. I'm not making an excuse; it just happens to be the way things unfolded. I was focused on not worrying, because worry doesn't pay dividends. All it does is empty you of your strength, and I needed all the power I could muster. That much Mindy and I agreed on. The source of that strength was where we differed. Even so, there were many times when my strength ebbed because of my stubbornness. But looking back, I have to admit that the smart choice would have been to get the damn feeding tube.

As a result of my refusal, I looked sick. Actually, I looked like I was dying, even though I wasn't. I was a frail and almost unrecognizable version of my former self. Despite that, once my treatment was done, I wanted to try to maintain a normal routine.

We returned to our home in Jackson Hole and did our best to resume business as usual. Mindy and I have always been very social, attending charity events and business gatherings. In late 2014, we went to a YPO event. Usually, I'm a very outgoing guy who loves being in the center of things, shaking hands and saying hello to everyone. This occasion felt different. There were about 150 people in attendance. Most knew about my diagnosis, and those who didn't could easily see something was wrong. When Mindy and I walked in, I saw at least half the room shift their eyes away from us. It was the strangest feeling to see people we knew look down or in another direction, as if they were uncomfortable. Did I have cooties? Those people didn't want to come near me. News flash: Cancer isn't contagious! And as if that wasn't bad enough, there were others who made a beeline for me, arms extended, to say, "Just giving you a hug," or "How ya doin'?" While they may have meant well, it felt very awkward.

I wasn't dying, but I wanted to in that moment. I can deal with confrontation a lot better than avoidance. What I learned was there is no right or wrong way to handle someone else's struggles. Everyone deals with crisis differently.

Finally, one of my buddies came over and said, "Great, thanks—now I can't tell you my best cancer jokes. You've ruined it." And he walked away.

Now, *that* I loved.

Let me give you some advice: When you don't know what to say to someone going through a struggle, acknowledge it and move on. Be yourself. Say, "Hey, sorry about the cancer thing. I'm sure you'll get through it, but can we talk about the Dodgers?" or whatever. Believe me, your friend will appreciate that gesture a lot more than the sad sympathy.

It's amazing to me how many people haven't dealt with loss or think they can't deal with death. Both are such pivotal parts of life. Everyone deals with loss or death differently. No one is wrong. It's just different.

When I was first diagnosed with cancer, I didn't want

people to feel sorry for me. In fact, what I really wanted was for them to think I was an idiot for getting it. To be clear, it wasn't my fault—I wasn't a smoker, and I didn't bring it on myself. I didn't want to tell anyone what I was going through, but if I had to, I preferred that my friends and colleagues laugh with me through my last breaths than cry for me.

Over the years, lots of people have come to me to share the news that they're battling cancer, too. They would tell me all about their journey and then say, "Nobody can know."

I get it.

That's how they want to handle their situation. And I respect that.

But that wasn't me. I wasn't hiding what I was going through, but I didn't want to broadcast it, either. At one point, Mindy wanted to set up a CaringBridge page. CaringBridge is a social network whose mission is to help keep loved ones connected during a health journey. To me, CaringBridge seemed as good as saying I was dying. It felt like a hospice platform, so I said no. I didn't want people to worry or think I was fading, even if it could be true. While I knew Mindy intended to keep people informed, the whole idea of it spooked me to my core.

You don't know my wife, but she's a very independent thinker, the perfect yin to my yang. She inherently understood that our family and friends would want to know what was going on. I knew there was no use protesting her actions, so the best I could do was say that I didn't care what she wrote as long as I didn't have to read it. In the end, instead of using

CaringBridge, she put together a private Facebook page, which I never once clicked on. I had no idea what Mindy posted or who was part of the group. I liked it that way.

One day I received a message from Sir Richard Branson. He asked if he could post parts of a blog entry Mindy wrote about laughter being the best medicine on his social media:

Laughter is the best medicine, or so the old saying goes. I have always found there to be some truth in this. This has never been more apt than with our good friends Glenn and Mindy Stearns. Glenn was battling cancer, and taking on the disease with his love by his side and a smile on his face. I'm delighted to say he is now well again. As Mark Twain said: "The human race has one really effective weapon, and that is laughter."

While Glenn was undergoing treatment, he and Mindy sent us a hilarious note about their recent experiences. I asked if they would be happy for me to share their wonderful words to make other people smile. "Share away," they said. "We're all about spreading hope with a laugh!"

Glenn maintained his legendary humour throughout his illness, and they joked about wishing he could have a strong margarita before beginning his treatment. "They have given him a strong sedative to help with that . . . not tequila.

"Not much can get him down. I think the biggest challenge will be giving up chicken wings and getting REST. The doctor says he will need that the most. Up until

this point, rest has not been a recurring word in Glenn's vocabulary.

"Right now he's gambling his odds of success with a backgammon app on his iPad. He has been doing this since we met with the game of the moment Texas Hold 'em, Blackjack, Angry Birds, Temple Run and now Backgammon. 'If I win this game, we're going to get married, if I win this game we're going to get that house, if I win this game we'll get through this financial crisis, if I win this game I'm going to get through this cancer.' Good news: he wins every time.

"Thank you for all of your love and prayers. We have been so touched by the outcry of support. Glenn just wants to get this out of the way so he can get back to living. He is still Glenn, he loves attention but not pity, and he doesn't want anyone feeling sorry for him. He's open about his battle and already telling stories about the ordeal so far. Please feel free to text, call, email, but please don't feel the need to walk on egg shells. The more normal the dialogue and exchange, the better."

A few months later, Glenn was given the all clear. The smiles seem to have worked. Anyway I hope Glenn and Mindy's story has made you smile. Sometimes all you have in this world is a smile and a friend. Sometimes, that's enough to get you through. As August Wilson said: "All you need in the world is love and laughter. That's all anybody needs. To have love in one hand and laughter in the other."

"You always laugh it off," he wrote to me. I had to smile. Sir Richard was right. He understood where I was coming from. No matter how big the obstacle, we always have a choice. Sir Richard, of all people, understood this, because he's my brother in mind, body, and spirt. He knows how to *live* life. And I feel the same.

Despite the unease some people felt when seeing me after my treatment, so many of my friends rallied around me during this time. They pulled off amazing and thoughtful shows of support. Lance Armstrong and Wayne Gretzky sent me videos wishing me well, which I really appreciated. So many other friends did, too. But it was during a trip to New Hampshire when Mike Ingram surprised me with a gift I'll never forget. I was in the back seat of his Escalade when he said a friend of his wanted to FaceTime with me. He handed me his iPhone, and it was none other than Rodney Atkins. He and his entire band were set up in a grassy field, where they began to play my song. At the time, my voice was pretty rough from my treatment, but I was able to muster a gravelly "Thank you" to Rodney and the guys.

"Glenn, we're thinking about you," he said.

I was choked up for sure. That call meant the world to me. And it reminded me:

> *If you're going through hell, keep on going.*
> *Don't slow down, if you're scared, don't show it.*
> *You might get out before the devil even knows you're there.*
> —RODNEY ATKINS

CHAPTER NINETEEN

PLANTING SEEDS

*The growth and development of people
is the highest calling of leadership.*
—Harvey S. Firestone

I THINK SUCCESSFUL people all come from some kind of pain. Their drive is fueled by an innate need to prove something. This is what separates the ordinary from the extraordinary.

I sold Stearns Lending around the time I was diagnosed with cancer. The sale enabled me to spend five years focusing solely on enjoying life with my family. For twelve months of that stretch, we traveled the world. I wouldn't change a moment of that time, not even the diagnosis. Within every storm lies a silver lining. If I hadn't been diagnosed with cancer, I can't imagine that I would have sold the company, let alone spent the kind of quality time with my wife, children, and loved ones that I did over the course of those years.

So, you might say I'm grateful for it all because it taught me some valuable lessons, opened some new doors, and gave me a gift I'll cherish forever.

I've always had a deep understanding that challenge and pain will pass, even if it takes time, even if it doesn't always end when we want it to. I've relished in challenge because I know it's temporary. I've tried to pass that on to my children. I want them to work hard, live with integrity, and make good choices. Like all kids, they don't always listen to what they're told, especially by a parent. Sometimes they need to come around to decisions on their own. I know I did.

When my family and I decided to travel around the world on our yacht, I wanted all my children to come with us. We planned to be gone for a year, too long not to see my older kids and too long to leave Taylor and Brooke. If we were going to do this, it was one for all and all for one. As I mentioned earlier, we asked Amber, the mother of my three boys, to come with us. She homeschooled our youngest daughters as we sailed.

My youngest son, Trevor, was about to go to college. I thought it would be so much better for him to come with us instead, so I talked him into taking a gap year. Trevor didn't come as a guest, though; he was going to be a member of the crew. That way he could work to earn money while on the boat. Because he was brought on in an entry-level position as a deckhand, he had to get his seaman's license.

We got on the boat in Monaco and spent the summer hitting all the European hot spots. We visited the French Riviera, the Amalfi Coast, and Sardinia. It was grand in every way. Our itinerary took us to twenty-six countries in the far corners of the world.

There were many times when the rest of the family enjoyed themselves while Trevor washed down the decks or polished the chrome. Being a deckhand means you're on call seven days a week, twenty-four hours a day. The entire staff worked constantly, and hard. The only break they got was when we left the boat for a few days. Then they could enjoy some much-needed time off.

When we traveled through the Suez Canal, the captain wanted our entire family to disembark, because pirates posed a real threat. They didn't want Trevor to stay aboard, either, for fear that he would be kidnapped if they discovered he was a family member.

Trevor chose to go back to California while the rest of us traveled to India, where we stayed for three weeks. The plan was to meet up in the Maldives for Christmas. When Trevor arrived, I could tell something was on his mind. He wears his emotions on his sleeve, so if something's bothering him, it's front and center. You just have to make him feel comfortable enough to tell you what it is.

After a few days, he sat down and told me that he didn't want to stay. He said he loved being on the journey with all of us, but he'd decided to take a job at McDonald's back in California, where he wanted to start college in the fall. When he was in California over the break, he stayed at Amber's house with his girlfriend. He must have thought that was better than another eight months of mopping the decks and cleaning bathrooms.

"Let me get this straight: you think the real world is where you get to go live in your mom's house for free; hang out with your girlfriend all day; eat whatever you want, whenever you want; and answer to no one? That's not going to happen," I said. I could feel my blood boiling. Who was this kid? I hadn't raised my children to act this way, and the mere thought of it pissed me off. The dialogue between us began to escalate, until it occurred to me that this was a teachable moment.

I've allowed myself to live my whole life on the edge, but I've never once jumped. I've let my fingers and toes dangle over that ledge, and I've gotten close—I've even threatened to jump—but I didn't. I've never once bailed on my responsibilities. This was a moment when Trevor had to decide whether jumping was really what he wanted to do. But first he needed to understand the parameters of that decision. I took a deep breath, leaned in, and said to him, "You haven't quit yet. It'll take about a week to book you a flight home, so why don't we do this: I'm going to think about what you've told me and figure out how I feel. If I respond right now, it won't end well. So let's meet again tomorrow. I can tell you my thoughts then. All I want you to do is listen. When I'm done saying my piece, we're going to separate and think about what I said. The next day we'll sit down together again, only this time you'll get to speak and I'll have to listen. Then we'll walk away one more time before I react. Throughout these talks, we'll both have a chance to share our feelings. We'll really be able to think this thing through, because you can't leave now anyway. We're stuck on the boat. Sound fair?"

"Yes, okay," Trevor agreed.

The next day we sat down together and I said, "I've thought it over, and I see three options: First, you can leave, but know that you'll be deserting your crew. They'll be stuck having to carry the extra load, and you'll set up a pattern for your future, where you bail whenever times get tough. You may tell yourself that this time things will be different son, but it's never different. There's always a good-enough reason to quit in life." I shared the story of my college professor telling me to quit school because of my dyslexia. I wanted him to know that if he quit, he would always be a quitter, and that just wasn't in our DNA. Besides, if he quit, I explained that he would never be able to get back on this boat with a shred of dignity, even as a guest.

"Can you imagine being a guest on this boat after you let down fifteen other people? You could never come on board and look those people in the eye, because you'll have disappointed every one of them. You dropped them on the other side of the world and went home. You think you'll come back next summer with a casual 'Hi, how ya doin'?' I don't think so. If you quit, you'll have burned that bridge," I warned him.

The second option was for Trevor to stay: "You can stay and be a resentful jerk, because that's what happens when you don't like what you're doing or being where you are. When you're doing something against your will, your attitude will likely get you fired. So, basically, you'll net the same result as if you'd left."

The third option was to figure out a way to compromise.

"Is there a way to not get *everything* you want but still get *some* of what you want? I don't know what that looks like, because that's up to you. To me, number one doesn't seem like a good option because you're not a quitter. Number two only sets you on a path of anger and misery whenever you don't get your way, so that doesn't seem like a good option, either. But compromise? That's what the world is all about, son. That's all I have to say."

And then I stopped talking. Trevor and I stood up without another word. He went back to work, and I hoped he'd heard what I was trying to convey.

I believe failing is a part of the journey of life. Those circumstances teach us more than any others. More important, those tiny setbacks don't have to define who we are. They're really nothing more than hiccups in life. If we dwell on the disappointment, that's exactly where we'll live. If, however, we don't interrupt patterns, we'll inevitably keep repeating them—and when that happens, it's easy to fall into a "poor me" state of mind. People stick to patterns because they're comfortable and familiar, so they feel good. The reality is, most of the time, they have the opposite effect. I'd spent most of my teenage years watching people I cared about stick to their cycles, and most of them ended up either dead or in jail. Sometimes those patterns teach you what *not* to do. They taught me to fight the urge to stay complacent and follow in my family's footsteps. I wanted more out of life. To do that, I had to get off that familiar, comfortable path. It wasn't until that day in the bar when I asked Parker to drive to California with me that

I understood this need to pivot. But ever since, the constant shifting has kept me moving forward.

Once you recognize a negative pattern and find the courage to change it, you'll be free of whatever chains have been holding you back in life. When you finally realize you're strong enough to break free of those behaviors, you'll discover the difference between failure and success.

So often I see parents, especially those who've achieved some level of success, put expectations on their kids that raise the bar impossibly high. Those are unfair and unrealistic shadows to live under. My priority as a parent has always been to first raise a good human being. I never worry about anything else, because I know good grades or winning blue ribbons won't create sustainable happiness—and every parent wants their children to be happy and content.

The next day, as agreed, Trevor and I sat together once more. This time, Trevor spoke and I listened.

"I thought it over, Dad. You're right. Option one doesn't work. If I leave these people, it's a bad thing. I know deserting them isn't a good idea. Option two—staying and being pissed off—is also not a good idea. So that leaves me with option three. Do you know how hard I work here? We work eighteen-hour days. I don't complain. I do the work even though it's demanding and the hours are long. So I was thinking that I need a raise."

"Wow," I said. It just came out of my mouth. I wasn't supposed to talk, but I couldn't help it.

"It's okay, Dad. You can talk." Trevor wasn't going to make me wait another day to say how I felt.

"You know what? I love that you're starting to understand leverage and when to use it, because this is the perfect opportunity. I give you a lot of credit for that. However, there's not enough money in the universe to buy your integrity. Your word is your bond. You committed to staying until July and paid a certain wage. You can keep or break that promise. So, I like your idea, but it isn't going to work. You've got to think of something else." I wasn't being confrontational; I was speaking from a place of love. If I wanted my son to learn what I was trying to teach him, browbeating him wasn't the answer. He had to come to his own conclusions.

Trevor hadn't expected my answer. I could see that. He thought about it for a while and came back with another compromise: if he didn't use any vacation time, he could take the entire month of June off and leave the boat early at the end of May.

That sounded like an awesome answer to me, and a doable compromise. I wasn't his boss, though—the captain was, so he needed to talk to him about it before I could agree to his resolution. The captain thought it was a great idea, and Trevor felt heard and valued.

I was proud of my son. He thought through his circumstances. He'd taken himself to the edge and almost jumped ship, but didn't. He was starting to think about actions and reactions, cause and effect. And I hoped he was beginning to understand that sometimes in life, things go the way they should instead of the way we wish—and because of that, it usually works out better than we could ever imagine.

We all have that voice in the back of our minds telling

us the right thing to do. Sometimes we listen, and sometimes we don't. Listening often reveals the harder thing to do, which makes it more difficult to act on. When you do those right things, though, you're planting seeds that can be harvested one day. There will come a time when I won't be able to help my son, but knowing I've planted those seeds gives me hope that he'll make the right decisions without me.

I believe good people are good because of what they do throughout their lives. It's how they live. When you continuously plant bad seeds, your actions will eventually catch up to you and you will fall. That's how life works. This was a wonderful time for my son to see how one's actions, even the small ones, always came back to either help or hinder.

Most people don't know their own potential, or, worse, they doubt it. The most important gift you can offer to people is the encouragement to believe in themselves. Planting seeds of hope doesn't require you to be bigger or more successful than others; you simply need to have enough confidence in yourself to build someone else up. Believing in another human being's potential is incredibly powerful. Encouragement like that can be difficult to receive, and the leap to fulfill such confidence in you can feel awfully big, but trust me: when someone says they believe in you, it can give you superhuman strength.

When I was a kid and people told me they thought I was going to be successful, I bought into it. It inspired me to want to do better. Even when I was falling away from that path, I never forgot those words. They still inspired me to want to prove that they were right.

CHAPTER TWENTY

YOU CAN'T GO BACKWARD IN TIME

I can't go back and change the hands of time,
but what I can do is create a new legacy.
—ERIC THOMAS

I MET JOHN ELWAY for the first time in 2003 on a hunting trip with Mike Ingram. We'd traveled to South Dakota to hunt pheasant. This trip was very similar to the one I'd taken with Robert Schuller. I always enjoyed these outings, because they gave me the opportunity to meet some very interesting people. Mike put these trips together to help connect people he believed needed to know one another.

Mike was a big land developer, and John was a partner on one of his deals. When I met him, I immediately thought back to that day in the bar in New Orleans, where I watched him play in the Super Bowl.

When you hunt pheasant, you walk the fields all day,

talking with the other people hunting with you and getting to know them better. Mike had a wonderful way of drawing stories out of people. On this trip, Tom Brokaw spoke the first night, I spoke the second night, and former vice president Dan Quayle spoke on the final night. My being sandwiched between those two men caught John's attention, and he offered to fly me home on his plane. We spent the entire flight talking and forging a friendship.

We hit it off right from the start. What surprised me the most was how down-to-earth he was. He didn't take himself seriously, which resonated with me. John shared a story about playing golf with Dan Quayle. Both of them are scratch golfers, and they were playing against two younger guys. Dan was losing, and was so frustrated that he pounded his club on the ground. When John asked him what was wrong, Dan responded, "Everyone wants to say they beat the vice president at golf."

John looked at him with a straight face and said, "Let's face it: we're both has-beens."

Years later, Mindy and I played a round of golf with Dan and his wife, Marilyn, in Fiji, and Dan suggested we play with only one club.

"You and Mindy pick your club first," he said, "and Marilyn and I will pick ours second."

We picked a 7-iron. Dan and Marilyn picked a putter.

I never knew you could putt a ball 150 yards.

But in the end, the Quayles were up by one. They were on the green, and we were off the green. Mindy chipped in a shot to put us one up, while Dan two-putted and lost.

It was great.

Yeah, everyone *does* like to beat the vice president!

In 2019, John Elway called and asked if I wanted to go to the Barrett-Jackson auto auction in Arizona. The auction was a week-long televised event, at which close to two thousand cars are typically sold. Elway was selling his Dodge Viper and thought it might be a lot of fun to be there and check out the other cars.

My son Trevor and I met John, his business partner Mitch Pierce, and some other guys from John's auto dealerships at the Burbank airport, where we boarded Mitch's plane and flew to Arizona. The entire flight, I couldn't stop thinking about my old car. I turned to the guys and said, "There's only one car I want. I hope I can find it at the auction."

I'd spent thirty-seven years regretting my decision to sell my '69 Camaro, and I'd always said if I could somehow find that car again, I would buy it. Through the years, I'd found many Rally Sport and Z28's, but never the elusive Rally Sport/Z28 package together. I was looking for a needle in a haystack because there were only twenty made. Fifty years had passed since that car rolled off the assembly line. What were the odds it was still on the road? Slim to none.

When we arrived at Barrett-Jackson, a group of people from the company came to greet John. We were ushered to a VIP area, where we received credentials that allowed us to walk around the place. The setup for the event is huge. The main tent, where the auction takes place, holds thousands of people, and the VIP area has additional seating. There are many other tents with cars on view as well.

"Mr. Elway, would you like to see your car?" one of the Barrett-Jackson people asked.

We made our way past several other tents as our escort walked us over to the one where John's car was. We had to descend a flight of stairs, and as we did, I looked up and spotted a blue-and-white Camaro.

I grabbed John and said, "Oh my God . . . that *can't* be my car."

My heart was racing with excitement, yet I didn't want to get my hopes up too high. I mean, what were the chances?

John's Viper was parked right next to the Camaro. I walked over to the Z28 and read the description that was pasted on the window: "Only 20 302 Z28s were produced in 1969, making it one of the most collectible muscle cars in today's marketplace."

And then I saw where the car was from.

Maryland.

I couldn't believe it.

It *was* my car.

Not just a car like mine, but *actually* my old car.

I had to have it.

I spoke to Craig Jackson, the CEO and chairman of Barrett-Jackson, and told him the story of my car. He called over Jerry MacNeish, a well-known Camaro expert, to verify that it was authentic. Not only could he verify it, but he was also the person who appraised it.

John's Viper was auctioned while I worked with Jerry.

I was told the car would go up for auction later that day.

Eight hours later, though, it still hadn't come up on the block. It was so far down the list that I wasn't sure it would happen that day. It was time to head out for dinner, so we left. We first stopped at Mitch's home in Paradise Valley to change. I didn't have anything to change into, so while the others were getting dressed, I turned on the television to see if I could find the auction.

We were scheduled to fly out later that night, me to Baltimore and everyone else returning to California. I was nervous because I hadn't heard anything about the car.

Suddenly, my phone rang. It was the woman I was looking at on TV. She asked if I wanted to bid.

"*YES!*" I shouted.

Bidding began.

I could see that another guy, who was standing next to the car, wanted it as much as I did. There was a three-second delay between the live bid and my phone bid, which was being shared with the television audience. We were going back and forth, furiously upping our bids. It was really exciting. And then I heard the auctioneer say, "Sold!" I took a deep breath. "To Glenn Stearns."

I could hardly believe it.

By this time, the guys had all gathered around. We were high-fiving each other and celebrating my winning bid.

I finally had my car back.

Life is funny. As I said earlier, it's all about timing.

And patience.

I'd waited thirty-seven years to find that car.

Whenever I've wanted something in my life, I didn't just think it; I spoke it aloud. I made it real, whether it was finding the perfect mate, achieving success, or looking for a needle in a haystack, like I did with my old Z28. I still do it. No matter what it is, if you put something out there in the universe, I believe you can manifest it. You can turn your dream into a reality. The results don't always come fast, making patience a very important trait. But if you believe in it, I truly think anything is achievable. Even starting over. There have been times in my life when things just aligned. I hadn't necessarily connected the dots then, but later the pattern made total sense. Is that manifestation, too? Maybe. I'm certain that when one door closes, another always opens.

Timing, patience, and manifestation had everything to do with my next steps in business, too.

When Blackstone bought Stearns Lending, they made the purchase because we were the best lender in the country. After the acquisition, they didn't utilize me in any capacity, even though I was the guy who'd built that company from the ground up—the one who knew it inside out. Sure, I didn't have the same pedigree as most of the guys in the Blackstone boardroom, but it didn't stop me from hitting it out of the park before they took over. I mean, that's why they bought the company, right?

I suppose it's human nature to ask, "What if I'd stayed in?" I'm certain I would have grown the company to three times the size it was then. And who knows what other roads it could have led me down?

I believe wholeheartedly that if I'd kept the company, it absolutely would not have filed for bankruptcy. More to the point, I'm convinced that we would have made a lot of money during that time. Those were good years in lending, and the company should have performed much better than it did in that climate. I know this from watching my friends and colleagues in the mortgage business really grow during that period. Was I keeping score? Maybe, if only to have something to measure. But I'll admit, it wasn't easy sitting on the bench when I'd been used to playing in every game for years.

Pondering my decision later was a lot like analyzing the buying and selling of a stock. Sometimes you get in at the right price but sell too early; other times you buy too high and take the hit. I knew it was no use struggling with the question, but it didn't make it any easier for me to ignore. Here's what I know for sure: you can never go back in time—and the truth is, I wouldn't want to. There are always lessons to be learned, even if they come slow and hard, and at a high price, like the Blackstone deal did.

When you've spent your life overcoming adversity, the silver lining is evident the day you realize that all those experiences have given you a protective suit of armor, a thick skin that's impervious to slings and arrows.

I've always been fascinated by people who idolize someone and then enjoy watching them fall. It's like a train wreck they just can't stop gawking at. For whatever reason, they have to look, even when they know they shouldn't. Whether it's happening to Tiger Woods or Lance Armstrong, a fall from grace is never easy to witness, and apparently even harder to turn away from. And that's partly how I felt watching the new management of Stearns Lending slowly knock down the house I'd built. I loved that company, and at first, I thought highly of the team running it after I left. But as incalculable damage was being done, I couldn't look away. The difference was that I didn't want to see it fall. I would've done anything to save the company, but my hands were tied. Believe me, I tried. I knew there were a lot of people, including colleagues and competitors, who were watching the demise and waiting in the wings to grab the spoils. I was very disappointed in them—and I was mad at myself for making the initial decision to sell, as it ultimately led to the dismantling of an amazing company.

Don't get me wrong—I'm really glad I took those years to travel and be with my family. Most people don't have the ability to do that. I'll forever be grateful for the memories and experiences we shared, and I'm equally thankful for the perspective it gave me. I didn't know it then, but I was tired. I'd been working at a breakneck pace for so long that I'd forgotten what it was like to just . . . *be still.*

When you're left alone with your thoughts, though, a lot of crazy ideas start to churn around in your head. One thought was pervasive: *What would it be like to go back in time and start all over again with nothing?* It's a strange fantasy for anyone to engage in, but for a guy like me, it was more of a curious daydream.

There were many days at sea when I began resurrecting an idea for a television show I'd had in my head for at least ten years. It was an experiment of sorts, to see if you could take a guy like me; strip him of everything he had except for a car, a phone, and one hundred dollars; and see if he could re-create himself and his success. I clearly envisioned the opening for the show: I would take off in my private helicopter from the two-hundred-foot yacht I was sitting on and find myself sleeping in an old, beat-up truck with nothing but a few bucks in my pocket and a cell phone. I thought this exploration of resilience might make compelling television. I also thought it would answer another big question that had been gnawing at me for some time: "Am I good, or did I just get lucky?"

Some guys hit the jackpot in business. I know this from experience. Others are gifted enough to earn their fortunes. I wasn't really convinced I fit either of those categories, but I was intrigued by the thought of really testing my mettle. By this time, my cancer was in remission, and I thought it might be fun to try my hand at something completely outside my wheelhouse.

I called friends to ask their opinion. I said, "If you could turn back the clock, go thirty-five years back in time and start all over again, would you?" If they said yes, my follow up question was, "What would you want to do?"

Both Elway and Branson had the same answer. "Hell no. I would never do that." I was a little surprised to hear that from these two guys, because both of them loved adventure and were fearless.

For me, the idea of snapping my fingers and suddenly having no name, no contacts, no friends, and no money was exciting. I thought it would be fun to challenge myself with the pressure of knowing the world might see me fail. It would be my version of *Naked and Afraid,* where all I would have with me was my experience and some clothes.

My first foray into television happened early in my mortgage career. It certainly wasn't planned. I was just a guy hacking loans and trying to figure out how to create a business. At the time, I was still very new to lending, so I was surprised when somebody asked me if I wanted to talk about the loan business on their local television show. I was thrilled for the opportunity. At the very least, I thought it might generate more leads.

The show was on late at night and was hosted by a local insurance salesman. Once a month, he would film a segment to air on this B-rated local access cable show that people could watch for free. It was a paid advertisement, but I didn't know that then. The first time I went in for my interview, I was really nervous. Afterward, I remember thinking, *That was easy.* I figured that even if I screwed up my answers, nobody was watching anyway, so no harm, no foul. I liked being on television, though—so much that I reached out to a publicist to discuss getting on more shows. I started pitching them ideas I had for segments about HUD and the one-hundred-dollar down payment loan that was very popular at the time. For certain properties, you could put down as little as that and end up owning the place. There were even homes that came with a 50 percent discount on the property if you were a teacher or a police officer. At the time, you could own a home for less money down than your first and last months' rent. A lot of people weren't aware of these government programs, so I started talking to anyone who would listen, especially news outlets.

The more I talked, the more coverage I began to get. It was great. Every time a story aired on a local news station, I would get hundreds and sometimes thousands of calls from people who wanted to get in on those deals. The news gave me instant credibility, because people generally believed what they saw on television—or at least they did back then. I buddied up to a few of the producers, who encouraged me to come up with more content. I didn't know anything about television or the entertainment business, other than it was a thing I could never be a bigger part of—or so I thought. I kept pitching ideas, and that kept me on the air. I couldn't figure out why other lenders weren't doing what I was doing. It was so simple, and it always resulted in new customers.

When you're in business, you've got to be willing to think outside the box and try new things, even if it makes you uncomfortable. It doesn't matter if you're a start-up or an established company—evolving is a never-ending pursuit. As I've said before, a lot of people don't like getting out of their comfort zones. They like the status quo, old-school way of doing things. And that's cool, because when you're the one thinking differently, the opportunities come to you like bees to honey.

As I grew in business, I became too busy to keep doing local news, but I had definitely been bitten by the entertainment bug. It wasn't until I met Mindy several years later that television would come back around in my life. Being a television personality, Mindy was a natural on camera. She would do her thing at work, and I would do mine. And I loved seeing her on the air.

About a year after we were married, one of my employees was a finalist on a new reality show called *The Real Gilligan's Island*. Contestants competed in challenges based on the plots of various episodes from the famous 1960s sitcom. At the time, the producers were looking to cast the Skipper. When my employee went in for his final call, he casually mentioned that his boss and his wife would be great participants, too. He described Mindy and me to the producers, and before he could finish, one of them said, "I know Mindy from KTLA, and I saw Glenn and Mindy's wedding on *Oprah*!"

Okay, so this is where I get to brag about my wife a little.

Long before Mindy and I met, she was living in Chicago, working as a dental hygienist. She and her mom loved Oprah and decided they wanted to go to a taping. Mindy's mom lived in Oregon, where Mindy grew up, so she flew in for it. Before Oprah came out, the audience wrangler asked if anyone had any special talents.

Mindy's mom elbowed Mindy and encouraged her to do her noises. So, as the audience clapped, Mindy made the sound of a crying baby. It was so loud that it could be heard over the crowd.

Curious, the wrangler called her up on stage, where Mindy proceeded to run through her entire repertoire. She barked like a dog, meowed like a cat, crowed like a rooster, and wailed like a car alarm. She had the audience in stitches. Mindy went back to her seat, where she excitedly awaited Oprah's entrance. As it turned out, Oprah had been watching Mindy do her thing from her dressing room.

So, when Oprah came out, she said, "I've been doing this show for years, and I've never heard anything quite like this. You in the pink, c'mon down here." She called Mindy back up on stage and asked her to crow and cry all over again—only this time it would be seen by people in the 130 countries where *The Oprah Winfrey Show* aired.

That was the start of a beautiful relationship, as Mindy became known by Oprah fans all over the world as "the Rooster Lady."

That day changed Mindy's life forever. It didn't take long for people to see her talent. Producers reached out and offered her jobs in television and radio, and she loved it. She was a natural, and audiences adored her upbeat, fun, quirky personality. Before long, *Entertainment Tonight* and *KTLA 5 News at 10* in Los Angeles had also offered her jobs as an entertainment reporter, which she eventually accepted. Her career in television really took off after that. Oprah never lost interest in the Rooster Lady, though. Mindy appeared on the show five times, and Oprah has called Mindy one of her all-time favorite guests.

Naturally, the producers of *Gilligan's Island* were interested. One called to say he would love to talk to us about the possibility of our doing their show. I was curious, so Mindy and I agreed to meet him on our way to the airport, as we were headed to Hawaii for a vacation. The production team was set up at a hotel, so we thought, *Why not?* When we got there, we sat in chairs across from the camera and crew while the producer interviewed us. We had a wonderful camaraderie right from the start. He said we would be perfect as their Howells, aka "the Millionaire and his wife."

We were flattered, of course, but we had a flight to catch. As we stood up to say our goodbyes, the producer asked if we could wait one more minute. We said we could, and he briefly left the room. When he came back, he motioned for us to follow him into another two-room suite, where Sherwood Schwartz, the creator of *Gilligan's Island* and *The Brady Bunch*, was sitting with Mike Fleiss, who created *The Bachelor* and other shows.

Sherwood and Mike both said they wanted us for the show and asked us to commit right then and there. I couldn't believe it. I knew people who'd waited hours just to be seen and never got a call back. Now here we were, being offered roles on the spot.

At first, Mindy and I were reluctant to say yes. I didn't think I wanted to take that much time off from work. But then they said we would be needed for only two weeks.

Two weeks? That I could do.

"Okay, sign us up!" I said.

We shook hands and left. When we returned a week later, we received a call from Lynn Spillman, who was the casting director for *The Amazing Race* and was married to one of Mindy's co-workers at KTLA. Through her husband Eric, she heard that we were going to be on *The Real Gilligan's Island*. She offered us the opportunity to do her show. She did her best to convince us that *The Amazing Race* would be a better opportunity for us, with more exposure and a bigger cash prize.

Again, Mindy and I were flattered. *The Amazing Race* was

a huge show, one we would've loved to take part in. We wanted to say yes, but we'd just given our word to Sherwood and Mike. We shook on it. There was no way we could back out, so we had to graciously decline the offer.

When we started filming *Gilligan's Island*, Mindy said, "I'll do anything to win, Glenn. But I *won't* eat a bunch of nasty stuff. No way, no how. As much of a foodie as I am, I have my limits." I completely understood. We'd walked into the production so fast that we didn't really think about it much beforehand. It wasn't until we arrived on the "island" that we learned we would be there for thirty days, not fourteen.

Damn.

We were in it now, though, so there was no turning back.

At the same time, we discovered that we would be competing against an identical set of castaways. In other words, rather than our competing against the Professor or Ginger right away, we would first be up against another pair of Howells. Our Skipper would also compete against another Skipper, our Mary Ann would be pitted against another Mary Ann, and so on. The idea was that we would compete to preserve the characters we were playing. Which of us would go? We battled it out to determine who would be eliminated. One by one, cast members left the island, until one last person was left standing.

And as if the matchup against the other set of Howells wasn't a big enough surprise, the producers made the competing castaways share a hut. The Gilligans shared a hut, the Mary Anns shared a hut, and the Gingers did, too. And, yes, so did both pairs of Howells.

Mindy and I bunked with Donna and Bill Beavens, from Louisville, Kentucky. They were an extremely conservative couple compared to us. From the first episode, we could tell they would make for some very compelling television. Donna was dramatic and opinionated about *everything*. Our first night in the hut, she talked about the horrors of the gay lifestyle and compared gay sex to having sex with snakes. She was slamming gay people, which didn't sit well with Mindy or me. Her husband stayed quiet, until he couldn't.

When he finally spoke, I hoped he would be a voice of reason. I really wanted Bill to rescue his wife, because I knew how bad this would look to viewers.

But no such luck. "It's true—they do have sex with snakes," Bill said.

I just about died. This wasn't going to end well for them, either during the show or after. I did what I could to salvage the conversation, but it was too late. The damage had been done.

Our elimination challenge against the Beavenses was an exotic food competition. The first thing I thought was, *Great. Mindy isn't going to do this.* I was wrong. We'd been in the game long enough for Mindy to overcome her fears and dive right in. She ate a wild boar heart. She also ate bee larvae—while some of the bees were actually hatching on the plate! I could see the baby bees wiggling around. Meanwhile, I ate a plate of live worms and chicken rectums. They tasted like, well, chicken. Sort of. The worms popped in my mouth, snapping like Pop Rocks.

The Beavenses had a very hard time eating any of the foods in front of them. Mindy and I crushed them in the competition. They were soon eliminated, and I can't say I was upset to see them go.

Being on the island was very challenging. We had to forage for our own food unless the producers provided it to us in a challenge. They secretly stashed bananas in trees for us to find, and occasionally we would crack open a coconut. They deliberately wanted us to be tired and hungry so we would be on edge. That all but guaranteed good television.

We quickly learned that creating alliances was critical to winning the challenges and, ultimately, the game. This was really an "every man for himself" show, but I knew from the start that without creating partnerships along the way, I would never emerge victorious. Like everything I do, I was in this to win—but not for me. I was in it for the charity I was playing for. Frankly, the cards were stacked in my favor from the start. I was the only person on the island who had experience building teams and negotiating every single day.

I understood that it was a lot easier to move the ball forward when everyone played as a team. If there was a rogue player, there would be unknowns you couldn't calculate for. I also understood the value of knowing your competition—who they were, what strengths and weaknesses they had, and how to use those attributes to achieve your ultimate goal.

The fact that I also had a lot of experience managing a variety of personalities gave me a distinct advantage in the game. Oftentimes, especially in business, you need to be chameleon-like—malleable and adaptable enough to your surroundings to survive. If you're not, you'll fall.

Kate Koth (who played one of the Mary Anns), Mindy, and I were left as the final three players. We'd built a strong rapport while we were on the island, and it was sad to think that only one of us would be the winner. Even so, we all played the game and wouldn't allow ourselves to lose sight of why we were there.

The night before the final competition, the producers came to tell me that my mom's sister, Joy, had died. I knew she was sick before we came to the island, and had been able to see her in the hospital one last time. They offered to put me on a plane that night, as the funeral was the next day. I asked when she'd died, and they told me it had happened two weeks earlier. They kept the news from me because they didn't think I would make it that far in the game. They assumed I would've been home by this time. It appeared that they were only telling me now so they could write me out of the finale. I was pissed—so angry, in fact, that I told them I didn't care if the game lasted another year. I would miss the funeral if I had to, because I wasn't leaving.

The next morning, one of the producers took me aside and said, "What do you think it's going to look like when the rich guy takes the two hundred fifty thousand dollars in prize money from Mary Ann? You're going to look like a jerk."

Well, that stopped me cold, because he might have been right. I actually considered throwing the final competition after that. But I hadn't spent all this time on the island just to throw the game. I didn't want to cheat to lose any more than I wanted to cheat to win. Plus, I really wanted to try to get my charity the money I was playing for.

The final competition was grueling. The first part of the challenge set the three of us on the beach, tasked with building a giant SOS out of boards that had been placed in a pile. Once the SOS was built, we were to use a shovel that was under the boards to dig up a box containing a torch. Mindy raced down the beach and had us both beat. She built her SOS so fast that she must have been ten seconds or more ahead of us. But when she finished, she couldn't find her shovel. She was confused, because Kate's and my shovels were under our piles of wood, but for whatever reason, hers was buried under the sand. She had to furiously dig it out, which significantly set her back. That's when I found myself taking the lead and never looking back. I dug up the box, ran toward the fire, lit the torch, and swam to the designated platform in the ocean to be rescued. Whoever got there first would be the winner. I beat Mindy by more than thirty seconds. To this day, it's a bone of contention between us. She adamantly believes that had her shovel been under the boards like ours she would have emerged victorious. Even so, she says she's glad I won, because if I'd lost, it would have been hard to live in our house with my deflated ego!

I won $250,000 and a brand-new 2005 Ford Mustang. Mindy and I donated the prize money to our favorite charity and matched it with another $250,000 of our own money. When it came time to get the car, I was told I could actually pick any Ford vehicle I wanted, so instead of the Mustang, I selected a truck. I knew my sons would get a lot of use out of it.

A few years later, I found myself thinking about resurrecting the TV show idea I'd had while we were on our sabbatical at sea. Mindy and I had great fun doing *The Real Gilligan's Island*, so why not give it another go? Besides, what else did I have to distract me from what was happening to Stearns Lending in my absence? Doing something new and different seemed like just what the doctor ordered.

For as long as I can remember, I would wake up in the morning and think, *Today may be the best I've got. If I don't do it today, when will I do it?*

Now, "it" can be anything—starting a business, buying a new car, beginning a new health regimen. The purpose of saying that to myself was to circumvent any excuses that might hold me back. Procrastination only steals time, and time is such a precious commodity. Like it or not, we all get older, every single day. Whatever you feel in the moment, you should do, because a year from now you may not feel like doing it. Don't put off until tomorrow what you know you can do today. And that's exactly how I was feeling about doing *Undercover Billionaire*.

CHAPTER TWENTY-ONE

BITTER OR BETTER

*All the adversity I've had in my life, all my troubles
and obstacles, have strengthened me. You may not realize
it when it happens, but a kick in the teeth may be
the best thing in the world for you.*
—WALT DISNEY

WHEN I DECIDED to do *Undercover Billionaire*, it wasn't
for the fame or recognition. For me, fame is a lot like riding
a motorcycle: if I hop on and open the throttle too much, I
know I'll take off too fast, and likely crash. I decided to do the
show because I believed the prospects would be limitless, and
that most people needed to be inspired to tap into their own
potential. Most of us don't have MBAs from Harvard or the
resources to make a company an instant success. I get that. I
didn't have either when I started out. But that doesn't mean we
lack the drive, passion, or commitment to do so.

My true motivation for doing *Undercover Billionaire* was twofold: I did it for my kids and to explore whether the American Dream was still alive. After the cancer, my young kids hadn't seen their dad work hard. I wanted them to see that life is about always moving forward, being strong, working hard and being proud.

I've always believed in the American Dream—and why wouldn't I? I'm walking, breathing, living proof that it once existed. If a scrappy guy like me can overcome the many obstacles that stood in my way and find success, anyone can.

After our appearance on *The Real Gilligan's Island*, several production companies approached Mindy and me to do another show. Over the years, we listened to some really great proposals. We would go to pitch meetings at various studios, but we were never the ones pitching the shows; the producers were. Each time they finished what they had to say, I would share my idea: what if I was dropped off in the middle of nowhere to see if I could start over again with nothing? The concept always appealed to me, and I thought it would appeal to a larger audience, too. But at the time, no one bit.

There were two production companies that consistently kept bringing us ideas. One was for a talk show featuring Mindy and me that sold to Paramount. They put us under contract for a year while it was being developed. We got pretty far down the road with them, but they were vacillating between our show and another new one called *The Doctors*. Ultimately, they went in that direction, and our show was shelved.

After coming to us with many different ideas that went

nowhere, the other production company circled back and said they'd pitched my concept to Discovery. They wanted to know if I was ready to go for it. Was this *really* something I wanted to do?

It was the proverbial dog catching the car. Now what?

Be careful what you wish for, because I had no idea what I was really getting myself into when I said yes.

We got the green light to get started in February 2018.

For those of you who've never watched *Undercover Billionaire*, the general premise was to turn $100 into $1 million in ninety days. I would be plunked down in Erie, Pennsylvania (a place I'd never been to), and given an alias, an old beater truck, a cell phone with no contacts, and one hundred dollars in cash. I couldn't use any of my connections, and I wasn't allowed to start a company similar to the one I'd built my career around—in other words, lending. The challenge was daunting. It felt like being at the bottom of Grand Teton, looking up and realizing that I had a very steep climb ahead of me if I wanted to reach the top.

Maybe I can do it, I thought.

I certainly wanted to give it my best shot.

Before going to Erie for the shoot, I'd scheduled trips to MD Anderson for a routine checkup and to Costa Rica to go fishing with friends. I breezed in for my checkup, thinking everything was A-okay. I explained that I was in a hurry to get out of there and asked if they could move up my appointment so I could get through as quickly as possible, which they did. When I got to Costa Rica, I received a call from the hospital.

They weren't calling to wish me a Happy Easter, however: they'd seen something on my scans that concerned them.

My cancer had come back in full force, and a few weeks later I was scheduled for surgery. The plan was to laser the tumor at the top of my epiglottis (the flap of cartilage that covers the opening of the windpipe) and put in a temporary feeding tube, which I would have for only a few weeks. Again, I refused the tube. This time, though, the doctors insisted. They said the surgery would require me to have one so I could eat, and that this would be the only time they could put it in. I still fought them, until I realized I had no choice. During the six-hour procedure, the surgeons also made the decision to cut out my epiglottis. Without that, food could easily travel to my lungs, which could cause all sorts of medical concerns. That's why they insisted on putting in the feeding tube, which, under the circumstances, became permanent. I'd gone into the hospital thinking I would be out that afternoon. I ended up staying for ten days.

I was scheduled to begin filming *Undercover Billionaire* in a few weeks. I didn't have time to be sick. The producers of the show did their best to document what was happening, making it a part of the story, although I know they were worried that the show might be in peril. As a way to keep the train on the tracks, I allowed them to film my surgery and stay in the hospital with me afterward. Tim Warren, one of the producers, kept asking Mindy for updates because he didn't think I was being totally up-front about things. I was telling him that I would definitely be ready to film in a few weeks, while Mindy was saying it wasn't happening. She was worried about my health, and I was worried about the commitment I'd made to Discovery and to our production team. I had enough experience in and around television to know that there's a window of opportunity that comes and then goes. You either hit that mark or it disappears. I wasn't worried about myself; I was concerned for all the people who'd committed to work on *Undercover Billionaire*. This was a job they were counting on. I didn't want to let anyone down, from the crew to the executives at the network.

Tim understood the danger in allowing me to pretend that I was strong enough to film. He and Mindy spoke about options for moving our start date out a few months. I kept insisting I would be well enough, but everyone knew the reality. Mindy was clear that I needed to get back to being myself. I needed to be strong for at least a month or two before I could even think about filming. No matter how good I said I felt, she stood firm, and so did Tim. He and I had quickly developed a good rapport. I knew he didn't want to feel responsible for putting me in harm's way, especially with the grueling schedule of shooting a reality show. Even when I fought them, I never doubted that he and Mindy were on my side.

Tim moved the start date to July, which seemed like a long-enough period of time to fully recover, but it wasn't. When July rolled around, I was still on morphine, which clouded my thinking. I knew I had to wean myself off the various medicines I'd been prescribed. Instead of doing it slowly, I went cold turkey and ended up in the ICU for five days. I couldn't even lift my head up, and I'd never felt that bad before (or since). That's when we scrapped the show. My health was more important than anything, even if it meant disappointing some people. Once I let go of the idea of doing the show, it took a lot of pressure off and allowed me to focus on healing.

Toward the end of 2018, Tim called once again to see how I was feeling. I told him I was great, but Mindy jumped in to say I still had healing to do. We talked about the possibility of aiming for February, which felt right to me. I said I thought I could be strong enough by then. I still had one surgery scheduled, though. In February 2019, doctors removed part of my hyoid bone, which anchors the muscles that aid the tongue in moving and swallowing. Removing my epiglottis had caused a loss of tissue around the bone, which was now poking into my throat; it felt like I'd swallowed a toothpick that became lodged there. It was very irritating and painful, so I welcomed the relief. I have been in and out of the hospital seven times since my surgery. I guess Mindy and Tim were right about extending the date.

Once I got on the other side of that debacle, I decided it was time to get the show on the road and finish what I'd started.

For the next three months, I scraped, bartered, and worked my way into establishing Underdog BBQ with a group of local entrepreneurs who wanted to do more than offer delicious barbecue and locally crafted beer. I wanted to build a brand that celebrated the underdogs of Erie, Pennsylvania. All the while, no one knew the real reason we were filming. Everyone we came into contact with believed I was taking part in a documentary film, not a reality show. It was the easiest way to explain the presence of the cameras and crew. When people think of reality TV, they sometimes expect the worst—that things are staged or reactions are forced for the drama—but that was the opposite of what we were going for. We wanted the people we worked with to be their authentic selves. Saying it was a documentary allowed that to happen.

I quickly realized that it's hard to have real perspective on how the rest of the world lives when you don't have to worry about your job, food, or rent every day. When those concerns disappear, you begin to think differently—faster, in some ways. When you have the luxury of not worrying, you forget the struggles and stresses most other people have to deal with on a daily basis. Being in Erie was a brutal reminder of the real-life fight being waged in cities all around the country. It instantly brought me back to the days of my youth, when I lived from paycheck to paycheck, needing to make every penny count. It's how most people live—in a constant state of *surviving* instead of *thriving*. The impact was immediate and surprising, because I felt connected to all of it in ways I hadn't in many years. I quickly became attuned to the fact that so many people can't shop for necessities or go out to dinner when they want to. I could feel what that was like, not just see it. I went to a soup kitchen to eat when I didn't have the money to buy food. The people there were so grateful to have a hot meal, and boy, I understood that. The world isn't an easy place to navigate, let alone to prosper in. It's really tough for a lot of people, especially for those without the resources or tools to help them along the way. I had so much more compassion for their struggles and their journey. I could understand it a lot better than I had in a long, long time. As difficult as the experience was, I was grateful for every eye-opening moment. It changed my way of seeing, thinking, and moving through the world.

If there were ever a group of people I related to, it was the team we assembled at Underdog BBQ during those ninety days. They said yes to opportunities and yes to life. They were authentic and driven, and didn't back down when things got challenging. I loved that. They had no idea who I really was or why I was starting the restaurant, and, frankly, it didn't matter. I was back in the trenches, doing what I loved to do most—building something from scratch. For ninety days, I got to pretend that I didn't know anyone who could help me in business, that I had no money, that I needed to rebuild, and that I was young again. One thing I insisted on when I was at the restaurant was that there be no free food or beer. I would pay for my order. I wanted to show the people there that we were paying, too. One of the reasons I set up a profit-sharing system for the Underdog BBQ team was because I knew that if they were invested in the bottom line, they would think twice about throwing out a pat of butter, comping their friends, or serving beer on the house. Every penny that flows out takes away from your profit. As you'll recall, this was a lesson I learned while working for "Ivan the Terrible." Despite how hard he was on me those many years ago, I never forgot what he taught me. Remarkably, Yvan and I remain very close friends.

Even if it was all in the name of entertainment, the

exercise was very real. I welcomed the discomfort because I craved starting anew, and that was part of the process. The challenge of building something from nothing and turning it into a profitable business was both daunting and enticing. The feelings were real. What happened was real, too.

We soon got into a healthy rhythm, and things started moving in the right direction. We encountered our share of obstacles. Each required me to fall back on what I knew about business, management, and leadership—all skills I was happy I had.

By the time I decided that my plan would be to open a barbecue restaurant, I'd found a vacant building that I thought would be ideal. When I first went to see it, there was old sports memorabilia hanging on the walls. As the Realtor was showing me the space, she pointed to a picture of someone I recognized and knew quite well. She said, "This guy was a legend. He broke Lou Gehrig's record."

Not wanting to appear as if I know too much about him, I asked, "Who is that again? He looks familiar."

"Cal Ripken Jr., from Baltimore."

"Yeah, that's right," I said, and walked on past the photo.

What she didn't know was that the night before, I'd secretly flown to Baltimore so Mindy and I could attend an event Cal had asked us to be at. He insisted we go. How was I supposed to say no to him? Mindy and I had first met Cal at the Preakness Stakes, where we instantly hit it off. He told me that I should look him up the next time I came to town. At the time, I was on the board of directors for Towson University and was scheduled to be back in that area a few months later. When I got in, I called him. He was extremely kind, and immediately invited me to come to his house.

In Maryland, Cal Ripken Jr. is the man. He's truly a legend. I'm not going to admit to being awestruck, but I won't deny it, either. We had an incredible day touring his home and his minor league baseball stadium in Aberdeen and eating Maryland crabs. Everywhere we went, people swarmed Cal. He was gracious with everyone, signing autographs and never losing his cool.

Inside Cal's home was a training room, complete with the original soaking tubs from Memorial Stadium in Baltimore. He explained that when they were knocking down the old place, he wanted the tubs he'd spent twenty years in. As we walked around the training room, he showed me his collection of memorabilia.

"Quick: Your house is on fire—what's the one item you would take with you from here?" I asked.

"It's just stuff. None of it is important. This is just something my wife put together for me." Then he said, "Well, I'd probably take that."

He pointed to something that looked like a piece of trash mounted on a board. But it wasn't trash.

He began telling me about the day he broke Lou Gehrig's record. He remembered it like it had just happened. As he told me the story, I felt as if I were there. After the fifth inning, a baseball game is deemed official, so before the start of the sixth inning, Cal's teammate Rafael Palmeiro pushed him to take a victory lap to celebrate his breaking the record. Cal said he felt hesitant. He wanted to acknowledge the moment, but there was a game to be finished. Even so, play was stopped for forty minutes while he took a victory lap, and it was then that he realized the magnitude of the moment. He talked about the people who were in the crowd—his old teachers, coaches, family members, and friends, all of whom he spotted in the stands as he made his way around the field. He said it meant so much to have them all there.

And then he said something I've never forgotten: "As great as that was, at the end of the game, it was like any other. I took off my uniform and ankle tape and threw them in the garbage, got dressed, signed some autographs, and headed home. My trainer for over twenty years took my ankle tape out of the garbage that night, mounted it on a board, and gave it to me. That was pretty cool." And, that was the very thing he would take in a fire.

I loved how humble he was. It inspired me to be more like him.

Later that night, after eating dinner together, Cal and I watched Rafael Palmeiro record his three-thousandth hit, which made him only the fourth player in major league history to produce at least five hundred homers and three thousand hits. When I left that evening, I was so invigorated that I decided to stop by a pub I used to frequent when I was in college. While I nursed a beer, I heard a man behind me say, "I'll never forget where I was the night Ralphie hit his three-thousandth ball!"

I desperately wanted to turn around and say, "Guess

where I was?" but I didn't. I couldn't help but smile, though, as this was a night for the record books in so many ways.

So, when Cal asked me to come to his fundraiser, I didn't think twice about it. I made the short flight from Erie to Baltimore after we were done filming that day and was back in Erie by 11:00 p.m., before anyone even knew I was gone.

Of course, I considered it a good omen for Underdog BBQ that Cal's photo hung on the wall of the space I wanted to lease.

There were times during filming when I really didn't like deceiving people about my identity. There was a Realtor who worked with our producers for a year before I arrived, showing them several locations around town that might be suitable for businesses. Since the producers didn't know what type of business I would gravitate toward—nor did I—they asked her to show them a wide range of vacant commercial properties. Not many of them were suitable for a restaurant. That Realtor did a lot of work in advance to get things teed up for my arrival.

The Realtor had grown suspicious about who I really was. When the producers presented her with an appearance release—a legal document allowing the network to use footage in which she appeared—she flipped out. It was a multiple-page document full of legal jargon that basically said they could do anything they wanted with the footage. She panicked and immediately worried that they might make her look bad, which of course wasn't their intent at all. Yet I appreciated her resistance. I understood her business very well, though she didn't know that. She decided right then and there that she was out of the "documentary." She said we wouldn't be permitted to film or even have cameras present when we met with her.

I took her aside and tried to calm her. I explained that I was the person they were most interested in filming and that I'd signed the same agreement they were asking her to sign. I tried to reassure her that the show was focused on positive outcomes, not throwing people under the bus.

But nope—she was done. She just wasn't comfortable, and I had to respect her decision.

As a last-ditch effort, I phoned her a few days later and asked if I could look at buildings *without* bringing any cameras or crew. I reiterated that the purpose of the filming was to capture the whole experience of starting a new business as it happened, and said that I understood where she was coming from, but because I knew she'd worked hard for over a year, I didn't want her to be left empty-handed.

"Fine, you can meet with me. But no cameras."

I brought Melinda, one of the producers, to the meeting, but I left the cameras behind. I thought that having Melinda there would be a good idea, in case the Realtor had questions I couldn't answer.

The Realtor and I engaged in a little small talk, but the air was thick with tension, mostly coming from her. Finally, she said, "Look, I don't know what this is. This could be anything from *Dateline* to a show for Discovery. [I hadn't told her that!] Either way, I have no idea who I'm dealing with or what they might do to me."

I told her I understood and diverted attention back to the reason we were there—to look at properties.

There was one she thought might be the perfect space. I enthusiastically said, "Great, could the owner of the building meet us there?" Whenever I embark on a real estate transaction, especially commercial real estate, I like to work with the decision maker to get the deal done. The more people there are in the middle, the more likely the deal will become muddled and fall apart. That's why I typically go right to the source. Now, this Realtor had no idea I knew what I was doing when it came to negotiating a real estate lease, let alone purchasing a property. She was under the impression that I didn't know anything at all. But you should never underestimate someone based solely on what you think you know about them. There's usually information you don't have—and in this case, there was *a lot* of information she was missing.

A few days later, we met in her office. The owner was there, as I'd requested. When I arrived, I asked the Realtor for several reports listing comparable rent costs, income for similar properties, and sales prices for buildings recently sold in the area. These were all standard requests for this type of transaction. Even though I'd asked her to prepare all this information several days earlier, she hadn't gathered any of it yet. She brought me nothing. When I pushed her, the Realtor pointed to the owner and said, "Why don't you ask him?"

I stopped cold, turned to her, and said, "I just want to know one thing: Do you work for him, or do you work for me?"

I knew that game. I'd gone out of my way to keep her in the deal. The producers easily could have found another Realtor who would happily comply with their requests. I figured that if I did the deal with her, even if it was off camera, she would still get the commission. She'd worked hard and, frankly, she deserved it. I'd tried to do the right thing. Unfortunately, she was so angry that she resisted my help, which was very disappointing.

I asked her one more time, "Do you work for him or me?"

That's when she stood up, pointed at me, and said, "I don't trust you. I don't trust any of you. I don't know who you really are. You won't give me any information."

"I did everything you asked me to do," I said. "I pulled out the cameras and asked you to represent me so you could get paid. Maybe I should have moved on, but I didn't. If you don't trust me, though, at the very least trust my intention to get you a commission for your efforts."

At this point, she was so unnerved that she was shaking. I hadn't meant to upset her, and I certainly didn't like how this was turning out. While she had every right to her feelings, I'd never had a transaction go south like this in all my thirty years in real estate. Nobody had ever kicked me out of their office, which was essentially what she was doing when she said she couldn't trust me. If the deal went through, I would see to it that she was paid. If it didn't, well, that's just the nature of the business. Either way, it was time to move on. We ended up making a deal without her.

The ninety days ended up being a compressed version of life. There were many highs and lows. There were several times I wanted to quit and even more times I couldn't have been prouder. In the end, it appeared that I fell short of my goal to build a business that met the $1 million mark—yet I didn't perceive this as a failure. What if I told you it wasn't my intention to hit that figure, and that instead I'd set a different goal for myself? The ninety days of pain and struggle allowed me to see that this endeavor wasn't about my ego or whether I met an arbitrary goal. It was more about connecting with individuals and motivating them to realize their own potential.

Here's another scenario to think about: What if I had exceeded my goal, and the business was estimated to be worth $5.5 million? How do you think people would have responded to that? I believe most people would have thought it was an impossible task—one they could never achieve themselves. Falling short of $1 million sent a message that working hard and building something of value doesn't have to hit a certain goal to be successful.

When Mindy and I filmed *The Real Gilligan's Island*, people were rooting for us throughout the show—but after I won, the tide turned, and people got angry. They vented on blogs, writing things like "The rich get richer" and "You took it away from Mary Ann, who needed the money." I'll never forget how that felt. Winning that show was important to me, but really so I could donate the winnings to charity. This time, though, it was more important that I inspire others and give people hope that they can achieve a goal—even a far-fetched one—by trying their best.

After the filming ended, I committed to staying involved in Underdog BBQ as a mentor and guide so I could help the team and the business grow. I also confided in my team that I'd been sick the entire time we were shooting. I shared that I ate through a feeding tube and wasn't able to enjoy the delicious barbecue they made every day. As you might imagine, they were shocked to learn who I was and the truth about why we were there in Erie.

I hadn't opened Underdog BBQ to be in the restaurant business. My real intention was to inspire others, including my kids. After the show, I realized the restaurant really belonged to the people of Erie, but especially those who had worked hard to launch and build it. And I thought they should own it. When Covid hit, our business went down by 66 percent. It was brutal, and very hard on the team. Mike, the general manager, fell short as a leader during the pandemic. It was disappointing to me, but it was also really disruptive for the other team members, who lost faith and trust in him. As hard as it was to say goodbye, the time had come to let him go.

Around this same time, I returned to Erie with the Discovery crew in tow to film *Undercover Billionaire: Comeback City*, which was about helping six businesses turn around in twenty-seven days. Why that amount of time? The average business has only twenty-seven days' worth of cash flow to survive on at any given time. One of the businesses I was there to help was Underdog BBQ.

When Mike left, I asked Ashley, who was running the kitchen, to step into the role of general manager. Her hard work and dedication helped the restaurant pivot. At first I wasn't sure she would be up to the task, but she came through in every way. She proved herself to have tremendous grit. When she took over, the business was valued at $425,000. I told the team that if we couldn't recover, I would sell—and I meant it. That motivated everyone to work hard, fast, and smart.

Nearly a month later, I sat with Ashley to go over the results. The appraiser said the restaurant was now worth $800,000. Ashley did a fantastic job leading her team.

After hearing that, her confidence shot up. I could see the relief on her face when she heard she'd hit her goal. Even so, she asked if I was still planning to sell the restaurant.

I hesitated for what felt like a minute or more, then said, "Yes, I am."

Ashley broke down crying. She believed we'd come to the end of the road.

I'm a big believer in promoting from within, and I'm an even bigger believer in giving people an opportunity they might otherwise never have. I wanted to find a local owner who could take the business to the next level.

I put the idea right out there: "I'd like to see if you'd like to buy it."

Ashley looked at me like I was nuts. "I can't afford to buy this restaurant," she said through her tears.

"Give me a check for a hundred bucks and we can call it even." I chose the same amount of money I'd landed in Erie with.

"Are you serious?" she asked.

I was. Very serious.

Ashley had earned it. I wanted her to be the founding

owner of the first location of what I hope will become a franchise operation across the country.

We broke the news to the rest of the team in the same way. I told them I was selling before letting them know that Ashley would be the new owner. It felt really good to pass the torch, and even better to know that these amazing people now had a business of their own to grow.

Before leaving Erie, I spent some time thinking about what all this had meant to me. For twenty years or more, people have kissed my ass in business. They wanted to give me loans or become my vendors because it was good for all parties. Everyone was looking for something from me. And oftentimes they got it.

When I was a kid, I didn't have that same clout. I came from very modest beginnings, and I understood what that felt like for a lot of the people I met in Erie. That was especially true when I found myself sleeping on other people's couches all over town. That's right—after freezing my butt off in the truck with no blanket or pillow that first night, I signed up for an app called Couchsurfing, which connected me with people who were willing to let a stranger sleep on their couch. I needed a warm place to lay my head, and the cameras that followed me were gone at night, so it was perfect.

One thing is for sure—when cameras are around, people tend to be on their best behavior. When those cameras are gone, however, there's no reason for anyone to shine or be someone they aren't. Every night I would sit in people's homes and get to know them one-on-one. At first they were strangers to me, and I was a stranger to them. They knew me only as Glenn Bryant, a guy from Maryland with no money and no job. I told them I'd battled cancer and was trying to start my own business. I said I wanted to make the best life for my family and felt that Erie was full of untapped opportunity. My story was *fairly* real, even if I didn't divulge that I was taping a reality show. On paper, it was a much greater risk for them to take me in than it was for me to knock on their doors, and yet I had the most amazing conversations with these people. Every single one was interested in getting to know me. Our conversations were deep, real, and rooted in life, not stuff. That felt so good. I left Erie a very humbled man, deeply appreciative of the time, people, and experiences I had there.

When the show wrapped, I was exhausted, relieved, and more convinced than ever that the American Dream is not only alive, it's ours for the taking. We'd done something extraordinary together in Erie, and it was a reminder to be grateful and that business is a gift meant to be shared. I was excited by what we'd accomplished and where I thought Underdog BBQ could go in the future.

On the day I was scheduled to leave, I had some unfinished business to take care of. On my way to the airport, I turned to Mindy and said, "I need to make a stop. Come with me." I motioned for her to follow me into an office building.

I wanted to see the Realtor I'd met during filming. I told the receptionist who I was there to see, and when the Realtor came to the lobby, I said, "Hi. I want to introduce myself. My name is Glenn Stearns, and this is my wife, Mindy. My last name isn't Bryant. I'm from California, and yes, I was doing more than a documentary. I couldn't say that to you when we met because I was under the same nondisclosure agreement we were asking you to sign. You were right, and you made a wild guess thinking the show was for Discovery, because it is. It's going to be an international show called *Undercover Billionaire*. I'm here today because I wanted to tell you the truth before you heard it from anyone else. This is who I am. I'm very sorry I couldn't reveal more information to you earlier. I know it bothered you. I just wanted to say thank you."

When I finished talking, I reached into the inside pocket of my jacket, pulled out a white envelope, and handed it to her. I didn't say another word—nor did she. Mindy and I turned and left. I was ready to go home.

I thought a lot about my experience in Erie. Without adversity, you can't possibly learn resilience; of this I'm certain. People who fight their way up from the bottom, gritty scrappers who refuse to take no for an answer or be held back by their circumstances, those who've been hit over and over again yet still scramble to their feet for another try—these are the people who know that no matter how far down you think you are, you can always rise up again. It also occurred to me then that I no longer thought about what happened with Stearns Lending. I had such a different perspective now. It wasn't about looking back; it was about how I was going to move forward.

Don't fear the "what ifs"—the inevitable mind game we all play, asking ourselves,

"What if I lose everything?"

"What if I fail?"

"What if I can't do it again?"

And so on.

Instead, believe you can. Believe you can start over, and over, and over again if you have to. Leadership expert John Maxwell calls this "turning obstacles into opportunities." Fearing loss and taking on the challenge to rebuild involve two very different patterns of thought. The latter is a mindset that actually comes from adversity—from living through loss, fear, and pain. I see it as a wonderful tool. It's like an invisible cloak of impenetrable skin. Wearing it, I tell myself, "I can always rebuild," and I never live in fear.

For a long time, I would tell people that I never wanted to relive 2007 and 2008, the years the financial crisis ravaged our industry. I thought those were the most painful years of my life. And then I was diagnosed with cancer. So yes, that gave me some deep perspective, for sure. Interestingly, when I was listing all the reasons why I wanted to beat this dreaded disease, the second thing I thought about after wanting to be around for Mindy and my children was, *I would love to relive those years.* Looking back, I realized that I'd never felt more alive. Having to confront the banks and figure out how I would survive the traps I'd set for myself was invigorating. I'm not convinced I understood that at the time, but I did a few years later.

Most people have to touch a burning flame to understand that it's hot; they can't just listen to other people say it is. They've got to get burned at least once. And when they do, hopefully, they'll never want to make the same mistake again.

It must be human nature to learn the hard way. If you're a parent, you get this. I know all my kids had to go that route. The apples certainly haven't fallen far from the tree.

It takes great maturity and wisdom to listen as someone else tries to dissuade you from touching that flame. Believe me, that kind of wisdom doesn't come easy—but it does come. And it's usually worth the wait. Remember this: when you think you've hit your lowest low, there's no place to go but up.

It wasn't long after we finished shooting *Undercover Billionaire* that I got the news that my old company was filing for bankruptcy. A momentary shock resonated through me when I heard about the Chapter 11, because I'd put my heart and soul into building Stearns Lending. As I mentioned earlier, when they filed, they wiped tens of millions in debt to me off their books, as well as my 30 percent share in the company, which amounted to well over $100 million in personal equity off my balance sheet. What I didn't mention was that when they sold off the servicing piece of the business, the company received millions of dollars in gains, which left me with a tax liability on my share of that income. And, to add insult to injury, through the bankruptcy, the relief of some of the bond debt triggered a debt forgiveness tax, which I was also responsible for. So yeah, it hurt—not just me but everyone. I kept thinking about all the people I'd left behind, those who'd helped me build my company over the years, and those who'd depended on their jobs to provide for their families. I was more concerned for their well-being than my own. That's why I had to start Kind Lending.

Here's what I understood: I had an opportunity to be *bitter* or *better*.

I chose *better*.

About *everything*.

I can't have regret about the doctor cutting out my epiglottis. That surely changed my life, but I refuse to think about it that way, because it's over. I can't look backward, ever. Have I gotten angry about my health challenges? You bet. I hate eating through a feeding tube. I would much rather be eating solid food than the liquids that are the staple of my diet now. I don't dwell on the negative, on things that didn't happen or could have happened. What's the point? I've weathered more storms and endured more pain while still functioning at a high level because I rarely let such things get to me. But every once in a while, they do. The only time I've ever lost my cool over my health issues was when Mindy and I were rushing out of the house to get to the emergency room for the tenth time in a year and a half because I wasn't feeling well. I didn't want to go.

We got in the car, and I asked her to drive so I could feed myself before we got there. She drove over a speed bump a little faster than usual, and the tube fell out. The white drink I was feeding myself with spilled all over the car and me. I lost it. "I don't want to do this. I hate that this is my life," Five seconds later, that feeling passed. I was mad, but more about the mess than the cause. When I took a moment to collect my thoughts, I was grateful to be alive, to have my tongue, to be able to speak. So what if I couldn't eat? I didn't want my wife, kids, or friends to worry about whether this was the day I was going to die. For a while, that was the only thing on their minds. *Would today be the day?*

No, it would not.

I recently picked up cooking. I cook for my family and friends two or three times a week. If I can't eat, I still want to be involved. I don't want people to feel sorry for me. What better way to serve them and feel the deep connection that sharing a meal brings to people? While I am not breaking bread with my friends, I am at least making the bread with my family and friends.

Having just come off production for *Undercover Billionaire*, I had a fresh outlook about life and business. For years, I'd worked myself to the bone. After doing the show, I was filled with renewed hope and the belief that business should and could be fun. It didn't have to be about making the most money. It could be about being happy, fulfilled, and excited by the unknown potential. Besides, there's also the old saying "Don't get angry, get even."

I was exhilarated just thinking about the next steps. Reinventing myself once again felt like a once-in-a-lifetime opportunity, one I wasn't willing to let pass by. I wanted to have fun doing it, too. I wanted to start a movement—one we would call the Kind Movement.

My purpose in starting Kind Lending was different than when I founded Stearns Lending. Then I was building a company that turned into a family—and a very large one at that. This time I wanted to start with building a family first. I wanted to make sure that the people who came to work with us knew they were important to the company. After all, every single broker has a choice about where they work. I felt I owed those who came to Kind Lending a new and better experience than they'd ever had before, because they were there to invest their time and talents in us. My aim was to provide an environment where they, as family members, could grow and prosper personally as the company grew and prospered. This time, my end goal was to build a business that disrupted an industry, not to create a business big enough to sell. My only exit strategy involves a pine box.

As soon as word got out that I was getting back into lending, so many of the people who'd worked with me before wanted in. I wasn't recruiting; they were *asking* to come back. Every position from the ground up matters in a company. Debbie, our receptionist, had been with us for twenty years. She always felt like a vital part of the company, and was enthusiastic about whatever I was planning next. Keely, my assistant of twenty-six years remained with me. Yvonne, my President was with me for eighteen years. And many more. That meant a lot to me. If every person in a company feels they matter, they'll move mountains. I'd demonstrated this before with Stearns Lending and Underdog BBQ. Now I was ready to do it again at Kind Lending, only better.

I was thrilled with our accomplishments in Erie, and thought, *If I could do that there, for the show, why not do it here, in real life?* I could restart and rebuild, only this time I could use my connections and surround myself with the talent I'd spent years cultivating. It would be a lot easier than it was for the show.

When Stearns announced their bankruptcy, they vacated most of the office space I'd called home for many years. It was important to me that I return to the same building, the same office, the same top floor, and that I remove the old Stearns Lending sign and put up the new Kind Lending one in its place.

I was all in.

No looking back.

No regrets.

There was just one last detail I had to attend to: I needed cubicles. So, I called the CEO of Stearns Lending and asked him what he was going to do with all the ones he had—yes, the same ones I once bought back from the very guy I'd hired to haul them away.

"What do you want to do with them?" he asked me.

"How about you sell them to me for one dollar?" I said. I knew it was a lot easier for him to say yes than it would be to disassemble them and have them carted off.

Been there, done that.

You can never really be sure where you are in a story. If my life has shown me anything, it's that what goes around always comes around. You may think you're at the end of your tale, but it could just be the beginning. You never really know. Expect the unexpected and you'll never be surprised. That goes for cubicles, old cars, divorces or just about anything you love in life.

Ironically, around the time Blackstone announced the bankruptcy, the CEO of Stearns Lending reached out to ask me if I would post a video on social media congratulating the company on thirty years of success. While I wasn't especially pleased with what they'd done after I left, I was damn proud of the people who'd helped make that business everything it was, so I said yes—though I never once mentioned Blackstone in the recorded message. Was it an ending? No. For me, it was just the beginning. A new start.

A lot of friends and colleagues called me in shock, asking why I would release such a positive video. "Aren't you in pain? Doesn't it hurt?"

Nope. I was really happy that something I'd created lasted so long.

In the end Blackstone rode out the biggest boom in mortgage banking history and sold Stearns Holdings in the first quarter of 2021 for a lot of money, which proved they *are* very smart and savvy businesspeople. I just happened to be on the wrong end of this deal.

The bankruptcy certainly could have been a catastrophic moment in my life, but I didn't give it that power. Whenever there's a huge event in your life, you can't help but feel pressure, but that isn't the time to fold. You might feel miserable, defeated, and hopeless, but you must stop and ask yourself, "What am I learning?" These are the times when growth will be the most substantial. These are the moments to think about everything you want to do and figure out how you'll get there, so that one day you can proudly look back on your decisions *and* the strength you displayed to persevere. If you live like that, you'll build a life and legacy worth every challenge that threatened to get in your way.

Not long after *Undercover Billionaire* aired, I received an email from my attorney informing me that Discovery wanted to do a second season. The network had the option to renew for another year, and they exercised it. At the time, I wasn't exactly sure how that would work, since my identity was now well-known.

The morning the email arrived, I was lying in bed with Mindy and my daughter Brooke. It made me feel good to receive that letter, but what really filled my bucket was knowing that people who watched the show got something from it, whether it was the inspiration to change their circumstances and rise above the challenges that were holding them back, or to start anew. I also appreciated that people found me down-to-earth and relatable.

Brooke then started looking at what people had written on social media about the show. I was never interested in reading any of that. At the time, I didn't fully understand the power of social media, nor did I understand the impact *Undercover Billionaire* had on people. There were thousands of comments on LinkedIn alone. Brooke began to read them aloud, one after another. Every message except two used the word "inspired" or "inspiring."

"Dad, there isn't a single hater in the bunch. Something's wrong. Everyone has a hater! There are so many haters in the world, especially on social media, and not one person said a bad thing." Brooke was both excited and confused.

"Of course people said good things about your dad," Mindy said.

"Mom, you don't get it. People are mean. They love to write, 'You suck. Your show sucks,'" Brooke said.

And she was right.

I'll admit, for a moment, that I was really proud of my decision to do the show, because my teenage daughter, who usually thinks I'm a dork, was glowing with pride for her old man. She read all those comments and loved it. In fact, on several occasions when I've been out with my children, people have come up to me to say how much they loved the show. And you know what? I like that my kids get to hear that. I want them to think their dad did something good, that my legacy is more than building a company—it's really about inspiring and motivating people. When they look back someday, I hope they'll see the good I tried to do in the world and not just read about the dumb stuff I have admitted doing while I was young and maturing. Especially my early beginnings. I cringe at how lost I really was as young man.

CHAPTER TWENTY-TWO

LETTING GO OF THE PAST

*"Always focus on the front windshield
and not the rearview mirror."*
—COLIN POWELL

SEVERAL YEARS AGO, I hosted a party on the Minderella to celebrate my friendships from grade school. A group of us spent three days reminiscing and getting caught up on forty years of life. The whole thing started on social media with an innocent invitation for a few old buddies to come fishing with me. One of the guys suggested we invite another of our classmates, but none of us knew how to reach him. That's when I contacted two women from our class who had put together a reunion ten years earlier. I explained that a few of us were going fishing in the Bahamas and that I was looking for a way to contact our friend. As soon as I threw the idea out there, one of the girls immediately responded, "Hell, yeah! I'm in!" She thought that I was extending a wider invitation. Shortly after she realized her mistake, she sent a follow-up. "Oh, I see. You weren't asking us ladies to go. You wanted his number. Let me see if I can find it for you." I thought about it for a minute and wrote back, "If your significant others don't mind you hanging out with four or five dudes you haven't seen in thirty-five or forty years, come on down. I'm totally fine with that."

They were in.

Before I knew it, the weekend grew into a get-together for forty old friends. Nearly our whole class came.

Mindy was very nervous about it. I hadn't seen most of these people since grade school. She questioned my motives. Why was I doing this for people I barely knew and hadn't been in contact with for years? Was I trying to show off? I didn't think so. Still, when I reflected on that time in my life, I recalled feeling really insecure, especially after failing fourth grade and watching my friends move ahead without me. I was left waiting in the wings. Those feelings persisted throughout grade school. Nevertheless, something inside told me this was the right thing to do. I could feel the vibe and I believed with every fiber of my being that the weekend was going to be extraordinary.

The Minderella couldn't accommodate forty people over-night; there just weren't enough beds for everyone to sleep. So we all met at the Atlantis, a resort in the Bahamas where our yacht was docked out front, along with our big fishing boat and our speed boat.

I had thrown a lot of parties prior to this weekend. What I had learned is that there's always a certain group in the crowd that just wants to have fun. They don't care about ice sculptures and extravagant settings. They would rather have a keg of beer and friends to party with. I can fall into that category as easily as I can a more elaborate celebration. My job that weekend was to strike the perfect balance and ensure that everyone had a memorable experience.

At the opening night party, we all met at five o'clock. I had a bar set up on the dock so we could have a drink before boarding. I had arranged for a Samba band to play and for a group of dancers wearing feather headdresses to entertain us as well. It felt like a Brazilian Mardi Gras. The band and dancers winded their way through the port and onto the dock before leading us all onto the Minderella where another band was playing. All of us danced, laughed, and had such a good time. As the night went on, I commandeered a microphone to thank everyone for coming. I wanted them to know how grateful I was to be with each and every person in attendance. I reminded everyone that we were headed to the Exumas bright and early the next morning and to be ready to leave by 6 a.m. Needless to say, more than a few of the forty guests who showed up the next morning paid a price on the open seas after a night of an open bar!

The next night, I hosted a concert for the group. My buddies Keith Harkin and Taylor Hicks were scheduled to perform at one of the four houses I had rented on Stanley Key. Before they took the stage, I asked my guests to gather around. When everyone was seated, I said, "Since we all went to Catholic school together, I am going to call this our confessional."

I could tell some of my old friends had no idea where this was going, so I continued by asking, "How many of you had things happen to you when you were younger that you've carried around all these years? Has anything bothered you that you've never spoken about?" I waited a beat for everyone to think and then I continued "You know what? I'm going to kick things off here.," I said. "When I flunked the fourth grade and was held back a year, you became my new fourth grade friends while my other classmates went on to the fifth grade. I'll confess, I felt pretty dumb. I was very insecure because I failed. When I entered eighth grade, I got a girl pregnant. Some of you told me you could no longer be my friend, that your parents didn't want you to talk to me anymore. That really hurt, because I didn't know what I did wrong. I was just a kid who was suddenly branded with a scarlet letter. It was kind of tough." I paused, took a deep breath, and then continued talking. "Don't get me wrong, all of this made me who I am today and I am grateful for every challenge that brought me here. So, until last night, no one knew this story. I told my wife what I am about to share with all of you now. Does anyone here know why I named my daughter Charlene?"

No one raised their hand.

"I named her that because of you, Charlene." I pointed to one of the ladies who was in our class. "You were always so nice, kind, and beautiful—inside and out. People admired you and I wanted my daughter to grow up to be just like you."

Charlene began to cry. She had no idea. Nobody did.

"I have one more thing I'd like to add." That's when I

asked a woman in the group to take a seat next to me. Growing up, she suffered from alopecia and was horribly teased for it. I turned to her and said, "I want to apologize to you. You were by far the most bullied girl in school. It must have been awful for you all those years, being brutally picked on and relentlessly tormented. I just want to say I am sorry for my part in making you feel bad." I couldn't remember if I had ever teased her or not—and it didn't much matter. What I knew for sure was that so many of the kids had, and that must have been awful for her.

I could see tears welling up in her eyes. I am sure she didn't expect my apology; however, it was something I had wanted to do for a long time. I asked if anyone else had something they'd like to say. One by one, the mic was passed around, with each person bearing their soul, sharing something they had been holding onto for all those years. Every single person there apologized to the woman we had teased as children. It must have been something for her to hear that from all of us.

I learned a lot about my classmates that night—stuff I didn't have a clue about back in the day. We all had so much going on in our lives. I realized that even the people who I thought lived a perfect life struggled with problems.

It felt good to let go of the past—the resentment, the remorse, whatever it was each of us were carrying around. I hadn't planned this, but I was so happy for the outcome. We ended up having four days of amazing discovery, rediscovery, and connection. It was wonderful, joyful, and something I knew none of us would ever forget.

About a year later, the doctors had noticed something on

my scans and wanted to put me under to make sure my cancer hadn't returned. Just as I was coming out of from my anesthesia, I opened my eyes and saw Mindy standing next to my bed. She had a look on her face, and immediately I could tell it wasn't good news.

"It came back." I said in a whisper.

She nodded her head yes.

I wanted to get out of there as fast as I could.

I ripped the IV out of my arm, got dressed and headed to the airport.

I wanted to fly to Baltimore. Keith Harkin was playing a show at a local pub that night. Everyone who had been on our trip to the Bahamas was going, and I wanted to be there too. The first person I ran into was the woman we had all apologized to in the Bahamas. She put her arms around me, gave me a great big hug and said, "Thank you. Glenn, you have no idea the weight that was lifted off my shoulders when we were on the boat. I didn't know I was carrying that with me until that night. It was like a gift. I hadn't realized how much those years impacted me until I was finally able to let it all go."

This woman is one of the strongest people I know. Having her share this with me meant so much. Especially that night, as I too was processing an unexpected change in my life.

I made it a point to go back to Baltimore and see those friends several times after that weekend. Our get togethers continued over the next few years, and in July of 2021, I invited them all to be my guest at our family ranch in Montana. I thought we could all ride horses, fish and explore the land.

We brought everyone on horseback and ATVs to one of my favorite spots for dinner. There's an old homestead from the 1800s with one window and barely a roof overhead. It's just an old, beautiful, gray slanted building in the middle of thousands of acres.

After dinner, we had a powwow. Ten Blackfeet Indians arrived wearing their traditional ceremonial clothing. They told us the story of their land and of their tribe. They danced, chanted, and shared their customs with us as the sun faded into the horizon and the night sky began to appear.

I asked Taylor Hicks to entertain our group just as he had done in the Bahamas years before. We sat around the giant campfire, which was made of lanterns to prevent us from accidentally setting any wildfires on the land.

We all reminisced, bonded, and had yet another amazing experience together. I could tell that each of us was proud of the relationships we had formed.

"Let's catch up," I said. "There are a few of you here who weren't with us the last time we all got together." I went on to describe the "confessional" and the incredible impact it had on all of us. And then I suggested that anyone who had something they wanted to get off their chest, could do just that.

"I'll start again." I offered.

I talked about becoming a father in the eighth grade, and then I conveyed the story of Amber getting pregnant and the words I had shared with her when she was deciding the fate of our unborn son. I also told them about the time I took that son, Skyler, to Las Vegas for his twenty-first birthday. I surprised him by flying in several of his friends, and then showing them the time of their lives for the rest of the weekend. Finally, I shared something Skyler said to me after the weekend was over. "Dad, I want to thank you for the best time. But, if it had just been the two of us, that would have been just as great."

I choked up as I bared my heart and soul that night. But I also understood that allowing myself to be vulnerable permitted everyone else there to be vulnerable too. Most of us live in a world full of shallow conversation. This was the opposite of that.

Once again, several people got up and spoke. They shared their stories and struggles with the group. There was no judgment. No defenses. Just love and camaraderie. We were all finding connection and purpose by realizing that everybody struggles sometimes. The exchange reminded us that life is fragile and not perfect. It was really touching to hear so many people express their appreciation for one another, and for Mindy and myself, for giving them a second chance to feel loved again.

You don't usually get a do-over in life. But we did. It was as if we were a bunch of fourteen-year-old children with the wisdom of fifty-seven-year-old adults. We were looking back so we could move forward lighter, happier, and with tremendous gratitude.

Here's what I know for sure. Life boils down to three things: People, love, and acceptance. It isn't about who has more money or less. It certainly isn't about the things you acquire along the way. It's about the people you live this life with, those you experience pain and joy with. And it's about knowing that you are loved and will be missed when you are gone.

THIS is the absolute definition of success.

We all have that capacity.

Those of us who had gathered at my home in Montana certainly had it that weekend, and it was wonderful.

CHAPTER TWENTY-THREE

BE REAL, HUMBLE, AND KIND

Life isn't about being rich, being popular, being highly educated, or being perfect. It's about being real, humble, and kind.
—Unknown

WHEN I WAS fifteen years old, I felt very self-conscious about being a new father. I really thought people in our community were judging me whenever they saw me. To be fair, I wasn't a model citizen back then. I suppose I gave some people reasons to feel the way they did. The angrier I got, the darker I became. I wasn't sure what my future held, but back then, it wasn't looking great. So many friends abandoned me after I had my daughter. They would come up to me and say, "My parents said I'm not allowed to talk to you anymore." It wasn't unusual to find the words "baby maker" scribbled in marker across my desk. It felt as though everyone was always looking at me with disgust and disdain.

One day our class went to confession. Usually, the priest would tell kids to say two Hail Marys or two Lord's Prayers for forgiveness of their sins. Not me. The priest gave me fifty Hail Marys and fifty Lord's Prayers, which I had to do in the pew in front of everyone. I was humiliated, saying them as fast as I could while the class waited. They all knew why I'd been given so much penance.

Although I wasn't a great student, there were two teachers in high school who took a liking to me. Because I attended Catholic school, I felt that most of my teachers looked down on me. I thought they saw me as nothing more than a delinquent kid with a baby. These two teachers did what they could to intervene, but frankly, I wasn't their problem. It also wasn't unusual for me to find myself in other kinds of trouble at school. I often had detention. I don't recall what I'd done this particular time, but I do remember being told I had detention on Saturday morning. *Great*, I thought. *I have to give up another weekend for school.*

I showed up at ten o'clock as required. Normally, there would be four or five other people there, but this time there was no one but me. Shortly after I arrived, Mr. Martinez and Mr. Duckwitz walked into the classroom where I was sitting.

"Glenn, come with us," they said. We got into their car and drove to Shakey's Pizza. They ordered a pie and a pitcher of beer. One of them poured a glass for each of us, and we talked about life. I know—it probably sounds strange that two teachers took an eighth grader to a restaurant and poured him a beer, and you would be right. Of course, today they'd surely lose their jobs.

No one had ever just sat me down and asked me the kinds of questions these two did that day. What were my dreams? Where did I see myself in the future? I was surprised when one of them said, "Glenn, you're going to get through this. You're going to be fine. We just want you to know we're here for you. We've got your back, son." Hearing those words of encouragement meant the world to me. There was nothing they could have said that would have had a greater impact. I'd been in such a dark place, and to have people validate me and say everything was going to be okay and that I shouldn't worry was an unexpected shot of confidence that I'd been missing since my dad assured me of the same thing. It was exactly what I needed at exactly the right time. I was lost, and they knew it. These two men showing me this type of kindness changed everything for me. Thinking back, I feel that this may have been the single most impactful meeting I've ever had. I look back on this one day and believe it started my climb up to becoming a more confident individual.

Confidence is a funny thing. If you lack confidence, you start to see yourself only through that lens. When my son Trevor was young, he was an outstanding athlete. He played soccer and baseball, and really excelled. By the time he reached second or third grade, Amber and I noticed that he had trouble reading. We had him tested for dyslexia, which he had. All his friends were beginning to take off academically, but Trevor struggled. He would tell himself he was stupid and that he couldn't do something before he even tried to do it. His self-esteem tanked so badly that it began to affect his athletic performance. He couldn't hit a baseball to save his life. He lost all his confidence. When you see someone in a downward spiral like that, you begin to understand how easy it is to latch on to those kinds of feelings. As a parent, it was difficult to watch my son suffer and feel so inadequate. He surely was a capable young man, only he didn't realize it at the time.

When you see yourself as having value, others see you that way, too. You can start to feel things getting better, which boosts your confidence. That's how you become someone like Michael Jordan, someone who's the greatest at what they do because they believe in themselves. It's the pathway to doing things you never dreamt were possible. You begin living and leading as the example you want to be. And of course, you put in the hard work that others aren't willing to do.

It wasn't unusual for me to fly off the handle when I was younger. There were so many times I stood on principle when I should have stopped and considered what the other person might be going through.

When my three boys were younger, Amber and I took them on a vacation. When we got back to California, I was exhausted. The flight home was brutal. My kids were yelling and screaming for nearly the entire flight. I wanted to kiss the ground when we landed. I went to fetch the car while Amber waited for our luggage. I was trying to secure the car seat when an airport police officer demanded that I move the car or she would give me a ticket. I was frazzled, irritable, and in no mood to be berated.

"Move the car!" she said in a very authoritarian tone.

"My family is gathering the rest of the luggage. I'm just putting in the car seat and will move when they come out."

"Move the car now, and circle back around!" she demanded.

My blood began to boil. Couldn't she see I had my hands full? I backed out of the car, slowly turned around, got right in her face, and yelled, "What happened in your life that made you so miserable?" I must have been two inches away from her when I said this. And then I just stopped talking, because I could see tears welling up in her eyes. She began to cry. I hadn't thought she would respond that way. I reached my arms out and hugged her, saying I was sorry over and over. She was being tough on me, but she didn't deserve my reaction. My hard day shouldn't have become hers. I felt horrible about my response. That interaction stayed with me over the years, although there were still many times when I found myself being unnecessarily adversarial because I believed I was right, even when I wasn't. There's a difference between *being* right and *having to be* right. It's taken me a long time to understand that fine line. I can't say I don't fall into those old ways from time to time, but these days I find myself choosing peace over drama.

I've always felt that great responsibility comes with success. Why? People look up to you, whether you want them to or not. They watch how you move through the world. Many years back, I went to a concert with my wife. One of the featured bands was already playing by the time we arrived. I wanted to see who was on stage, so I ran up a flight of stairs that I thought led to our seats. Unfortunately, they were the wrong stairs.

"Tickets, please," the burly security guard said.

I handed him our tickets.

"Your seats are on the other side of the arena. You've got to go around."

"I just want to see—"

He cut me off before I could finish my sentence. "No, you have to go around," he insisted.

Something about the way he spoke rubbed me wrong. I puffed out my chest and said, "Why do you have to be such a jerk?"

Then I just turned around and walked away before he had a chance to respond. I was terribly frustrated. As Mindy and I made our way around the arena, I couldn't shake the feeling of how wrong my actions were. It had been years since I'd reacted like that. We were halfway to our seats when I turned and walked back.

I approached the security guard, put out my hand, and said, "Sir, what I did wasn't right. As a matter of fact, *I* was the jerk. I shouldn't have said that."

"You know, Glenn . . ."

Oh no. He knew my name. *How does he know my name?* I thought.

"I've seen you on television. I thought you were such a cool guy. And then you said that to me, and I thought, *Wow, guess I was wrong.* But then you came back and told me you're sorry, which proves to me you really are a good guy."

We all have our moments. I'm not perfect; far from it. But I know when someone's wrong, and I know when I am, too. This time it was me. He was just doing his job.

BE REAL, HUMBLE, AND KIND

Until that night, it had never really occurred to me that anyone would recognize me. I don't live in the public eye, and frankly, I don't really want to. I've enjoyed my brushes with fame. It would be disingenuous if I didn't admit that. However, I understand the downside of living under the microscope, and this run-in was just a small taste of what that can feel like.

Whether I liked it or not, having a child at a young age made me feel vulnerable. But looking back, I believe that being judged and feeling like an outcast forced me to build an inner strength and a better understanding of how others feel. This book isn't about being perfect. If it were, I would be the wrong guy to write it. It's about being human. I didn't get here by being perfect. I've scraped my way through life. I'm still scraping my way through, but now I wear kid gloves instead of boxing gloves. I've put away the talons. That maturity and awareness took conditioning, time, and some really powerful role models.

In 2005, a local chapter of the Entrepreneurs' Organization (EO) invited Sir Richard Branson to speak to their group. EO is for young entrepreneurs, many of whom later become members of YPO. The group really wanted Sir Richard for their event, but his fee was way over their budget. Although I'm not a member of EO, I believe in young entrepreneurs and their spirit. I didn't want them to lose out on hearing from someone like Sir Richard Branson, so I said I would cover the deficit.

Although we're good friends today, I didn't know Sir Richard at the time, but I greatly respected him. Much to my surprise, he said he wanted to meet with me for sponsoring their event. I invited him to dinner at my house, and he graciously accepted. Sir Richard arrived with one member of EO and her husband. No entourage, no fanfare. We had an amazing night, swapping stories of life and business. We instantly bonded; it was as if we'd known each other our entire lives. We also drank a lot of wine. Luckily, he had a car and a driver, so there was no concern about tying one on. Just past midnight, Sir Richard said it was time for him to head out. I walked him to his waiting car to say good night and thanked him for coming to the EO event and to my home. As he got into the car, the driver attempted to turn on the engine, but the battery was dead.

"Mr. Branson, I'm so sorry," the driver said. "I must have left a light on while you were inside the home. I'll take care of this right away, sir."

In that moment, I felt like I was in the Matrix, because everything froze. I observed his face, looked at his eyes, watched his breathing. What would Mr. Suave do when things didn't go his way after having some drinks? Was he about to berate this man? Was he going to cuss? Would he take a deep breath and roll his eyes?

Instead of getting angry, Sir Richard turned to me, shrugged his shoulders and with that charming Branson smile, he said, "Well, Glenn, looks like we need another bottle of wine!"

And that's just what we did: we headed back into the house, opened a bottle of port, and waited.

The driver knew he'd made a mistake; Sir Richard didn't need to point it out. He understood that the guy already felt bad enough. So, he made the best of an unfortunate circumstance. Before we knew it, my doorbell rang. It was the driver.

"Well, looks like everything is fixed. Off I go," Sir Richard said.

As he drove away, I thought, *How cool is he?*

I once asked John Elway what he did when he got sacked five or six times in a row. I was curious about how he reacted. Did he yell at his offensive linemen in the huddle? He said that some guys yelled and screamed and did whatever else it took to get their teammates fired up enough to protect the quarterback, but he wasn't one of those guys. Instead, he would always crack a joke and ask, "Are you mad at me? Did I do something wrong?" He understood that the players already felt bad. He didn't need to pile on.

I greatly admire Sir Richard and John, not just for their athletic and business success but for their examples of how important it is to be kind. So, when I do happen to slip, as I sometimes do, I try to recover quickly by owning my mistake. Some people get stuck in their ego and pride, but there's a lot of grace in owning up. While some might think showing vulnerability is a weakness, I see it as a strength.

Several years ago, Kevin Hall, a good friend of mine, wrote the book *Aspire.* It's all about discovering your purpose through the power of words. He was an original partner in Franklin Quest, makers of the Franklin Day Planner. Kevin has been recognized for his groundbreaking approach to uncovering the hidden, and often secret, meanings of words. He's also credited with creating—and trademarking—the original slogan for the 2002 Olympic Winter Games, "Light the Fire Within." When he wrote *Aspire*, Kevin felt adrift. Despite his success, he wasn't sure where he was going with his life. He decided to go to Vienna to look for Viktor Frankl's family. He wanted to sit down with them and understand how their grandfather had such an optimistic view of the world despite what he went through during the Second World War. He wanted to know how he held on to hope under such horrific conditions, how he didn't let his circumstances break his spirit.

When he arrived in Vienna, Kevin set out to explore the city on foot. He walked along the old cobblestone streets, purposely getting lost. He felt as though his mind and spirit were lost, too. He wandered into a tiny gift shop full of tchotchkes and antiques. He was looking around when the shopkeeper said, "I see you are wearing a pin on your lapel of clasped hands."

"Yes; it's Viktor Frankl's hands of forgiveness," Kevin responded.

"Why do you have that?" the shopkeeper inquired.

"I'm here in Vienna to seek out the meaning of my life," Kevin explained.

"Would you have lunch with me?" the shopkeeper asked.

Kevin immediately agreed, and the two men headed to a local café. When they sat down together, Kevin told the man that he was working on a book about the power and meaning of words.

"Do you know the word *Genshai*?" the shopkeeper asked Kevin, who shook his head no. "Genshai is an ancient Hindi word. It means 'never treat others—or yourself—in a way that makes them feel small.'"

Kevin loved the word. It struck him like an arrow to the heart.

After lunch, the shopkeeper took Kevin back to his store. When they arrived, he unlocked the door and motioned for Kevin to enter, saying, "Come, I have something I want to show you."

The shopkeeper walked behind his desk and pulled a large, leatherbound tome from a stack of old books. "This is my Book of Greats," he said as he opened to the first page and showed it to Kevin. "This is where the Dalai Lama signed. And here is Ray Charles and Mother Teresa." There were hundreds of names in the book.

"I want to show you something else," the shopkeeper continued as he turned to a specific page somewhere in the middle of the book. There, on the page was Viktor Frankl's name.

"This is the man you seek, right?"

Kevin got closer and saw that it was indeed Frankl's signature.

"Yes, it is." Kevin could hardly believe it.

The shopkeeper pulled a pen from a cup on his desk, handed it to Kevin, and said, "I'd like you to sign my Book of Greats."

Taken aback, Kevin said he couldn't do it. He didn't feel worthy of signing such an important book. "Sign it," the shopkeeper insisted. But Kevin declined.

He left the store without signing.

When he returned to the United States, he couldn't shake that day in the store from his thoughts. It bothered him that he hadn't felt "worthy" of signing the book. He thought about it for months until he finally bought another plane ticket and flew back to Austria.

He returned to the store, walked through the door, and said to the shopkeeper, "Do you remember me?"

"Yes, of course I do," the shopkeeper said with a smile.

"I brought my pen, and if it's okay with you, I'd like to sign your Book of Greats," Kevin said.

The shopkeeper grinned, opened the book, and happily let him sign it. When he closed the book, he looked Kevin in the eye and said, "I would like to give you my Book of Greats, because I would like you to go around the world and share Genshai. Help people realize the power of such a word."

Needless to say, Kevin was floored by this gesture, and by the responsibility the man was bestowing upon him. He took the book, held it close, and said, "It would be my great honor."

Not long after that experience, Kevin came to California to give a speech to my employees. "I want to tell you a story," he began, and shared this remarkable experience with my team. At the end of his presentation, he announced that he'd brought the Book of Greats with him that day. He invited me to come up on stage and sign it in front of my entire company. I opened the book and intentionally went to the page with Viktor Frankl's signature, where many other signatures now appeared. I signed my name right next to his. I don't know why I did that.

Maybe I felt understood by his message of not letting anything break our spirit. That was a privilege I've never forgotten.

Six months later, I got a call from Kevin, who was in Texas giving a speech to two thousand dentists. He'd told his story about Vienna, Victor Frankl, and the Book of Greats. When he finished, he called Steve Bilt, the CEO of Smile Brands, the company that was hosting the event up onto the stage to sign the book, just as he'd done with me months before.

Like me, Steve signed on the same page Frankl had.

Afterward, Kevin was backstage talking to Steve. "Ironically, you're only the second CEO I've ever had sign this book, and you both signed the same page," he said.

Kevin started to describe the first CEO who signed the book to Steve. As he spoke, a smile came over Steve's face.

He stopped Kevin right there. "Before you tell me his name, let me tell you who I think it is, because he's one of my best friends in the world. Is it Glenn Stearns?"

Steve is indeed one of my best friends.

Steve signed his name two inches to the other side of Viktor Frankl's signature. He swears he didn't see my signature. There are so many signatures in the book, names of amazing and inspiring people from all over the world. We were all blown away by the synchronicity.

A few months later, I happened to be talking with Kevin and mentioned that I was going to Necker Island to host one of the events I'd planned to benefit the Horatio Alger Association. This was the same event where Michael Johns performed.

While we were at Necker Island, a package was delivered

with my name on it. I wasn't expecting anything, so imagine my surprise when I found the Book of Greats inside with a note that asked if I would spread the word of Genshai and have our speakers sign it. Would I? You bet I would, and then some.

When it was my turn to speak at the event, I pulled the book out of a large canvas bag and began explaining "Genshai" to the group. After all, this was the reason the shopkeeper had entrusted Kevin with his Book of Greats. I told every part of the story, and then I had Sir Richard Branson, Michael Johns, and the students from Horatio Alger sign it. Those kids were absolutely worthy and deserved to be included in the Book of Greats.

I really appreciate the meaning and purpose of the Book of Greats and the powerful concept of Genshai. We are *all* equal. We should never treat people as if they're small or make them feel less than, including ourselves. The irony in having Michael sign the book was that he always felt small, even when he appeared to be larger than life. Once the demons took over, he was never able to break free from those feelings.

In 2017, while traveling around the world, I flew back to Los Angeles for an important meeting. Before I boarded the flight, a young woman sat next to me in the terminal. We struck up a conversation, talking about art, movies, and books. I told her some of my favorites, which of course included Viktor Frankl's *Man's Search for Meaning*. I never saw the woman again, though occasionally she would text to say hello. I would hear from her about every six months, and her notes usually said something along the lines of "Not sure why, but for some reason I was thinking of you today." About a year later, she sent me a note with the same remark, but this one came with a photo of a diary entry she'd made in 1987, twenty years before we met. It read, "I grasped the meaning of the greatest secret that human poetry and human thought and belief have to impart: The salvation of man is through love and in love." I didn't recognize the quote or put a lot of thought into it; I was just grateful that she'd shared something so meaningful with me.

Later that evening, I walked into our cabin on the boat, and Mindy stopped me in my tracks and said, "Glenn, I have to read you something: 'I grasped the meaning of the greatest secret that human poetry and human thought and belief have to impart: The salvation of man is through love—"

"'And in love,'" I said, finishing the sentence.

Mindy turned to me and said, "How do you know that?"

I told her about the text I'd just received. What were the odds? Incalculable, I'm sure. This sentence from *Man's Search for Meaning* is so powerful that it moved both my wife and a complete stranger to want to share it with me—and on the same day! Now, that's remarkable. I don't always understand the significance in these kinds of synchronicities, but the world aligns even if we can't see the patterns. Imagine what could be done if we all had *that* gift.

None of us got to where we are today by accident. Everything is connected. Good decisions and bad ones, who we choose to surround ourselves with, and the way we treat others all matter. There's an art to putting yourself in someone else's shoes. Mr. Duckwitz and Mr. Martinez showed me that. When my vulnerability led them to talk to me that day at Shakey's, they taught me that truth. Ever since then, I've been more than willing to share my true self with others, because it leads to deeper, and more meaningful and trusting relationships.

In psychology, putting ourselves in someone else's shoes is known as "attunement," meaning you aim to understand what the other person feels, not what you feel. It's a form of deep empathy for others. I always want to understand why someone is the way they are. What happened in their life to create who they became? I think back to my old boss Yvan and how his years of growing up during the war, when everything was taken from him, made him the man he was. When you attune to others, you quickly realize that most things aren't about you, they're about them. Their reactions are learned. Habitual. When you know that, it's a lot easier to accept people for who they are instead of who we want them to be. It also makes it easier to not take offense, because you understand that it isn't personal. The next time something like this happens to you, stop and ask yourself, "Is this because of something I did, or is something else going on in their world that I may not be aware of?" How can you show that person empathy and compassion? Can you overlook your own feelings and attempt to see things through their eyes? Is there anything you can do to help that person? Ask yourself, "What is this person saying? Why are they reacting this way?" The faster you can put yourself in their shoes, the less likely you are to feel hurt or offended by their actions.

I think a lot of the disappointment we sometimes feel in others comes from their not living up to the expectations we place on them. This is where trouble lives, because something that usually has very little to do with you suddenly becomes all about you, and not the other person. Your defenses are up, and rational thinking goes right out the window. Here's what I know for sure: When I do or say something I'm not proud of, the best course of action for me is to own my mistake. I apologize right away and admit that my reaction was about the bad day I'm having, a confrontation I had with someone, stress at work—whatever the reason. Let the other person know that your behavior is on you and not them. And act fast; don't let these things linger, because that's how molehills become mountains.

In 2010 Domino's Pizza put out a commercial that declared, "Our Pizza Sucks." They used counterintuitive marketing and salvaged the company's fortunes. That's exactly how I've operated for my entire life.

There's great power in coming from a humble position. It gets you a lot farther than strong-arming people. Sure, there may be times when that approach is necessary, but I've found that being vulnerable, showing your human side, usually draws people in and helps build deep bonds, which are necessary when you're growing a relationship or a company. If you come from a shallow place in business or in life, people won't go as far for you, because they don't have as much at stake in the relationship. When you go deep and get vulnerable, people feel trusted and have a stronger connection to you, so they're willing to sacrifice more.

Being vulnerable involves being truthful. As a parent, I've tried to teach my children that they'll never get in trouble for telling the truth. They know lying and deception won't be tolerated. It's up to me to be consistent with that philosophy, so if any of my children do something I don't agree with, as long as they're honest, there isn't as big a price to pay as when they're not. It's like a game of truth or dare: Tell me the truth and we're all good. Lie to me? Well, that's not going to end well.

Our behavior and our actions matter. Do you want to be a hothead or a calm and thoughtful person? Are you fair-minded or are you a cheat? As I matured, I wanted to set a higher standard, to inspire others to live up to their greatest potential. I used to regret pushing people to reveal their real selves; now I encourage it. I want people to believe in themselves while realizing that it's perfectly okay to be flawed. Embrace your potential, and don't cling to your flaws. My typical approach is *build, burn, build*, meaning that I compliment people, provide constructive criticism, and then build them back up again. If I'm going to lay into someone, I always start off by talking about their strengths. Then I lean into the ways they could do their job smarter, faster, or more efficiently. Finally, I end by offering them encouragement and acknowledging that all people make mistakes. I never want to break anyone. We all screw up. We're human. Coming to this understanding was a difference maker for me. It helped me change my ways at certain points in life, and now it defines how we are building Kind Lending.

No one gave me a blueprint for conquering the abundance of challenges that were set in my path. And that's okay, because it was those challenges that gave me the grit, resilience, and confidence to know I could get through anything.

I've had zero regrets since getting back into lending. My only thought has been that I have no second thoughts. While I've learned throughout the years that overconfidence often means I'm missing something, that's not the case now, at least as far as I can tell. Here's why. My greatest confidence comes from knowing that things won't go perfectly. They never do. But my history has taught me that I have the capacity to deal with whatever comes up along the way.

I think there's a big difference between fighting and surviving. Until writing this book, I hadn't thought of myself as someone who fought his way out of anything. Sure, I had a history of fighting, but to me it was more about surviving those battles. It never occurred to me that I was actually fighting for, well, anything. It's only when you get to a place in life where you understand what a true fight is that you can really grasp the distinction.

I had a friend in high school named Phil. He and I lost touch over the years, especially after I moved to California. A few years ago, I received word that Phil was dying of cancer and the doctors had given up on him. Hearing this broke my heart, especially after coming off my own battle with cancer, where quitting was never an option. I called MD Anderson to see if they could get Phil into a particular program there where doctors were getting very good results treating his type of cancer. For a while, it looked like they'd made great strides. Phil was doing well, and there was hope. Unfortunately, his cancer came back with a vengeance.

Friends of his reached out to me, thanking me for what

I'd done by opening the door to the doctors at MD Anderson. One after another, I received calls saying how special Phil was to everyone and how much he meant to so many. We would occasionally run into each other at MD Anderson, which gave us some one-on-one time to spend together. When we walked around the hospital, the doctors and nurses all seemed to know Phil, as if he'd somehow touched their lives, too.

I was curious about Phil's secret. How could one man affect so many other people?

The more time I spent with him, the more I began to see that he was one of the most authentic men I'd ever known. He would listen to you as if you were the only person in the room. He cared deeply about whomever he was speaking with. He never missed an opportunity to follow up on a conversation, send a handwritten note, or bring up something that reminded him of the talk we'd had. He sent me photos of himself fishing, because we spoke about that all the time.

The night after buying back the Z28 I'd owned and cherished in high school, I flew from Phoenix to Baltimore and immediately drove to Phil's house. He was just returning from hospice that morning, having decided to spend his last days at home. I waited for his family to get him into bed before I walked through the door. When I entered his room, Phil was attached to an oxygen machine and his little dog was lying next to him. I climbed into bed with him, put my arm around Phil and blurted, "I got my car back!"

His eyes opened really wide. "You did?" he said with a strained voice.

You see, everyone in high school knew my car. It was legendary.

"Last night, I found my Z28 at the Barrett-Jackson auction. And that damn April Caputo! I had to pay sixty times what I sold it for!" I said.

Phil laughed his butt off. It felt good to crack him up one last time before his sendoff. Our conversation lasted for forty-five minutes. We spoke about the same things we always did, fishing, family and friends. And then Phil stopped.

"Listen—just to get serious for a minute. I don't want to put my family through this. I've lived a great life. I'm not afraid. I'm ready to go. I don't want to hang on and make people feel uncomfortable," he said in a voice barely above a whisper as he gasped for air.

"I don't blame you," I said.

I stood up, stroked his hair, and walked out of the room.

Phil's wife and a few friends had gathered, as the end was near. After a few minutes, his wife popped her head out of the room and said, "Glenn?"

I thought this was it.

"Phil said you better not forget that big fat kiss you promised him."

I had to smile. You see, when I'd told Phil I was stopping by that day, I assured him that I wasn't coming to say goodbye; I was coming to give him a big fat kiss. I swore that was all I wanted to do.

When I went back into his room, Phil was clear-eyed. He teased me, saying, "I would've tracked you down, buddy."

That's when I approached his bed, bent over, and planted a final kiss on his forehead. "I love you, Phil."

"I love you, Glenn."

We knew it was the last time we would see each other.

I walked out of the room smiling. Why? That was the way I wanted to go someday.

Phil died later that day.

And then I got it. I understood why so many people thought this guy was magical.

He left his mark.

I saw peace in his eyes that day. There was no more pain.

I grinned all the way to the airport. I'd been in rare air; I'd been touched by someone very special—someone who'd been put on this earth to make a difference. In the film *It's a Wonderful Life*, Clarence says of George Bailey, "Strange, isn't it? Each man's life touches so many other lives. When he isn't around, he leaves an awful hole, doesn't he?" Phil was the closest person I'd ever met to George Bailey. He absolutely lived a wonderful life.

During his final years, Phil and I shared a deep connection and an understanding of how cancer can be a gift that teaches us what's really important—to love those who mean the most to us. I was asked to give a eulogy at Phil's celebration of life ceremony. What I most wanted to convey to those who'd gathered at the church that day was why he'd made such an impact on so many of us.

At the end of my remarks, I said, "Sometimes Phil and I would just be still. We wouldn't speak a word." I paused, took a deep breath, and added, "Be still and know that I am God. Psalms 46:10."

Give it up to God.

Whatever is going to be will be. It's in His hands.

When I finished, the pastor started his sermon by quoting the same scripture I had. We hadn't talked about it. I'd never met the pastor until that day. He said he had just selected it the day before.

In life and business, you can either be with the people in the balcony or the people in the basement. Here's what I mean by that: you can choose to wallow in your challenges, use hard times as an excuse, and let your circumstances beat you down. There are a lot of people who believe that misery loves company; those are the basement people. They're always willing to pull you down to where they live rather than build you up.

The balcony people, on the other hand, are those who want to see you succeed. They lend a helping hand to pull you out and up. They're always on your side.

That was Phil.

He was one of the richest men I knew, because in the end, wealth isn't about how much money you have, the house you live in, the stuff you've accumulated; it's about your relationships. It's about being fulfilled. It's about choosing happiness. And it's about the legacy you leave behind.

It's not up to anyone but you to decide how you want to live. You must believe in your capability to take a punch or two and in your willingness to pull yourself up, dust yourself off, and get back in the ring.

I don't always know how things come to be in life—they just do. Understanding that is a gift. It's provided me with the confidence to navigate every turn thus far, and to accept that a bend in the road is not the end of the road.

One of life's greatest advantages comes from knowing that your biggest mistakes can bring about your greatest successes. If you know that, there's no fear in moving forward, even without a game plan. Everything works out. I don't just think it; I *know* it.

CHAPTER TWENTY-FOUR

HERE WE GO AGAIN

"I laugh, that there's a certain kind of cyclical nature to life and that I don't have to worry because whatever isn't there right now, it's coming back again."
— WALTER MOSLEY

SOME OF THE sharpest minds in business have the ability to see what's coming from a distance. Sometimes, they spot it before anybody else does, giving them a head start. Not many could have foreseen Covid. . .or the biggest refinancing boom in the history of housing that followed on its heels.

Kind Lending was still a start-up company when the pandemic hit. After Covid forced business closures, event cancellations, and people to work from home, the government responded to the resulting economic downturn by offering all kinds of stimulus. What changed the game for our industry was when the Federal Reserve lowered the rate it charged banks for loans from its discount window by 2 percentage points. That had *never* been done before. As a result, every single home loan that could be refinanced was up for refinancing. You would think that it was a great time to be in the mortgage business, and it was. . . until it wasn't.

Most lenders doubled or even tripled their employee base, thus doubling or tripling their volume. To put it in perspective, the year I left the industry, Stearns Lending had one of its bigger years, generating $148 million in pretax profit. During the refi boom, there were companies that netted a billion dollars in a single quarter. In a good year, you might make 120 basis points. During the boom, many lending companies were making 450 basis points. That's 4.5 percent on each loan, which was insane.

Our industry had gotten bigger than it had ever been, and it happened practically overnight. As with anything, though, the bigger something gets, the farther it can fall. When a mortgage company starts receiving that many applications, they have to process and underwrite them. They also need the capacity to fund the loans. As a result, a lot of lenders' credit lines started running out. They obviously couldn't hang a sign outside their door saying, "We don't want any more business," so they tried to slow the market by raising rates. Because the industry heated up so fast, everyone raised their rates at the same time so that increase had little to no effect. The business kept coming in because there was nowhere else to go. The end result was that each loan funded became extremely lucrative.

Kind Lending came into the market with all that wind

at our backs. We were new, and we were small. We didn't have any of the capacity issues other companies were struggling with. We could write loans in two days, whereas everyone else was taking up to thirty days.

Since we were just entering the market, I had expected to lose $8 to $10 million in the first year. Instead, we made between $12 and $15 million. It was a complete windfall. I never anticipated that happening. I was grateful for that, but remember what I just said; what gets big, sometimes falls hard.

Many people were telling me, "Glenn, you have the best timing," and I would say, "Oh, thanks." But in the back of my mind, I was thinking, *If I had the best timing, I would have been in this business a year earlier.* I would have had my software already developed and all my loan documents set up. My support systems would have been fully integrated. I would have had my "mousetrap" all figured out. But I was brand new. I was just plugging in. Even so, I was doing $250 to $300 million of production a month. We funded a billion dollars in just five months. No one had ever climbed that fast.

From the time Stearns had filed bankruptcy to the time we were up and running was less than six months. This time-frame only happened because of my good friends Rick and Patty Arvielo at New American Funding. They helped me get my start as a division of their company. The plan was to spin off my company in a year or so, after I got my credit lines, my state approvals and licenses, and my operation fully func-tioning. Rick and Patty are wonderful people and at that time, our businesses were good complements. They were on the retail side, dealing directly with the consumer, while we were on the wholesale side, dealing with the brokers.

When I owned Stearns Lending, we were the largest joint venture partner in the country. We had numerous joint ventures with real estate companies, builders, and relocation companies. As soon as we entered the market under Kind Lending, we had several opportunities to joint venture again. One such prospect was with eXp Realty. Since it was founded in 2009, the company has grown to include eighty thousand real estate professionals and they are still expanding. From the start, they operated solely in the cloud so agents could work from anywhere they wanted, and the company also offered attractive revenue- and equity-sharing opportunities. I met up with Glenn Sanford, the founder and chairman of the company, at an event that Grant Cardone was hosting, called the 10X Growth Conference. Grant had also starred in his own season of *Undercover Billionaire* after me. I was his Executive Producer.

Glenn and I hit it off at the conference. At one point, he shared his plans to start a mortgage venture. That's when Glenn said to me, " Why don't you and I partner 50/50?" I found eXp to be an amazing company and, quite frankly, one of the best models I've ever seen. I was all in. I wanted to work with this forward-thinking pioneer in the real estate industry.

In no time at all we were up in Roche Harbor, Washington, on Glenn's boat as news broke in the media about eXp World Holdings and Kind Lending launching our new venture, Success Lending. It would take about six months or more for the new company to be fully established. In the meantime, the news of our newly formed joint venture did not go over well with Rick and Patty at New American Funding. In their minds, they had just let the preverbal fox into the henhouse.

"Glenn, why are you getting into retail now? We are getting so much push back from our staff. We need you to break away and be on your own immediately." Rick said.

Unfortunately, when we left New American, we were still not ready with IT, accounting, human resources, employee insurance and many other necessary functions. Given the breakneck pace of the market, we were dropping balls left and right. I was always that guy who never had anybody quit on him—that guy whose team was beyond loyal. Now our people were saying, "Look, I've got to go." These were people who had been with me at my old company—people who were deeply integrated into the business. From their perspective, there were just too many demands being placed on them as Kind Lending was still getting off the ground.

By now it was April or May of 2021. The competition had caught up. They went from thirty days of underwriting, to fifteen, to ten, to five, until they were down to two days of underwriting just like us. They had capacity again. They started to think, "Okay, I need to feed the machine. If we're making 450 basis points—4.5 percent on every loan— and we were used to making 1.2 percent, we can afford to lower our margin down to 400 basis points to keep getting business." Well, other lenders started doing the same thing. Soon enough, they were down to 300 basis points. Normally you might lower or raise the margin by five basis points, but now they were lowering it by fifty points a day until they are down to just thirty or forty basis points. They couldn't manufacture a loan for the amount they were charging. They were *losing* money on every loan. But all these companies had hundreds of millions of dollars in the bank. If they had to lose some of it to keep their team, they could do it. I, on the other hand, was still a little guy. I didn't have hundreds of millions of dollars of profits because I wasn't early enough to capture my piece of the pie. So suddenly, we were dragged into the deep end of the pool. We were starting to lose $2 million, $3 million, $4 million a month.

When it rains it pours. By August 2021, the head of our east coast operations, our Executive Vice President of Production, many of our IT people and a few of our largest originators left. By October, the majority of our marketing team, our COO, and the head of our project management team left as well. The COO's departure was a big blow. I even offered her the CEO title, but she still opted to leave. Blood was in the water. We were on a sinking ship.

I didn't know how I could possibly manage because everyone else had hundreds of millions or billions of dollars in their arsenal to ride this market out and we didn't. Most people are willing to bleed for a little while, until either they can't anymore or they say, "Uncle" and bail. But if you hang in long enough, as people leave the market you can pick up some of their share.

In my past life, when we were the number one lender in the country, we operated with an abundance mentality. As owners, we had mutual respect for one another. But the top wholesaler in this market didn't work that way. If we were at forty basis points of gross margin, he'd say, "Let's go to twenty." He squeezed until more people went out of business. I was left with no other choice than to start slashing the people I had left. We kept getting leaner and leaner.

By January of 2022, it was announced that Stearns Lending was closing down. That's right, my former company, still bearing my name, was shuttering their wholesale business. While I was disappointed, I placed my attention on picking up the salespeople we knew before. This gave us a little bump up in business and we stopped falling as fast as the market was falling.

A few more companies went under after that. Even Loan Depot, which was huge, announced they were closing their wholesale business. They lost nearly $500 millions dollars in the first three quarters of 2022. Many of the companies tapping out were the ones that had gone public two years earlier in the middle of the refinance boom. Some had lost 80 to 90 percent of their stock value. Because they were public, the pressure on them was enormous. The ones that weren't out already had to start dismantling their machines. Wholesale lending became the canary in the coal mine. If you're on the retail side, you get the loan, you keep it, and you fund it. But on the wholesale side, brokers have loans in their pipeline. They can send them anywhere they want, so when times get tight, they usually send them to the best price in town. Wholesalers will often undercut each other just to get those loans. Brokers who are smart know that good business has a lot to do with good service too, but in the grand scheme of things, brokers can switch on a dime and before you know it, the volume has slipped away from you.

The craziness had gone on long enough, and now *everyone* was in pain. Ninety percent of the refinances had gone away. What was left was all purchase money—people buying homes.

And everyone was fighting over those loans. But as each wholesaler closed, we picked up a few of their salespeople, more of their business, and a few brokers as well, until we were doing better. In fact, we started having some of our best months ever, while others were still on the downswing. Over a ninety-day period, while our competitors were in survival mode, slashing thousands of jobs, we added 150 new jobs. Once again, we were going against the current. We were actually in a growth mode. We were taking our shot while the big guys were distracted, burdened by all these issues.

In many ways, this was a real déjà vu moment. I had seen this movie before. It was exactly what had happened with our company in 2007 and 2008. The hunt for business was turning into the survival of the fittest again. People were comparing what was happening in the moment to what had happened back then, during the most horrible time in our business. Only they were saying that this time was worse. Fortunately, though, we weren't feeling as much pain as most. Don't get me wrong, we still were losing a lot of money each month, but at least we weren't losing $4 million a month. As far as I was concerned, we were definitely moving in the right direction.

Throughout all of this, we had started to make a name

for ourselves. People whose infrastructure had just been taken away from them at their company were coming to us because we were now building infrastructure. They'd say, "You just added more underwriters?" and then they'd laugh. They were so happy for the support to do their jobs. We were in an entirely different place mentally than we had been before, and an entirely different place than our competitors for sure. We were on the tractor, gaining ground. After such a long haul it was exciting to see and experience. At one of the saddest and most difficult times in our business, we had hope.

Now realize, we weren't doing well because we were better than other people. Sure, our management style is one that fits people well. It's a servant-leadership style that prioritizes the greater good, even in the middle of a major market freefall. But more than anything else, we owed our success to timing and having the courage to pull the trigger. As I said at the outset of this book, I have always had timing. Good timing or bad timing, I've always had *some kind of timing*.

It's the irony of my life. Back in 2000, when another of my companies felt like a sinking ship for a while, my CFO would call me with news of the latest problem saying, "Captain, there's water coming over the bow," and I'd say, "Bail, bail, bail." We'd laugh because what else could we do? We were drowning in bills. We didn't know which ones to pay first. When he finally said one day that he had to abandon ship and he wasn't joking, I said, "I'm sorry you feel that way. I promise you one thing: you will always have a job here, but you'll be in accounts payable when you return." Some years after he quit, he did come back to work for us, and as predicted, he wasn't anywhere close to being CFO. We had highly experienced people in those positions by then. Many of the people that left us in 2021 have asked to come back. Market conditions at the time, made it very difficult to rehire them. Plus, we were able to hire really great people in their place. There is a price to pay for those who choose not to fight through the pain.

One of the lessons in all of this is that in times of crisis when we think things are happening *to* us, they are really happening *for* us. We were much better off than we had been. Finally, we had the talent, the attitude, and the momentum.

After rebuilding, if I saw people stressing out, I made it a point to say, "Look, you have a choice. You are going to be stressed out right now no matter where you are. Do you want to be stressed because you may lose your job or do you want to be stressed because you are working really hard and wearing multiple hats?" Either way, it isn't an easy ride. I expected people to understand that they had to bust their ass.

Let's face it. When we are under pressure it comes down to two ways to spend our energy. How will you fight your way through this or how do you exit the situation with the least amount of damage. Fight or flight.

During the filming of *Undercover Billionaire*, I remember sitting at the Barbecue Fest trying to think of a perfect way out because I thought I was destined to humiliate myself in front of the entire the world. Instead, I fought through my self-doubt and pulled off one of my greatest personal accomplishments.

During the most difficult days at Kind Lending, it wasn't

just me thinking maybe I should get out; my financial advisors were telling me to cut and run. I have found that after I go through my initial, "Oh Shit" moment, I start using the energy I'm spending on figuring a way *out* of my situation to actually figure a way *through* my situation. I believe there are lots of times in our lives when we start thinking about quitting a little too early.

Look, as I'm writing this chapter, our industry is facing the most serious challenges it has ever faced. I have not made it through the fire yet. I don't know how this is going to end. But whenever I get to the place where I'm contemplating what will look best for me—to fail or to give up—something usually happens that gives me a glimmer of hope and I inevitably say, "You know what? I'm not going to quit. This is going to be the best part of the story. I'm going to make it through this." And then I gain momentum from thinking positively again.

I believe that everything in life is cyclical. Everything always comes full circle. I know from experience that one day I can be on top of the world feeling as if nothing can ever knock me down, and then the next day something will come along and do just that. I can fall to the bottom of the deepest crevasse and think that I'll never be able to make it out, but then life will eventually start to feel good again. I ascend to the top, drop to the middle, and then I am at the bottom again. It's just a constant cycle. If everyone were to look at their life, they would also see their own cycles of happiness, mediocrity, sadness, happiness, mediocrity, and so on. You can attach the stress of business, family, health, or whatever else to those cycles, but the movements are the same: you build something up, put energy into it, and then maybe you let it go and it falls. I think the only thing that stays the same is change.

My father taught me about cycles. He loved to explain that nothing lasts forever. I think that was his way of laying the groundwork for his ultimate exit. My father became ill in December of 2021. He had made the choice not to get vaccinated against Covid and he subsequently contracted the virus around Christmastime.

Before we knew he was sick, we drove from our home in Jackson Hole back to California. We took three separate cars and stopped at Zion National Park and a few other places along the way. Skye, Trevor, and Colby were in the car with my dad and me, and we had some of the funniest exchanges with him ever. He plugged in his iPhone so we could listen to all this great music from the fifties. Every time he would put it on play, it would skip to the next song. He couldn't figure out what was wrong. This went on for much of the ride. I finally let him in on the secret. I had a button on my steering wheel that skipped a track ahead. He couldn't believe it. "You've been messing with me," he said. And I was laughing until I was crying. The kids were in on it too. We teased him, saying it was just a little elder abuse. It was so easy, it was like shooting fish in a barrel. We filmed a lot of it and could see he loved it. He was laughing too.

Once years ago, I played a similar trick on my son, Skyler. I would turn the seat heaters on and play The Average White Band song, "Pick up the Pieces." I love that song. It's one of my all-time favorites. Every time I sang the lyrics though, I'd change them ever so slightly to, "Ass on fire.... ass on fire," as the seat beneath him heated up. We did the same thing to my dad on this trip. We were cracking up.

I confessed, "I have been cooking your ass for over twenty minutes."

I didn't realize it until later, but he never caught on because he had a bad fever. I kept thinking, "I wonder why he doesn't feel it." My dad never complained, so I didn't know at first. I couldn't tell that he was as sick as he was.

When we realized what was going on, we had doctors from Hoag Hospital in Newport Beach come to the house. Nine out of twelve family members got Covid at that time too. I was spared and so were my two sons.

My dad was ultimately hospitalized. His heart, liver, and everything else was healthy, but his lungs weren't. The doctors were trying everything. They even tried stem-cell therapy to regenerate his lungs. They did everything they could to help him heal for nearly four months, but his condition just kept getting worse, until eventually he was put on a ventilator. Looking at his scans, the doctors were convinced the situation would only decline from there. When we heard that news, I turned to my sister and said, "We're done. You know, he doesn't want to live like this." Sue agreed.

We gathered the family together, and we each told my dad what he meant to us. He had been fighting this virus for 120 days. He was exhausted. I have no idea what he was thinking at the time, but to see the whole family come together to give their regards that way had to signal to him that his time was coming to an end. After all the family members expressed their love for him, it was my turn.

Earlier that week, I had given a speech in Phoenix to a thousand loan officers from all over the country. After the address, I was walking through the crowd, stopping to talk and take pictures with people, when this guy came up to me and said, "Glenn, I just want to tell you, your dad is a hero." I was surprised. I thought, "My dad? My dad is from Maryland, and this is Phoenix." He continued, " I know your dad. Do you know how many lives he saved through AA in Maryland? I'm part of that system, and I can tell you, this man is a legend.".

I was taken aback. "Well, that's so great to hear," I said. And it really was. I couldn't wait to get back and tell my dad that a perfect stranger had approached me to say what a wonderful man he was.

I told dad what an amazing father, teacher, mentor, and role model he was to me and others. I let him know how proud I was of him. I reminded him that it isn't how you start, but how you finish. And then I said, "I love you." He mouthed back, "I love you too." Those were the last words he ever said.

Sometime after he passed, I was talking with my sister and I said, "Dad sure was a sleeper. I never thought I'd miss the guy."

Man, was I wrong.

I wondered about how that happened. Here was a guy I didn't want to have anything to do with after I turned eighteen.

I thought he was a boring man. I don't even think he had graduated high school. Yet, years later, he was reciting philosophers like Carl Jung and quoting people like Mark Twain.

> *"When I was a boy of fourteen, my father was so ignorant I*
> *could hardly stand to have the old man around. But when*
> *I got to be twenty-one, I was astonished at how much he*
> *had learned in seven years."*
> —Mark Twain

My dad used to repeat this quote to me all the time. If you think about it, this was exactly our relationship. And I've never forgotten those words. I missed his stories, though I'd heard them a million times. I missed his absolute "yes" for life too. During the last ten years of his life, his response was always "yes." He went skiing with us when he couldn't even walk anymore, he took a college course to get a scuba license! He jumped out of a helicopter in the middle of the Indian Ocean.

My point in telling you all of this is that my dad came full circle. He may have started at the bottom, and spent a long stretch of time there, but look at where he took his life after achieving sobriety. He ended it at the top. No matter how far down you fall—no matter how hard the landing is at rock bottom—there is always the prospect of pulling yourself up, making something of yourself, and inspiring others.

Life really is just about timing. . . . and inteGRITy.

ACKNOWLEDGEMENTS

WHILE THIS BOOK reflects a lifetime of adventures and misadventures, it would require a special thank you to every person who has ever crossed my path and taught me a life lesson, big or small, intentionally or unintentionally, fairly or not. But given the limited space here, and with all good intention, I will keep the list more intimate.

Among my earliest influences, I wish to thank the two people who gave me life and in their own way, each inspired me to grow: my mother and my father, Janet and Gilbert Stearns. What a life it's been! Each has made indelible impressions on me in different ways and at different times. As much as I carry their DNA within me, I also carry their spirit and love of life. I also wish to thank my sister, Sue; my ride-or-die friend since childhood, Shane, and those who had my back when I least expected it, including such teachers as Mr. Martinez, Mr. Duckwitz, and Dru Bagwell. I also wish to thank one of my first employers, Yvan Humbert. His early example helped to shape my understanding of business and my ultimate work ethic.

I owe an enormous debt of gratitude as well to all those

who helped build and sustain the success of my companies. I've always made it a point to keep strong women around me. First, my mother who gave me character, resilience and humility. Next, I want to thank Kathy and Amber for their fearlessness and willingness to jump blindly into the future. Through their choice, they created miracles that changed my life forever. To Katherine Le and Yvonne Ketchum, my two Presidents, who have led two of my biggest companies, in what has traditionally been considered a man's world, you are simply the best at the job. And to Keely Gilmore, who knows more about me than anyone. Your loyalty and professionalism is second to none. You make me look so organized and make it seem like I never forget a thing, when it's really you sweeping up behind me, catching everything that falls out of my head. You make your job look easy, even when I know it's not.

I also need to thank all the people at Stearns Lending and Kind Lending. I've always seen, valued, and appreciated your exceptionalism. I am also grateful to those who were involved in my various television endeavors, including the respective cast and crew of *The Real Gilligan's Island* and *Undercover Billionaire*. Big love goes especially to the extraordinary team at Underdog BBQ for embracing the entrepreneurial spirit and for sharing the adrenaline rush with me of founding a startup business again.

Very special thanks are in order for the mentors who showed me the way toward a deeper, more gratifying kind of success than the attainment of monetary wealth. I am deeply grateful for the wisdom, altruism, generosity, and friendship of Julia and George Argyros, Richard Branson, Larry Bridges,

ACKNOWLEDGEMENTS

Robert Day, John Elway, Foster Freiss, Mike Hayde, Mike Ingram, Chuck Martin, Harry Rinker, Dr. Robert Schuller, Ron Simon, Tom Tucker, Dennis Washington and Richard Watts. Although Richard is my longtime attorney, he is someone who has greatly impacted my life on a very deep level.

To the esteemed members of YPO; The Young Presidents Organization and my confidential forum and the Horatio Alger Association. I've had the good fortune to meet and know many of you. Both organizations and the people involved have enriched my life and spirit in ways too great to adequately put into words.

My heartfelt appreciation also extends to Mel Klein, Dr. Ron DePinho, Dr. Weber, Chris Haggerman, Dr. Neil Gross, Dr. Renata Ferrarato, Jancy Janes and the unparalleled medical team at MD Anderson. It is an understatement to say that they saved my life and gave me the opportunity to proceed with renewed purpose. A special thank you to Dr. Gigi El Bayoumi at George Washington University Hospital. She continues to help, heal and inspire me and my family.

And, of course, my undying love and gratitude goes to those who bring daily blessings to my life. My wife Mindy has been my rock and my safe harbor in troubled times. Mindy is my witness to this amazing and often challenging life. She keeps my stories straight and even helped edit this book. She is my spirited companion for all time, until we view our final sunset on a beach. Each and every one of my children—Charlene, Skyler, Colby, Trevor, Brooke and Taylor- are all I could have ever hoped for and more. You all make me so proud to be your dad. I am also inordinately proud to be grandfather to my two beautiful grandchildren, Jaden and McKenna. I must say that I am extremely grateful to all of my children's mothers-- Kathy, Amber, and Mindy-- for the many ways in which they continue to make our beautiful blended family whole. I am also very appreciative of my loving in-laws, Joyce and Dr. Eric Burbano. And, Marty and Kaili Burbano, your example of unconditional family love is unparalleled.

Finally, this book would not be possible without the extraordinary efforts and talents of my publishing team. Laura Morton, you are the consummate professional, offering just the right words, advice, wisdom, and support. I have enjoyed your humor throughout this process and greatly value our continuing friendship. Adam Mitchell, thank you for working tirelessly on hours…and hours of transcripts. Hope Innelli, your perspective, skilled editing, and deep commitment to honoring my voice are most appreciated. Benjamin Holmes, you are a master of detail. Thank you for copyediting and fact-checking this book with such care. Len Prince, you captured my soul in the brilliant images you took for the cover of this book. You never cease to amaze. Bruce Gore and Bill Kersey, I am thrilled with the final cover and interior design. Jonathan Merkh, I couldn't have asked for a better publisher. My compliments to you and your team at Forefront Books for all the ways you've supported this venture. Special thanks as well to the Sales and Marketing team at Simon and Schuster.

And last, but not least, I'd be remiss if I didn't thank *you*, the reader. I'm grateful you picked up this book and hope you've found some benefit in its pages.